Picturing Japaneseness

Film and Culture
John Belton, General Editor

Film and Culture
A series of Columbia University Press
Edited by John Belton

Picturing Japaneseness

Monumental Style,

National Identity,

Japanese Film

Darrell William Davis

Columbia University Press *New York*

Columbia University Press
New York   Chichester, West Sussex
Copyright © 1996 Columbia University Press
All rights reserved

The publisher gratefully acknowledges support toward publication given by
the Japan Foundation.

Library of Congress Cataloging-in-Publication Data
  Davis, Darrell William.
    Picturing Japaneseness : monumental style, national identity, Japanese film /
    Darrell William Davis.
      p.   cm. — (Film and culture)
    Filmography: p.
    Includes bibliographical references and index.
    ISBN 0-231-10230-5 (cloth) —ISBN 0-231-10231-3 (pbk.)
    1. Motion pictures—Political aspects—Japan. 2. Motion pictures—Social aspects—Japan.
    3. Motion pictures in propaganda—Japan. 4. National characteristics, Japanese.   I. Title.
    II. Series.
  PN1993.5.J3D38   1996
  791.43'0952'09043—dc20   95-22747
                                                                      CIP

Casebound editions of Columbia University Press books are printed on permanent and
durable acid-free paper.

Printed in the United States of America

c 10 9 8 7 6 5 4 3 2 1
p 10 9 8 7 6 5 4 3 2 1

Contents

     Narrative Structure and Characterization   132
     Style: The Primacy of Perception   147
          Garden of Stone   149
          The Poverty of Drama   159
          Perceptual Address   161
7   Historical Uses and Misuses: The Janus Face(s) of
     The Abe Clan (1938)   181
     Historical Appropriations   185
     Narration and Technique   193

8   Other Manifestations of the Monumental Style   219
     Monumentalism, Orientalism, and Gate of Hell (1953) 219
     Kurosawa's Theatrical Appropriations: Kagemusha (1980)
     and Ran (1985)   227
     Conclusions   244

     Selected Bibliography   279
     Filmography   291
     Index   295

Acknowledgments

Many thanks to the Getty Center for the History of Art and the Humanities for ten months of unparalleled postdoctoral privilege. I also thank my colleagues at the Yamagata International Documentary Film Festival for an intellectually enriching year of programming and writing. Special thanks to A. A. Gerow, Ono Seiko, Yano Kazuyuki, and Fukushima Yukio for their encouragement and challenging questions. The Kawakita Memorial Film Archives provided me with many rare stills, which the Getty Center generously paid for. *Mahalo* to Honolulu's East-West Center, and in particular to Wimal Dissanayake and Paul Clark, for providing me with over a year of support in my research and writing. Among my colleagues there, Naomi Tonooka and Linda Ehrlich read large parts of the manuscript and offered valuable suggestions. Clyde Nishimoto and Matthew Bernstein both provided close, insightful readings of my chapter on Kurosawa. For moral and intellectual support, as well as wee hour discourses on the crosses we must bear, I thank Rone Williams and Yueh-Yu Yeh. Donald Richie, David Desser, and Dudley Andrew have given much encouragement and guidance through the years. James Brandon of the University of Hawaii stimulated my thinking about *Chushingura* and Takie Sugiyama Lebra asked pointed questions of my interpretation of "modern girls" (*moga*). Peter B. High gave generously of his time and his manuscripts on prewar and wartime Japanese film. At the Library of Congress, Kathryn Loughney and Joe Balian were always available and attentive to the needs of bewildered researchers.

At the University of Wisconsin-Madison department of Communication Arts there is a tradition of historical film scholarship whose rigor is matched only by the imagination (and sometimes fanaticism) with which that scholarship is pursued. Thanks to Teresa Becker for providing a conference paper hot off the press. I gratefully acknowledge Wisconsin alumnus Donald Kirihara, whose monumental study of Mizoguchi is an indispensable reference and standard for my own work. I salute my colleague and friend T. R. White for his incorrigible sense of humor, a precious asset to the long-distance writer. I thank Professors Tino Balio, Donald Crafton, Vance Kepley Jr., and Tom Gunning whose historical exactitude and rhetorical sophistication have been a constant inspiration. I owe a deep debt to Professor David Bordwell, who made the mistake of introducing a new term for discussion in a Japanese film seminar one day in the mid-1980s: the *monumental style*. As my advisor, he has had to live with it ever since.

At Columbia University Press, thanks to John Belton for initiating consideration of this book for the Film and Culture series, to Jennifer Crewe, Publisher for the Humanities, and to Susan Pensak, who gives new meaning to the term *close reading*.

Finally, I wish to thank Abé Mark Nornes, who is indefatigable in his commitment to Japanese film culture and a model of sustained, spirited curiosity about all things Japanese. The people here acknowledged and the sources consulted have been a constant inspiration to this work—without which it could not be done—nevertheless, errors of fact and emphasis are entirely my own.

This book is dedicated to my parents, whose missionary zeal in postwar Japan brought me up in (to) a world whose alien familiarity has never ceased to attract and to captivate.

Picturing Japaneseness

1

Moving Pictures of Japaneseness

In the last decade or so the subject of Japanese identity has spawned a virtual cottage industry of speculations, research projects, and academic debate on both sides of the Pacific. In the U.S. such strenuous efforts of explication and demythologizing have not been seen since Ruth Benedict's *The Chrysanthemum and the Sword* (1946).[1] Contemporary works of Japanese demythologizing usually react to what is seen as an alarming proliferation of *nihonjinron*, or theories of Japanese identity, currently produced and consumed in Japan with almost compulsive relish.[2] Exchanges on the identity of the Japanese have indisputable importance in Japan-America relations as images of the "inscrutable Oriental" give way to visions of Japanese piracy on the high seas of technology, finance, and international trade. Japanese, in turn, marvel at the seemingly limitless American capacity for making excuses and accusations that the rules for entering Japanese markets are stacked against them, particularly when American economic clout is so formidable in other parts of the world. We can learn much from studies of mutual images of peoples and nations because these images are a common denominator of international relations and have a marked effect on the realpolitik of international diplomacy.[3]

But the following work is not about Western visions of Japan nor Western opinions of the Japanese self-concept. It is an attempt to define a particular Japanese vision of itself as it materialized at a certain time, in a certain medium. I wish to ask a central question about how this historical moment, the years leading up to Pearl Harbor, and the medium, film, impinge upon the question of Japanese identity.

Between 1936 and 1941, there were strenuous efforts made to express, and define, what makes Japanese people and life so Japanese. This had been an ongoing pursuit since the Meiji restoration (1868) when the Japanese islands were unceremoniously dragged from the seventeenth into the twentieth century. Defining Japaneseness in the late 1930s, however, became an institutionalized activity, as it is today. Writers, artists, journalists, company men, neighborhood associations, student activists, women's groups, boys' and girls' clubs were all organized for the express purpose of delineating the outlines of an authentic Japanese essence. Mass media, particularly the highly capitalized film, radio and mass circulation newspaper industries, were consolidated and encouraged to generate representations of Japanese culture and behavior. These pictures of Japaneseness were prescriptive: they were offered as models to be emulated and they were subject to approval by the authorities, primarily the Home Ministry and the Army.

The film industry produced some of the most vivid evocations of ideal Japanese life and behavior. There was a lot of "ordinary" propaganda put out at this time, hortatory newsreels and culture films typical of wartime. But there were also films that expressed more subtle and durable renditions of Japaneseness. They are sophisticated appropriations of feudal Japanese narratives and aesthetics, integrating these traditions into the basic textures of their style. They are superior films and enduring works of art. These films I have grouped together and designated the monumental style because they invest a form of spirituality in traditional Japanese heritage and embody a monument to a certain Japanese aura. The question I want to ask concerns the relation between the monumental style, its embodiment in the film medium, and the historical moment that called it forth. Which factor, the medium or the moment, has prior explanatory claim for the rise of this most powerful evocation of Japanese identity? What purposes does the monumental style serve with respect to the prewar militarist context, to the history of Japanese film, and to the workings of the individual monumental film? Answering this question requires some historical backtracking.

The 1930s was a time when the stakes in defining "Japaneseness" were never higher. Due to escalating military involvement in Manchuria and China, the balance of power in Northeast Asia (and eventually the entire East Pacific rim) depended upon the durability of the imperial Japanese aura. This aura, first conceived as a means for mobilizing support for the Meiji restoration, incubated into a near mythological elaboration during the formative decades of Japan's first sustained contact with the outside world. The rudiments of Japanese aura consist in the emperor ideology, the family-state, and the unbroken lineage of the two that ultimately functions as a cosmology, a story about the origins of the (Japanese) world. In the late nineteenth century the emperor ideology was formally promulgated, along with a Confucian notion of the family-state as the continuation of an imperial line that extends to the Sun Goddess. The 1882 Imperial Rescript to Soldiers and Sailors, recited by soldiers in the Pacific War, and the 1890 Imperial Rescript on Education, memorized by generations of schoolchildren, are prototypes of a state-sanctioned ideology of Japanese identity.[4]

By the beginning of the Showa era in 1926, the mystique of Japanese identity was undergoing a revival as it was adapted to the relatively new mass media of radio and film. Cinema, especially talking pictures, presented the most vivid pictures yet of what it meant to be Japanese. The accessibility of cinema was attached to calls for a "Showa restoration" to complete the process of imperial consolidation started in Meiji but allegedly derailed by the machinations of oligarchs and capitalists. Japan's occupation of Manchuria in 1931 marked the beginning of a gradual withdrawal from the community of democratic nations, along with a gradual escalation of nationalism and xenophobia.

At the same time, the movies started to talk and an occasion presented itself for politically utilizing the power of cinema to express the imperial Japanese aura. As 1930s nationalism gradually intensified, cinematic pictures of Japaneseness became less fluid. Samurai films began to shed the unself-conscious flamboyance of earlier *chambara* potboilers, in which ill-mannered swordslingers jumped into pitched battles with flashing, clanging (*chan, chan! bara, bara!*) swords. Cosmopolitan urban Japanese, whose heroes were Harold Lloyd no less than Bando Tsumasaburo, were addicted to Western music, clothes, and movies throughout the early 1930s.[5] The ways in which their preoccupations were woven into the social fabric and into the film industry are described in chapter 3.

Harold Lloyd's *Fuku no Kami*
(*For Heaven's Sake*, 1926).
Private collection.

In the late 1930s prewesternized Japanese tradition became something to be guarded, respected, and eventually fixed into a quite rigid portrait of traditional Japanese life, with all the spontaneousness of a stuffed trophy. Japaneseness itself was codified, meticulously packaged, and carefully distributed throughout the empire to sustain people in their support of the war in China. The films that fulfilled this function most clearly were *kokusaku* (national policy) films. They show an idealized, official picture of Japanese life and behavior in the 1930s as it was seen by ministries of education, culture and propaganda. Kokusaku films also exhibit an idealized, official picture of traditional Japan set in Tokugawa history (*jidai geki,* "historical period drama") and within this group are films in the monumental style.

    The monumental style was a backlash against "excessive" Westernization as well as a response to the nationalism mandated by the war regime. These films are important for the clarity of their pictures of Japaneseness, but also for their innovations in film style. Filmmakers took up the challenge of expressing an unadulterated Japanese ethos in a medium inextri-

Bando Tsumasaburo as the
blind swordsman in *Mumeijigoku*
(*Hell of Darkness*, Shochiku,
1926). Private collection.

cably linked to Western technology and style. The simplistic didacticism
of propaganda techniques was used in newsreels, documentaries, and patriotic pictures, but the most prestigious kokusaku films, including those in
the monumental style, tried to complement their indigenous subject matter with a unique style.

Tanizaki Jun'ichiro precisely summed up the difficulty of synthesizing
Japanese aesthetics with Western technology in his classic 1933 elegy for
traditional Japanese sensibilities, *In'ei Raisan* (*In Praise of Shadows*).[6] His statement on the problem that the monumental style tried to solve is so eloquent that it deserves quotation at length:

> One need only compare American, French, and German films
> to see how greatly nuances of shading and coloration can vary
> in motion pictures. In the photographic image itself, to say
> nothing of the acting and the script, there somehow emerge
> differences in national character. If this is true even when iden-

tical equipment, chemicals, and film are used, how much better
our own photographic technology might have suited our com-
plexion, our facial features, our climate, our land. And had we
invented the phonograph and the radio, how much more faithfully they would reproduce the special character of our voices
and our music. Japanese music is above all a music of reticence,
of atmosphere. When recorded, or amplified by a loudspeaker,
the greater part of its charm is lost. In conversation, too, we prefer the soft voice, the understatement. Most important of all are
the pauses. Yet the phonograph and radio render these moments
of silence utterly lifeless. And so we distort the arts themselves
to curry favor for them with the machines. These machines are
the inventions of Westerners, and are, as we might expect, well
suited to Western arts. But precisely on this account they put
our own arts at a great disadvantage.

   Tanizaki precisely identifies the cross-cultural conundrum of film and
other reproductive technologies. The recording of images on film is the
solution to a long series of Western problems, from the invention of flexible celluloid to the fixing of photochemical impressions on a treated surface to the mathematical calculations of perspective drawing. The artistic application of such technology is bound to be clumsy, says Tanizaki,
in a culture whose artistic practices have nothing to do with the technical problems of the West. How can Japanese film expect to produce
pleasing works out of a mongrel pastiche of cultural and technological
incompatibles? Tanizaki, however, underestimated the ingenuity of Japanese filmmakers.
   What is remarkable about the monumental style is its "bending" of the
language of classical Western cinema to accommodate the undulations of
classical Japanese design and behavior. These textual features contrast with
the usual Japanese proclivity for lopping off Japanese practices to accommodate a Western coffin. In technique as well as subject matter the films
aim to return the lost advantage to Japanese arts. The films enact a canonization of history, an emphasis on indigenous art forms and design, and a
corresponding technical repertoire of long takes and long shots, very slow
camera movements, and a highly ceremonial manner of blocking, acting,
and set design. The monumental style sets out to transform Japanese tradition from a cultural legacy into a sacrament. Though its intended social
mission is propagandistic, its uncompromising rigor and severe moral
geometry outstrips its motivational utility for audiences used to chambara
and Hollywood melodrama. The monumental style is less propagandistic

than hieratic. Its textual features, then, show a remarkable adaptation of Western technology to Japanese forms of expression.

As films that express a prototypical version of "Japanism" in a mass medium, the monumental style's social functions are no less interesting. First, commercial cinema needs a mass audience, and cinematic pictures of Japaneseness were screened for rank-and-file Japanese, not just elite readers of cultural discourse. This is what gives the films a political utility and makes the monumental style a bearer of "transitive" Japaneseness, a matter of being Japanese *for* some purpose rather than just being Japanese. The Japanese mystique expressed by these films was one designed to galvanize support for the war. These films construct a role to be filled by one who is proud of his or her heritage and willing to sacrifice anything for Japan and the emperor. The monumental style lays out a space for a specific, essentially religious purpose of inspiring the faithful and fortifying the rectitude of their belief.

Second, the capital needed to make and distribute films is so great that any film industry will be organized and rationalized to maximize economy of means. Resources were so short in the Japan of the late 1930s, furthermore, that the film industry was drastically consolidated. The huge expense and corresponding influence of commercial cinema resulted in the state standing watch over studio heads with little more than market share on their minds. The National Mobilization Law of 1938 and the Film Law of 1939, as explained in chapter 3, allowed the Army and Home Ministry to set up a system of enhanced profitability through enhanced patriotism. In this way profit motive was utilized as a carrot for studios to use precensorship to ensure that its creative staff automatically incorporated politically acceptable sentiments. The studios would act on behalf of the state rather than championing artistic freedom on behalf of its artists. But most prominent directors, writers, and actors were already on government committees set up to activate war-conscious creative work (e.g., Mizoguchi Kenji). Though Mizoguchi's *Zangiku Monogatari* (*Story of the Last Chrysanthemum,* 1939) can hardly be called a war film, its style and ideology are consistent with the self-sacrifice called for on the homefront and its Ministry of Education award enhanced its market penetration.

Now, back to the central framing question of this discussion, the question that concerns the relation between textual features and the social functions of the monumental style. Can textual analysis of film style tell us something about the contextual conditions of stylistic change? Does analysis of film style reveal hitherto unnoticed aspects of historical context? The question implies a reversal of the assumption that historical context (social and intertextual) reveals something about individual artistic texts. Can we also assume the opposite? Does the work performed by artistic texts, like films, reveal something about their historical context that we would not otherwise know? Film history is usually practiced using a kind of parallelism, establishing connections between fictional worlds onscreen (texts) and the actual world contained in primary documents from the same period (contexts). It is deeply satisfying when we "discover" correspondences between film imagery and documented historical fact—when it looks as if film indeed reflects history. However, this sells film short. Films are themselves primary documents of history, and can reveal things about their time that other historical records might not. Their value surpasses the illustrative chores they are usually made to perform. This is crucial in a time of authoritarian control, when official print documentation of the period is tightly regulated and unrelentingly consistent. What satisfaction is there in discovering that propaganda films reflect the ultranationalistic ideology of the late 1930s? However, on finding masterpieces of aesthetic experimentation worthy of modernist cinema in any period or nation, made under the auspices of an authoritarian regime, this gives pause. Historically, the political climate in the late 1930s was repressive, and we expect its cultural products to go along: blunt, repressive morality tales admonishing subjects to love Japan and hate the enemy. We can find such films among Japanese propaganda, if that is what we seek, but can we also find films that perturb our received ideas not only about propaganda but about the broader political climate as well? This is not a question of film practice that somehow escapes or resists authoritarian directives but a willingness to allow artistic works to feed back into our historical frameworks. "History is never simply the surviving records of the past," Tom Gunning writes, "but always a creative and imaginative act of trying to understand the past, a belief that it says something to us."[7]

Can texts modify, even transform contextual horizon? The answer is yes, as long as we keep in mind that imperialist propaganda provided the occasion, or the arena, for the innovation of the monumental style. But that is not a sufficient condition for explaining its cinematic peculiarities. Simply identifying provenance is not the same as providing a functional explanation. There is something unique, or at least special, about the monumental style as it relates to other media and to other films. The stylistic figures of the monumental style *express* an imaginary Japaneseness, but just because the expression of these images was mandated by the authorities does not mean we have understood how monumental style works *in* and *on film*.

My argument rests on the assumption that specifically filmic representations of Japanese identity in the 1930s can reveal the composition of that identity—its structure, function, and intended effects—in ways that are not visible to more conventional historical investigations. Because of what film is—a sophisticated modern technology infused with Western modes of representation—a premodern, indigenous national identity was articulated and dispatched against the very modernity (and perhaps modernism) embedded in that technology. Monumental style is a major embodiment of this reiteration.

The monumental style works primarily with clusters of techniques and episodes, or stylistic complexes. It is impossible to define the style by reference to techniques alone, or to characteristic subjects alone, but by specific recurring combinations between the two. Most prominently, monumental style will find ways to incorporate traditional aesthetics into the films, not just as setting but as basic building blocks of the film's stylistic patterning. *Genroku Chushingura* (chapter 6) is the best example of this, especially in its articulation of space through the long take and camera movement. Sacramental depictions of the Japanese family system is another stylistic complex in the monumental style, and again it is Mizoguchi who weaves images and techniques of a Meiji kabuki family in *Story of the Last Chrysanthemum* (chapter 5). A Tokugawa family is the focus of Kumagai Hisatora's adaptation of Mori Ogai's *The Abe Clan*, one of the most notorious of the kokusaku history films; I have analyzed it in terms of its reconstitution of Tokugawa and Taisho history for use during the height of the war with China in 1938 (chapter 7). Finally, chapter 8 concerns postwar appropriations of Japanese history in specifically filmic terms. The stylistic features of monumentalism persisted long after the death of the ideology that gave it birth. In the early 1950s Kinugasa Teinosuke expropriates his own monumental work for presentation to the postwar American and European art cinema audience. Monumental techniques and issues persist through the 1980s and the present, when Kurosawa cannibalizes his earlier theatrical appropriations.

The dyad of film and history, technology and tradition, textual features and social function will reappear throughout this study. The tension here is also an institutional one that involves the study of an artistic medium as against the study of a national culture. It is important to maintain the fruitfulness of this dialectic rather than try to subsume one term to the other. The monumental style must, in the first instance, be defined according to its historical and ideological moorings, but how can we apprehend that historical moment, let alone come to some affinity with it, without picturing Japaneseness through the monumental style and imagining how it and similar expressions affect us? For this we need to analyze the narrative and stylistic patterning of the films using the sharpest tools available to film scholars. The monumental style is rooted in nationalist ideology of the late 1930s, but the history of that period is manifested aesthetically in its artifacts. *Picturing Japaneseness* is addressed both to historians of Japanese culture and film historians, in hopes that the former will find material rich in confirmation and confounding of historical generalities and the latter will discover specific texts and approaches to a historically overlooked national cinema.

Chapter 2 introduces the history and composition of national cinema as a problematic concept seemingly difficult to sustain in light of recent political upheavals and new historical work on early cinema and popular culture. As elusive as the national can be, I believe it is necessary not only as a heuristic device but as a construct made more real, not less, by its use by ruling elites and working subjects alike. While it is fashionable to mark the 1990s as a postnational age of fin-de-siècle anxiety, we will continue to see nationality provide much needed stability in the uncertainties of political and intellectual life. Chapter 3 presents historical information on the social and industrial background of the monumental style, while chapters 4–8 are devoted primarily to in-depth film analysis. These analyses are meant to "talk" to the historical material presented first, but the arguments about the films are intrinsic to each one individually. The films are not used instrumentally as vehicles of claims made about the urban culture or political changes taking place in the 1930s. The films are the primary object and sources of this study, including not only the classic monumental texts chosen for extended analysis but also the fifty-two prewar films from the Library of Congress that form a background to the emergence of the monumental style (see filmography). For historical background I have relied mostly on English language secondary sources, and primary historical documents that are available in English (the *Japan Times and Advertiser, Cinema Yearbook of Japan,* et al.). As is customary, Japanese names will appear surname first, with rare exceptions for well-known individuals (e.g., Sessue Hayakawa, Nagisa Oshima).

The stylistic complexes of the monumental style—appropriations of Japanese aesthetics, Tokugawa history, and the family system—add up to a powerful invocation of a sacred Japanese heritage. In the end, it is an appeal to the holiness of Japan, over against the secular blandishments of Western materialistic corruption. The monumental style is nothing if not a cinematic spiritualization of Japanese identity. In working with monumental style we are working with "home movies" of how nationalist ideologies of the late 1930s saw, or wanted to see, Japanese identity. This study seeks to expose how that spiritualization works, both onscreen and off. As one historian puts it, "Identity is not discovered, but constructed, and the Japanese are now reengaged in that enterprise."[8] We should not suppose that the Japanese ever ceased, or will cease, to be engaged in that enterprise.

2

In the Postnational Neighborhood There Are No Foreigners (Knock on Wood): Nation as Cine-Superstition

Japanese gangsters and global corporation [sic] have replaced nations and battle each other for the new gold of this future, information.

Laurence B. Chollet, "Second Sight"

"Nationalism" is the pathology of modern developmental history, as inescapable as "neurosis" in the individual, with much the same essential ambiguity attaching to it, a similar built-in capacity for descent into dementia, rooted in the dilemmas of helplessness thrust upon most of the world (the equivalent of infantilism for societies) and largely incurable.

Tom Nairn, *The Breakup of Britain*

Tom Nairn's fanciful characterization of nationalism as a kind of puerile regression must appear far different in a post-cold war light than when first written in the mid 1970s. Nationalism no longer has the vaguely rustic associations of the fundamentalist, now that so many imperial curtains have come down and nationalisms of every stripe are commonplace. Even a study of Japanese imperial cinema looks much less obscure in this light than when I first began in the mid-1980s. Since the breakup of the Soviet empire was so precipitous, it has left us scanning the historical horizon for signs of further temblors. A consciousness has taken hold attending to the diachronic and the developmental, the fast currents of politics and culture that daily augur further change. Today, ideas about nationality usually congregate around its cultural constructedness, like those about sexuality, gender, and race. Naturally, the contingency, and sometimes the arbitrariness of nationality is often invoked within the same lines of thought, particularly now when long-established geopolitical frameworks are in such disarray. It follows, then, that there is a millenarianist tinge to current writing about the national generally and national cinemas particularly. Much recent writing about national cinema assumes a stance of anticipated ("planned"?) obsolescence, and sometimes nostalgia, as a way to demythologize a cultural construction already on its last legs. What follows below are reflections on the historical situation of national cinema as a pulse-taking on ideas and visualizations of the national itself (anticipating apparitions of the postnational as a corollary to the postmodern). This is followed by an account of the critical provenance of the concept of national cinema, and a brief discussion of early Japanese cinema and its coveting of a national singularity. Throughout these reflections I try to maintain a bifocal historical vision emphasizing a contemporary anachronism: a mutual awareness of inheritance and legacy that tries to preserve a creative contingency to historical "progress."

There is something regressive about the postmodern atmosphere in which nationality is sometimes interrogated. Because the temporal equivalent of cut-and-paste pastiche is a montage of disparate historical moments, there is no moment to snip that is not already past. If modernism has a nostalgic side, lamenting the disappearance of Victorian verities and the virtual certitude of apocalypse, then postmodernism is carefully paranoid. Time marches on, as linear teleologies of historical progress are cheerfully jettisoned. Social formations of late capitalism may be moving irrevocably into a cul-de-sac, or they could be uneasily settling into a purgatory whose makeshiftness is daily more apparent. Another way of saying this is to take note of the suspicion that the provisional is permanent.

Take the case of nations as an example of postmodern imaginary geography. Exploration, appropriation, exploitation, colonialism, migration, war, holocaust, reconstruction, and reexploration of new markets are all-too-familiar activities that have led to the establishment and to the anticipated obsolescence of the nation-state. The imagined imminent disappearance of the nation-state fuels a feverish scholarly attention to the activities that constitute the formation of nations not just as political entities but as daily ways of interpellated socialization.[1] The alacrity with which we pursue the national is in proportion to the provisionality of the postnational. A fixation on the past is the only response to an inexplicable future. But there is no mourning of lost bearings. In contrast to the otherwise paranoid strain of postmodernity, postnational criticism of the nation-state is affirmative, emancipatory, even euphoric.[2]

Many writers have theorized the paranoid aspect of nationalism, the xenophobic intolerance of difference and impurity.[3] Because of a fixation at a narcissistic stage of development, the nation, the neighborhood, the family, and one's "personal space" can all be subject to virulent delusions of invasion by the Other. One reason this is a fruitful avenue of research is the almost compulsive insistence with which nationalism has masqueraded as the family and, sometimes, the individual body writ large.[4]

Current criticism of the national affirms the breakdown of such tenacious forms of imaginary coherence. Underway is a vigorous program of historiographical rewriting, which salvages shards of "high" nationalism for clues to postnational forms of affiliation and subject-formation. Despite, or because of, the explosion of post-cold war nationalisms, nationalism is often analyzed retrospectively, as if from a postnational lookout coolly surveying terrain that has already been traversed. However, the affirmation and euphoria that sometimes accompanies postnational theory and criticism is a refraction of the paranoia at the heart of nationalism and postmodernism alike. As we rewrite history to expose the cultural mechanisms of nationalization, we also efface other contemporary interpellations, or "hailings," rendered invisible by our retrospective preoccupations. "Underneath the ripples created by fashion," writes Kurt Forster,

> the thrust of history keeps changing the past, blocking one segment from view while raising another from obscurity. Recovery and repression occur in the communicating vessels of contemporary interests. At any moment the historical dynamics involve loss as well as discovery.[5]

Postmodern historiography delights in exposing the imaginary coherence of outmoded sexual, class, or national identities, but it is no less narcissistic than its objects. Because it is fixated on the archaeology of imaginary identities, postmodern subjectivity imagines itself as its object: fragmentary, dispersed, vestigial.

Moving images, film, video, and television, are canonical fodder for elaborations of the postmodern. Postmodern criticism of film and video is not only institutionalized in the academy and the museum, but film and video also serve as master tropes for other kinds of new historiography in the arts, humanities, and social sciences. Reconceptualizing the history of national cinema, therefore, should serve to mark some stages of the way to our current postmodern stage of perpetual provisionality.

This autumn morning I awoke to a radio report on the 1993 General Agreement on Tariffs and Trade that announced the suspension of further discussion between the U.S. and the European Community. There had been a deadlock with France over U.S. penetration of the French film and television market. The impasse consisted in the inability of the French and American delegation to see each other's positions, because of the incompatible terms with which each described their object. The Americans wanted more freedom for U.S. production companies to make and distribute American products in France, while the French saw this as debilitating to the French film industry and leading to the corruption of French culture. President Bill Clinton agreed to conclude the talks without further reference to the issue, gladly wrapping up the sessions with relief for the trade concessions already extracted. Representatives of the American entertainment industry were devastated. What could national culture possibly have to do with entertainment?

A Certain Euphoria

At a recent film conference entitled "National Cinemas Revisited,"[6] Martine Danan chaired a panel where she gave a paper called "The New Hollywave: France's Post-National Cinema." In it she considered the paradox of recent French cinema: an industry flourishing thanks to strong state support and a high international profile, but doing so at the expense of its distinctive regional and linguistic differences. New globally oriented French films are high-budget affairs with internationally recognized stars, cofinanced by companies in two or more countries, and often released in English, the dominant language of international entertainment. The French New Wave of the 1960s slouches toward Hollywood.

Danan saw the victory as Pyrrhic if the French film industry sacrificed what made it French (language, topicality, national traditions and aspirations) in order to appeal to audiences in Los Angeles, Tokyo, and Peoria. While maintaining a certain ironic ruefulness toward this state of affairs, her study of French postnational cinema augured a need for the resituation of film criticism along the lines of global capitalism. As the tang and bite of national distinctiveness fades from the screen, so the critic's palate must be adjusted to discern new, hitherto untasted cosmopolitan flavors.[7] This idea was typical of many of the panels at the conference: since the collapse of the three-world cosmology of the cold war, national identities have become unfixed, mutable, and open to redefinition. National film criticism should therefore take stock of this postnational fluidity and concentrate its energies on understanding, and perhaps encouraging, postnational film practice for its liberating potential.

Two issues stand out here, old and new. The old issue, dating from the

1920s, is the various ways and means of resisting Hollywood blandishments so that a healthy national cinema can be cultivated. This involves cultural policies like protectionism, quotas, incentives for talent, and investments in production and distribution. The new issue is a critical one: to what extent must contemporary criticism and theory follow the transnational styles forged by the global capitalist juggernaut that Hollywood thinks it commands, and probably does?[8] Given that historical criticism constructs national cinemas from a canon of nationally significant texts, tracking emerging "new waves" and pronouncing this or that period a golden age, does criticism exacerbate the homogenizing of national difference? Is national cinema already dead, or has postnational film criticism killed it?

Criticism of national cinema must resist the homogenizing tendencies of postnational critical paradigms, argued film historian and theorist Dudley Andrew, and to consider whether national and postnational cinema can coexist, whether national culture and global capitalism can coexist is already to propose a judgment on what kind of scholarship film historians and critics do.[9]

In this view national cinema and culture needs to be reconceived according to noncompetitive cultural values. Most writing on national cinema conceives it oppositionally against the background of a presumably non-national norm, i.e., Hollywood, the movie version of the classic realist text. "International cinema" always carries the mark of the national; here nationality is an issue, as opposed to a correspondingly unmarked notion of film (meaning Hollywood entertainment film). Until now Hollywood was the great Other against which national cinemas had to struggle to define and defend themselves. With the advent of the postnational the collision of these values (always to the advantage of the dominant background, Hollywood) is transcended. From now on Hollywood is less the altar from which emanate high-concept American-style opiates for the masses (against which genuinely national cinemas struggle in vain) than a memory, a postnational mode of production and marketing that generates its own masses as fodder for its economic maintenance.[10] This does not mean Hollywood, the place, the reputation, and the legacy, ceases to exist any more than genuinely French, Italian, Japanese, and Indian cinema fades away just because their most visible and lucrative films may be international coproductions. It remains only for scholars of national cinema to open their eyes and seek out the detours, cul-de-sacs, idiosyncracies, and contradictions within national cinemas and not be blinded by the glare of a homogenizing postnational Holly-wave.

As scholars and consumers of international film and culture, we are implicated in the languishing and death of national cinema, if it is in fact in its final throes. "Minerva's owl flies at dusk," as Eric Hobsbawm has it, and the recent explosion of literature on the nation and national cinema may be an antemortem toll for national cinema's demise.[11] In the postnational landscape, and especially in postcolonial regions, the obsolescence of nationality appears imminent because cultural and personal identities are now so often forged between and across national borders. With the pre-dominance of exile and diaspora, not to mention the electronic circulation of capital under the shell game of corporate multinationals, nationality has become mutable and mobile, like gender and class (race remains a more intransigent factor). Nationality now being subject to negotiation, rather than an ineluctable birthright, intellectuals champion this new opportunity for self-invention, particularly when it offers a chance to overthrow oppressive, outmoded categories of affiliation.

But this lugubrious dirge for the death of national cinema is reminiscent of the death of God or, more recently, the end of History. As a form of anticipatory nostalgia, it signals the ascendancy of a new era of criticism as commentary/commemoration/inauguration of an age of postnational cul-ture. There is a certain euphoria with which scholars relish postcolonial apocalypse in Hong Kong cinema, the amnesiac reconstructions of erst-while (sub)national identities, and the (dis)locations of hyphenated Amer-ican identities. The dominant rhetoric is one of barely restrained delirium. Everything is in crisis, in flux, up for grabs in a vertigo of postmodern frag-mentation (an unprecedented opportunity to wipe the slate clean). Had the simulation and pastiche of postnational cinema not been born of global capitalism, then postmodern criticism would have had to invent it. Judging from the hostility that greeted Dudley Andrew's anxiety over the future of national cinema studies (a jeremiad that called on the scholarly community to reconsider its celebrations of the fruits of global capitalism), one might be forgiven for thinking that this congregation had an interest in the aban-donment of some presumably outmoded paradigm.[12]

Like the "mourning" of prohibition in the early 1930s, the revisiting of national cinema is really the commemoration of an era coming to a close. It is the memorial gesture itself, however, that closes it. Postnational crit-icism is a perlocutionary, rearward anticipation of a visit to a new terri-tory configured by the inadequacies of outmoded tools. It is as if we were rushing toward some as yet unknown destination full speed in reverse, one eye on the rearview mirror and the other on a nineteenth-century survey map.

The characterization of postnational criticism as nearly hysterical farewell to geopolitical civilization as we know it is itself slightly hyperbolic. But there continue to be thousands of human casualties in struggles over the redrawing of nations and ethnic identities. This is reality, not hyperbole. Wherever there are ongoing "salvage" operations of national, or pseudonational, hegemony, there is tension and violence, not just in the Balkans, the Middle East, Tibet, and Somalia. When so many people die within the shifting fault lines of national and ethnic definitions, it is too soon to celebrate the postnational as a liberating process or state of affairs.[13] To clarify our current provisional situation, we might better retrace our past formulations and uses of the concept of national cinema.

Bringing National Cinema Back Home

If the foregoing emphasizes the historical ambivalence of postnational criticism, I would like to be schematic here and sketch out three ways to think of national cinema. These are not full-fledged models so much as assumptions people, and critics, use when talking about films, literature, and cultural artifacts of countries other than their own.[14] We usually conjure up specific images from books, movies/television, and newspapers when the conversation turns to national culture, particularly in a lack of personal acquaintance with the countries discussed. These images are intertextual raw material we employ to grapple with questions of nation, nationalism, and national cinema. The following models are the frameworks, or schemata, with which this raw material can be organized and tested against the flood of new material that deluges us every day. They are the *reflectionist,* the *dialogic,* and the *contamination* models.

The reflectionist model dates from the 1960s, the "golden age" of national cinemas.[15] This period saw major "new waves" from cadres of independent directors in France, Germany, Brazil, and Japan. With the onset of the student movement these New Wave directors, like Jean-Luc Godard and Nagisa Oshima, were politically engaged, and created films, production teams, and audiences outside the commercial mainstream. The New German Cinema of Rainer Werner Fassbinder, Wim Wenders, and Alexander Kluge rode a similar wave of protest and activism. Roman Polanski and Andrzej Wajda were making their first works in Poland. In Eastern Europe directors Dusan Makaveyev, Jiri Menzel, Milos Forman, and Miklos Jancsó made scathing, subversive works in Yugoslavia and Czechoslovakia before and after the Soviet occupation of Prague in 1968. Sergei Paradjanov and Andrei Tarkovsky made their best early films in the same period even though it often took years for the Soviet authorities to allow their work to be screened. In India, Africa, the Caribbean, Latin America, and the U.S.

films were made and shown to audiences galvanized by the possibility of economic and artistic alternatives.[16]

The reflectionist model of national cinema emerged because film critics were poised to write about this explosion of cinematic experimentation in relation to the social and political cultures from which it arose. New ways of talking and writing about film were devised not only to elucidate the provenance of the films but also to analyze the infinite variety of cinematic expressions used to represent the cultural landscape onscreen.

Granted, national styles and characteristics had been duly noted and discussed since the silent era, and Siegfried Kracauer's *From Caligari to Hitler* (1947) is based upon a specifically national analysis of film subjects and themes. But it was in the 1960s, with the European art cinema, that formal traits were explicitly linked with national artistic traditions. Rather than emphasizing the recurrence of certain imagery within a national rubric, critics now explored the national associations of representational modes and conventions, mediated by the artistic choices of auteurs. Kracauer never emphasized auteurs or their formal choices.

In grappling with the difficulties of international films, critics needed to draw a distinction between conventions used by filmmakers through their national artistic traditions and those invented through directorial signature. To appreciate Mizoguchi's wrenching stories of sacrificial women, for instance, it was helpful to know that he was updating nineteenth-century melodramas called *shimpa* as well as pursuing his ongoing personal obsession with the "gait and swoon" of the Japanese woman oppressed.[17] The delineation of national and personal style went hand in hand. While it was auteurism (*Cahiers du cinema*, Andrew Sarris, Robin Wood, et al.) that captured the industry's and the public's attention, the fact that auteurs had national affiliation established another field for classification, analysis, and distribution. If artists have citizenship, then art movies do too.

It did not take very long for the European art cinema to become established as a movement, thanks to the auteurist policy that championed it. With the accumulation of serious criticism, festival retrospectives, independent distribution, and journals (and university film courses),[18] the European and American film industries gradually retooled to accommodate the financing and distribution of art films. After a while even the most casual moviegoers learned to ask the questions, "Who directed it?" with "What country is it from?" close behind (especially if that country was not Western European and the director's name was difficult to say).

The dialogic model of national cinema is one that emphasizes its similarities and differences to other works, usually from Western cinema. For instance, a reflectionist model would see Brazilian film in culturally specific terms: a representation of Sao Paulo or the *favellas* first and a film by Hector Babenco second. A dialogic model, on the other hand, might analyze *Pixote* (1981) in terms of Italian neorealism, Luis Buñuel, and perhaps film noir. Even better, it would bring up less proximate references to Gabriel García Márquez and Cervantes, resulting in an intertextual conversation of allusion and influence that conveys the dialectic of artistic process.[19] (Mikhail Bakhtin's account of heterogeneous speech, or heteroglossia, is an important after-the-fact theoretical prop for this model of national cinema.)[20]

A dialogic model takes for granted the internationalization of art cinema. It is hard to imagine how a dialogic model could arise without the reflectionist before it, not only because it is a stance of mediation or bridging that seeks out comparative relations between different cultures but also because its objects are in themselves thoroughly heterogeneous. The model is dialogic because films like *Tampopo* (Japan, Juzo Itami, 1986), *The Road Warrior* (Australia, George Miller, 1981), *The Icicle Thief* (Italy, Maurizio Nichetti, 1989), and *Brazil* (U.K., Terry Gilliam, 1985) are, in their very conception, dialogic. Films like these could not have been made without the institutionalization of national cinema inaugurated by the European art cinema.

While the formative years of national cinema and the reflectionist model provided vast reserves of cultural material for (Western) criticism to work through,[21] the last fifteen years have seen a galvanizing and cross-fertilization through the perpetuating institutions of home video, transnational broadcasting, and international film festivals. (N.B.: a popular base of university film courses supported by noncommercial distribution and serious film criticism is no longer the factor that it was in the 1960s and 1970s.)

The contamination model posits an international consciousness inseminating the film industries of all countries from the moment of their inception.[22] National cinemas do not lose their distinctiveness because of a lapse from some prior Edenic national identity. The contamination model sees cinema as an institution that is profoundly, inescapably *inter*national. Comparative histories of the birth of cinema indicate that tinkerers, scientists, and artists in America, England, France, Germany, and Russia were working on similar technical problems (pull-through mechanism/shutter, intermittent motion, flexible film stock) at about the same time (1870–1895).[23] Furthermore, their work was hastened by an awareness of their counterparts in other countries, as in the rivalry between Edison in America, Lumière in France, and Robert Paul in England.[24]

If the birth and initial growth of motion pictures was a competitive affair

between inventors and entrepreneurs in different countries, national cinemas are not born pristine and later become poly-, trans-, or internationalized, like some long-lost stone age tribe, but are "always already" touched
by other cultures. This is evident from all the places that were almost
instantaneously exposed to Lumière's cinematographe:

> Starting in February [1895] in London, an avalanche of foreign
> *cinématographe* premieres began. Within six months after the
> Paris opening the *cinématographe* was launched by the Lumière
> organization in England, Belgium, Holland, Germany, Austria,
> Hungary, Switzerland, Spain, Italy, Serbia, Russia, Sweden, the
> United States—and soon thereafter in Algeria, Tunisia, Egypt,
> Turkey, India, Australia, Indochina, Japan, Mexico. Within two
> years Lumière operators were roaming on every continent
> except Antarctica.[25]

The colonialist catalog quoted here reveals not only (the intended)
active cinematographe "roaming on every continent" but also, at the
moment of exposure, an automatic, passive inscription of cinematographic
modes with marks and striations from other places. The avalanche
metaphor is unsuitable, because avalanches are not affected by the topog-
raphy they engulf.

National cinema is a promiscuous notion, both historically and conceptually. The idea of national cinema as expression of a distinct sovereign
identity is a relatively recent one, compared with the unhampered flow of
films across national boundaries for twenty years before World War I.[26]
From the beginning cinema was incorrigibly cross-cultural, or at least
cross-national. This is what led film industries in France, Germany, Japan,
England, and other countries in the 1920s to protect their domestic markets, to discourage talent from emigrating, and to articulate the idea of
national cinema as a bulwark *against* the encroachments of Hollywood,
Moscow, or Paris.[27] National cinema is not just some limpid reflection of
personality or politics. We could then reconceive the nation as an effect of
technologies and institutions like cinema, rather than a preexisting thing
that expresses itself by cinematic means.[28] The concept of "national cinema" itself, if at first sight it appears slightly aloof and spinsterish, was actually devised to guard the integrity of a home identity against the fear of rav-
ishment by irresistible barbarians.[29] It is as if the national defined itself
through cultural technologies that anticipated, or even initiated, its own
future dilution or contamination: "One might go so far as to say that the
state imagined its local adversaries, as in an ominous prophetic dream, well

before they came into historical existence," in Benedict Anderson's words.[30]

Of the three models sketched above, it is the oldest one, the reflectionist, that is the most hermetic. It should not be too surprising that the model from the "golden age" of national cinema should be the one that seeks the purest possible distillation of national form and *Geist* in cinema. The other two, dialogic and contamination, routinely assume the existence and the necessity, respectively, of narrative and stylistic miscegenation between national cultures and across media.

Because national cinema is necessarily defined against a background set, all three models construct a form of alterity, which functions as a foil to set off the primary concept. All three engage and construct "Hollywood" as a mode of production. By Hollywood I mean a streamlined system of industrial production, distribution, and marketing. This system has a centrifugal effect on consumption (an ever widening circle of influence on audiences) and a corresponding centripetal vortex for talent and technical expertise. Others call this the "Institutional Mode of Representation" or "Classical Hollywood Cinema."[31] While these terms differ in their connotations, they both basically refer to American(-style) cinema in its most orthodox commercial manifestation as mainstream studio entertainment.

It bears repeating that "Hollywood" is not the same as Hollywood, the movie town in Los Angeles. The streamlined factory system of the vertically integrated Hollywood of old is visible more in Hong Kong and Bombay than in Hollywood. Ironically, the further one gets from the geographical Hollywood the less likely exceptions to it can be found.[32] Still, there is a "language" of conventional formulae and industrial protocols, forged in the 1920s—in Hollywood, U.S.A.—and codified in the 1930s, that still functions in some form as the lingua franca of cinematic discourse. This is what I mean by Hollywood: as shorthand or, perhaps, metonymy for an almost universally understood code of moving imagery and industrial organization.[33]

Imagine a Hollywood deluge as universal code, not just as foreign profiteer, and one has a better sense of what motivates the jealous circumscription of national identity through cinema. The potential loss of traditional folklore, linguistic specificity, and "national ethos" is enough to mobilize efforts to protect the home identity through national articulation and codification. It is galling enough to contemplate profits flowing out into the coffers of foreign investors, but the thought that the accumulated experience of generations, and the forms that contain them will be forsaken—not necessarily through racist programs of suppression, but through mere expediency—this is a powerful threat. The national, naturally, becomes a site of contestation, a power struggle, but it is only through contestation that it emerges as an articulated identity.

Hollywood is not the only Other, but it is the most universal. National cinemas react against other arts from the past, like the kabuki stage from which the earliest Japanese films emerged or disreputable ethnic ancestors from which a "true" national cinema might wish to dissociate itself. In the case of Indonesian cinema a racial amnesia disavows any kinship with a film industry run by ethnic Others. Indonesian film historians have dated the beginning of their national cinema in 1950, when Usmar Ismail ("the father of Indonesian cinema") made the first non-Chinese Indonesian film. Chinese Indonesians, however, had been making films since 1929.[34] These were not considered Indonesian films because their producers were not considered true, i.e., ethnic Malay, Indonesians. The same periodization of disavowal is at work in accounts of the Malaysian film industry. Nevertheless, the Chinese are credited with the precedent for making films almost exclusively about the upper classes. These films from the 1930s were supposed to distract attention from the (putatively Chinese) exploitation of the (usually Malay) working classes. When a "true" Indonesian film industry started up in the 1950s, it nevertheless continued to follow the bad habit of making only upper-class melodrama.[35]

Hollywood, the supranational institutionalized discourse of economic, representational, and social exchange, functions and is recognized as a language of central administration. That is to say, it is a language of power. Its efficiency as industrial organization and immediacy as visual and narrative legibility makes it almost irresistible to consumers and investors alike. In the movement toward a postnational world (actively promoted by Hollywood industrial policies and textual practices), it is functionally analogous to the King's English, High German, Central Thai, and Examination Chinese in their respective periods, and, following this analogy, we might call this discourse the royal code of moving pictures.[36]

Though all three models, reflectionist, dialogic, and contamination, are useful depending on texts and historical periods, I believe they are convincing to the extent that they do not reify, i.e., to materialize, for the purpose of disavowing, the royal code. The reason why a postnational, postcolonial critical position is so attractive is that it consigns the old, royal order firmly to the past.[37] But as with the repressed, it returns with a vengeance when it has been disavowed, transcended, and supposedly eliminated.

It is the reflectionist model, the most hermetic and exclusivist of the three, that reacts most strongly against the royal code yet backhandedly reinforces it. Historically, national cinema stepped into a vacuum left by

Hollywood in the 1960s, when the American film industry was in some disarray. The European art cinema, non-Western cinemas, and independent productions came into their own when the royal code was unraveling. The dialogic and contamination models, however, are more pluralistic, less oppositional in the way they conceive of national cinemas.

In order for languages of power to work as tools of administrative centralization, there must be a state of relatively unfettered capitalism, a new technology capable of simultaneous communication to a market of thousands, perhaps millions, and "the fatality of human linguistic diversity."[38] These are three factors stipulated by Benedict Anderson in his analysis of language, power, and the rise of national consciousness in the sixteenth century as forerunners of "imagined communities." To continue this metaphor of the royal code, it was the *general* condition of irremediable linguistic diversity" that was crucial. "Particular languages can die or be wiped out," writes Benedict, "but there was and is no possibility of humankind's general linguistic unification."[39] Precisely because spoken languages were irremediably diverse and numerous, came the establishment of central print languages for purposes of administrative control.

It is intriguing to speculate on the fatality of human *perceptual* diversity as a consequence of the invention of motion pictures in the nineteenth century. Could there have been perceptual "vernaculars," traces of which can be seen in films made before the Nickelodeon, that were completely overrun by the universalizing path of the royal code? In the beginning there was "terror in the aisles," as apocryphal patrons ran "howling and fleeing in impotent terror before the power of the machine," i.e., from Lumière's oncoming *Arrival of a Train at the Station.* [40] This putative confusion of the imaginary with the real could hardly serve as the basis for a visual Esperanto, as D. W. Griffith had hoped, let alone a centralizing language of power.

The royal road to universality required a "linearization of the iconographic signifier" (Noel Burch), which came with Griffith's codification of continuity editing (selectively adapted from Dickens's narrative parallelism) along with the insertion of expository and dialogue titles.[41] In the 1920s film industries around the world consolidated around national affiliation, as Hollywood came to threaten war-torn domestic film industries. Finally, the linguistic linearization of cinema arrived with the perfection of synchronized dialogue in the late 1920s, which solidified the position of film industries on national and nationalist grids. By the 1930s national cinemas were actively engaged in the propaganda and hostilities of what would become World War II. This further refined received perceptions of national distinctiveness (stereotypes), a process especially striking in Japanese cinema and that of the other wartime combatants.

The fatality of human perceptual diversity is fulfilled, then, in a royal process of linearizing, rationalizing, and "refining" cinema to make it more like a diegetic language.[42] As cinemas around the world contracted toward national specificity, they often became more like one another. To husband cinema within the national was but another step in the institutionalization of movies as middle-class amusements that coveted the mantle of artistry.[43] Cinema as national is doubly rationalized: at once standardization of movies in their production protocols and prophylaxis against outside depredation. A process that included the adaptation of high literature and drama, the narrative elegance of the Griffith codes, and the absorption of spectators' attention in the "invisible" continuity system was extended by the alignment of film along national coordinates. Furthermore, the efficacy of film as propaganda, together with aggressive and defensive struggles for foreign markets between the two world wars, elevated its status as a powerful shaper of popular perception. What was once an ephemeral fairground amusement had proven itself capable of public (i.e., national) service. During World War I, this statement was issued by President Woodrow Wilson on the formation of a film division within the Creel Committee:

> It is in my mind not only to bring the motion-picture industry into the fullest and most effective contact with the nation's needs, but to give some measure of official recognition to this increasingly important factor in the development of our national life. The film has come to rank as the very highest medium for the dissemination of public intelligence, and since it speaks a universal language, it lends itself importantly to the presentation of America's plans and purposes.[44]

But to return to Lumière's train, the prototypical astonishment of those nineteenth-century spectators may not have been a quaint confusion or naïveté. It may have been wonder at the *power* of a new illusion, the latest in a long line of fairground amusements like the camera obscura, stereopticon, and magic lantern. Instead of a primitive confusion, this reveals "a cinema of attractions" that has its own slightly shady history running alongside and beneath the royal code: "If the first spectators screamed," writes Tom Gunning, "it was to acknowledge the power of the apparatus to sweep away a prior and firmly entrenched sense of reality."[45]

The special power of the apparatus is where the irremediable diversity of human perception is remedied. It has the peculiar power to amaze, shock, sometimes repulse, and confound. With the irresistible technological virtuosity of "special effects," the impossible is there, before our eyes. This is an appeal that is primal, older than pleasures of narrative absorption, deeper than raptures at the sight of our favorite star. It is the stark confrontation of human perception with inanimate animation, an immaculate perception once found only in miracles and epiphanies.

Stars have nationalities, but the biggest, like Chaplin or Garbo, are beyond that. The mothlight attraction to spectacle, like the thrill of the roller-coaster and the surprise of a hologram, is "beneath" nationality, because it appeals primarily to the body. A national cinema is made up of films and people that have foreign fingerprints all over them—fingerprints not only from other countries, but from "foreign" arts, enterprises, and personal histories. Break a national cinema down far (and far back) enough, and it is all foreign. The best way to speak of national cinema, I believe, is to find inimitable styles in which these common elements are selected, combined, and polished to fulfill some national wish.

Sonno Joi: *Revere the Emperor, Out With the Barbarians*

I will not dwell on the cliché that holds Japanese cinema to be a limit case in otherness, only to recollect Ruth Benedict's opening statement in *The Chrysanthemum and the Sword*: "The Japanese were the most alien enemy the U.S. had ever fought in an all-out struggle."[46] And also, perhaps, to parallel the belatedness of the West's "discovery" of Japanese cinema with the relative tardiness of Japan's forced accommodation to Western technology and ideology. The Westernization of Japanese politics and culture accelerates throughout the twentieth century; in the 1930s it does not abate so much as expresses itself in ethnocentric terms. World War II served to "realienate" Japan all over again (launching countless Western careers), just when Japanese military-industrial might was attaining an intolerable likeness to the Great Powers of western imperialism. This is unlike centuries-old forms of colonial domination, which, however brutal they may be, do not have the novelty of being alien, except as alien to human rights. Notice, too, the symptomatic emphasis on the barbarian in the nineteenth-century slogan for the shogun's overthrow and the restoration of the imperial state (not "Down with the shogun"). With the cry of *Sonno Joi* (Revere the emperor, expel the barbarians), Meiji restorationists ushered in an unprecedented deluge of barbarian ways and means.

If this deluge began around 1860 and included the enthusiastic reception of movies at the turn of the century as one of its most incorrigible aspects, a comprehensive survey of Japanese film appeared only one hundred years later. This was Joseph Anderson and Donald Richie's *The Japanese Film: Art and Industry*. This book, along with Noel Burch's *To the Distant Observer: Form and Meaning in the Japanese Cinema* (1979), remains, after all these years, the standard English language history of Japanese film.

Anderson, Richie, and Burch all try to explain Japanese film as an outgrowth of a preexistent, relatively unchanging essence. Anderson and Richie, working within a traditional reflectionist model, want to naturalize Japanese film by performing a hermeneutic operation, demystifying what the uninitiated take to be its obscurities and weaknesses. They situate Japanese differences in a psychosocial realm and reconcile them to Western thinking by conforming them to principles congenial to Western aesthetics (e.g., realism, psychological depth, poetic values specific to Japan, etc.).

If Anderson and Richie try to naturalize Japanese film by arguing for its specifically Japanese "realism," Burch finds in it a material critique of Hollywood. This shows Burch to be using a dialogic model of national cinema. He finds in Japanese film a repository of alternative film techniques (fragmentation and materiality of the signifier, nonlinear narrative structures, polysemy and intertextuality), which coalesces with his anti-Hollywood, avant-garde agenda. In fact, Burch's construction of a Japanese mode of representation takes shape largely as a denial or at least a departure from basic features of Western representation (making it redolent of ethnocentrism).

While Burch works within a dialogic model, it is striking that Japanese film is used as a stick with which to beat the royal horse of Hollywood, which Burch refers to as the previously named institutional mode of representation. Although it is clearly a dialogic, oppositional model of national cinema, Burch's book is a limit case in the hypostasizing of the royal code. Of swish-pans and dissolves, those "flashy" techniques beloved by the sword fight movies of the early 1930s, Burch writes, they are what "makes these films appear so 'deconstructive' of the codes that dominate our cinema. . . . The bourgeois codes are *thrifty*. . . . *What was a mass cultural attitude in Japan was a deeply subversive vanguard practice in the Occident*."[47] He stands in awe of a mass popular cinema that is so profligate, extravagant, even incoherent. Most important, it exemplifies the radical distancing devices of the Western avant-garde. So he establishes a new canon of Japanese masterpieces (from the 1930s, but with many of the same directors celebrated before) absorbed into the poststructuralist critique of logocentric Western culture.

But what if the makers of those sword fight potboilers got those swish-pans and dissolves from Douglas Fairbanks, Mack Sennett, and Harold Lloyd? It is well known that American slapstick comedy, Westerns, and action programmers played very well to Japanese audiences as early as 1915 and that Japanese directors of sword fight movies borrowed liberally from their gags and technical tricks.[48] This is consistent with Burch's position that these films selectively and rather haphazardly appropriated Western devices, but to argue that their effect was to deconstruct Western codes of composition and narrative legibility really tells us nothing of Japanese cinema, i.e., how it functioned in Japan.

More revealing is to consider the reception of these films, imagining the circumstances of their exhibition and excavating contemporary public discussions of their effects. To be sure, Burch is only one in a long, venerable line of Westerners (Burch aligns himself with Roland Barthes's *L'Empire des signes*) who find in the Orient some provocation or confirmation of their own ideas, dreams, and pursuits. Frank Lloyd Wright's autobiography is a case in point:

> I saw the native home in Japan as a supreme study in elimination—not only of dirt, but the elimination of the insignificant. So the Japanese house naturally fascinated me and I would spend hours taking it all to pieces, and putting it together again. I saw nothing meaningless in the Japanese home and could find very little added in the way of ornament because all *ornament* as we call it, they get out of the way. The necessary things are done by bringing out and polishing the beauty of the simple materials they used in making the building. Again, you see, a kind of cleanliness.
>
> At last I had found one country on earth where simplicity, as natural, is supreme. The floors of these Japanese homes are all made to live on—to sleep on, to kneel and eat from, to kneel upon soft silken mats and meditate upon. On which to play the flute, or to make love. . . . Strangely enough, I found this ancient Japanese dwelling to be a perfect example of the modern standardizing I had myself been working on.[49]

Frank Lloyd Wright's enthusiasm for the modularity of Japanese design is helpful as an intervention into Western architectural history, but "elimination of the insignificant" cannot serve as an immanent description of Japanese design within its own history and practices.

Consider Herbert Muschamp's acid assessment of the Orientalist misappropriation of modular Japanese design by the international style: "It seems very high, very pure. . . . [But] History is already laughing up its sleeve at the material prostitution of Eastern ideas by the West, the art of kidnapping empty forms of which Wright was an early master. The temple wind chimes that provide one man with cosmic inspiration are the source of his neighbor's insomnia."[50] Muschamp's tittering "History" is presumably Western architectural history, which in hindsight cannot reproduce the once exotic allure of the East any more than emotions recollected in tranquillity by a homesick Asian picture bride now "home" in the States with her American GI.

How, then, did Japanese filmmakers and critics regard the incipient Japaneseness of their movies in the years before the Great Kanto Earthquake of 1923? In a prophetic gesture they decided to sell it abroad. Although it sounds incredible in hindsight, some Japanese producers hoped to attract hordes of enthralled Caucasian spectators in the same way that Hollywood and European spectaculars sold millions of tickets in Tokyo and Osaka. Embarrassed by the comparison between Japanese and foreign products, filmmaker-producer Kaeriyama Norimasa and others started a campaign, the *Jun'eigageki undo*, or Pure Film Movement. According to A. A. Gerow, who has done remarkable cultural studies on Taisho film history, the Japanese Pure Film Movement was an early formulation of a protonational cinema concept.[51] The movement above all wished to dissociate Japanese film from its reliance on the staple of Japanese photoplays, canned kabuki theater. During the " 'teens, they sought to introduce close-ups, actresses rather than female impersonators, and dynamic action sequences to rivet audiences' eyes to the screen, adopting universal editing patterns understandable by 'anyone, anywhere.' "[52] They reviled the *benshi* (screenside lecturers) as holdovers from the days of the *yose* variety hall, who sometimes dominated the images with their unpredictable commentary, jokes, and voiceovers. At the same time some magazines actually ran articles in English fawning over the *benshi* as picturesque curiosities from old Japan, with plaintive appeals to foreign readers not to write off Japanese movies.

These efforts to court an international market met with alarm and ridicule within the established domestic market. Dominated by exhibition chains and a powerful benshi lobby, Kaeriyama and his supporters were "ahead of their time," as a reflectionist model like *The Japanese Film* has it, but they actually mirrored other projections of the nation, particularly that of Hollywood. "What then constituted a true Japanese cinema to reformers was one able to expand into new territory and compete in foreign markets," writes Gerow. "Recognition by the foreign Other was then essential."[53] To become Japanese, Japanese cinema had to make overtures to foreign recognition as a prelude to seduction of foreign markets. The films had to shed their provincial trappings and put on the "high-class" garb (*kokyu*) of the universal commodity—the royal code.

Adolph Zukor formed the Famous Players company in 1912 to borrow ready-made respectability from legitimate theater. But the Pure Film Movement aimed to give Japanese film respectability through cinematic specificity, to dissociate cinema from kabuki theater while maintaining the ties to period settings and samurai characters that gave it national specificity. Kabuki films, which dominated the Japanese film industry from 1900 to 1910, were inimical to the recasting of the Japanese industry as a national cinema because they were "canned" for consumption by the masses. Kabuki films and *kyugeki* (early sword fight films) were doubly adulterated because of their contamination by the stage and by their working-class audience who could not afford to attend legitimate kabuki performances. At the same time samurai dramas were singled out as potential carriers of Japanese distinction, partly to counteract the "insulting" influence of Sessue Hayakawa.[54]

Subsequently, studios held up Hollywood and European spectaculars as cinematic standards par excellence, yet retained firm control of the burgeoning film industry in domestic hands. Both Shochiku and Taikatsu studios were formed expressly to emulate the filmmaking practice (and profits) of foreign companies.[55] Upon Shochiku's formation in 1920, it proclaimed, "The main purpose of this company will be the production of artistic films resembling the latest and most flourishing styles of the Occidental cinema; it will distribute these both at home and abroad; it will introduce the true state of our national life to foreign countries; and it will assist in international reconciliation both here and abroad."[56] This was a declaration of independence from the old-fashioned kabuki staples of Nikkatsu.

After the Great Kanto Earthquake of 1923, Hollywood silents were wildly popular, so much so that a boycott called to protest the anti-Asian U.S. immigration act of 1924 failed after just a few days.[57] Yet both Nikkatsu and Shochiku were able to exploit that popularity to form vertically integrated structures that capitalized on the exploding demand for film—to the detriment of the foreign companies who had initially fueled the postquake boom. Shochiku (having taken over Taikatsu), Nikkatsu, P.C.L., Toho, and scores of smaller companies continued to exploit the "showcase" status of foreign cinema throughout the 1920s and 1930s, especially in the gradual conversion to sound, but they were always poised to limit foreign competition while simultaneously capitalizing on the creative tensions between Japanese and Western films. Writes Kirihara, "Japanese filmmakers found great rewards in pursuing technical, formal, and stylistic standards of foreign filmmaking while differentiating their productions enough to allow for interpretations of 'Japaneseness.'"[58]

Japanese filmmakers also came to distinguish their work from the stage. In contrast to developments in Western cinema, whose pretensions to mimic the legitimate stage came relatively late, Japanese film was identified with the stage from the beginning.

The benshi, whose position in traditional theater is absolutely central, was the most important and tenacious legacy from this primary conflation of stage and screen. "With such constant availability of spoken commentary," writes Richie, "it was not necessary for the infant Japanese cinema to invent continuity."[59] The ubiquitous benshi, along with the Japanese audience's widespread familiarity with the theatrical repertoire, helps explain why Japanese film form did not evolve through the gradual self-sufficiency of the narrative track, the direction taken by Griffith.[60]

"In short, these [kabuki] films do not narrate for themselves," writes Komatsu Hiroshi. "Responding to the meanings always provided from the outside, the narratives freely attach themselves to the images in these films. This open-ended early Japanese cinema kept the Western concept of fiction at a distance."[61] Richie says that as a result, Japanese film technique consistently lagged at least ten years behind that of the West.[62] He also speculates that the incipient confusion of stage and screen was a way to accommodate a foreign technology within the familiar conventions of traditional theater, an accommodation that accounts for the inordinate popularity of period films. As Tanizaki noted, cinema is a Western technology stamped from its very inception with a formal-ideological complex inalienably remote from Japanese artistic concerns. What better way to lessen that distance, to domesticate the yawning gulf between Japanese dramaturgy and Western technology, than to film kabuki plays and later, adapt traditional period stories and conventions to the new medium? This was one way; the other, closely related, was the institutionalization of the benshi as a force of narrative standardization. "Rather than developing a mode of representation that relied on the film producer to supply a self-sufficient narrative," writes Komatsu, "the benshi's position was greatly strengthened instead."[63]

From 1908 kabuki films started to give way to *shimpa* films. These staged melodramas from the Meiji period, often foreign adaptations, tried to update what was considered anachronistic "feudalism" in kabuki theater. By 1908, though, shimpa stage theater was hidebound and dated, and some Western techniques, especially the crosscut chase sequence, were introduced into shimpa films. In 1912 there was a boom in chase scenes influenced by the popularity of the French detective movie *Zigomar*.[64] Shimpa films were one way in which Japanese films struggled to incorporate Western theatrical techniques; another was the chain-drama (*rensa geki*), in which a story is linked by both live theatrical and filmed sequences. Actors would exchange lines onstage, then, when some active stage business was called for, the drama would shift to a new location—a speeding car, say, or the grounds of a mansion—only the players would appear onscreen in filmed portions that had been shot earlier. Like the original kabuki films, chain-drama films were conceived only as parts of larger theatrical wholes secured by actors delivering lines on a live stage.[65] There were new-style *kyugeki* films, like *The Scene of Miyamoto Musashi's Elimination of the Baboons*, using a mechanical baboon, *The Kumagai Fan Store*, and *Hosokawa Covered With Blood*, all released in late 1908. These too were "exerpt" films that lifted scenes from popular serialized novels and required benshi commentary to fill in the narrative context.[66]

Kabuki films, then, were the original "canned theater" against which shimpa, chain-drama, and the new-style kyugeki films reacted by updating their subject matter and technique. But they all had in common the status of "digests" of longer narratives whose background was outlined by benshi or the audience's prior familiarity with the story.

Oddly enough, it is the 1910 *Chushingura, The Loyal Forty-Seven Retainers*, starring Onoe Matsunosuke, that is one of the first releases to approximate a self-contained kabuki play, although it was not made with this in mind.[67] Rather, the Yokota company strung together a series of short episodes that had been shot and released earlier. This resulted in a long composite pro-

Onoe Matsunosuke in
Kannon Daigoro (1916).
Private collection.

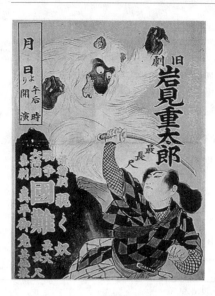

Onoe Matsunosuke in *Iwami
Jutaro* (1917). Private collection.

gram, a total of almost three hours, of collected episodes of the *Chushingura*
saga presented in its correct theatrical order. The irony of this is that the
most conservative genre of Japanese film was one of the first to make the
transition to a coherent feature-length narrative, but, in so doing, was
motivated by a greater fidelity to the original kabuki theatrical experience.

Moreover, Onoe Matsunosuke, a kyugeki actor, was Japan's first real
movie star, whose popularity did not wane until after the First World War.
Richie says "His popularity became so great that between 1909 and 1911
he and [Shozo] Makino made almost 170 films together, including the
popular *Jiraiya*, and the first film version of the kabuki, *Sukeroku*."[68] Again,
it is the hidebound, foot-dragging kabuki film that produces another milestone in the development of Japanese cinema, the bona fide star. It is as if
the films least interested in modernizing their subject matter and technique
were the most likely to initiate some kind of change, motivated by product
differentiation and prospects of greater commodity value.

In this light, we should consider the Japanese embrace of American
action films from the 1920s. These had enough grassroots popularity that
avant-garde theater troupes, like the *Shinkokugeki* (New National Theater),
sought to increase its appeal by taking some lessons from American films,
adapting some features of the Western, the adventure film, and slapstick
into its sword fight sequences. These plays were adapted to the screen in
the 1920s and formed the basis for the pre-World War II *jidai geki* film tradition. Further from the "cutting edge" were shimpa and *shingeki* theater

(contemporary Western plays), along with the degraded, old-fashioned kyugeki, whose star system and narrative familiarity made it so popular onscreen.

The styles of Douglas Fairbanks, Thomas Ince, and William S. Hart, as well as Cyrano de Bergerac, Jean Valjean, and Zigomar, entered Japanese film through the front door and the back: as fashionable theatrical troupes incorporated the latest Western rages, including film tricks, into their adaptations and acting, creaky kabuki films were turned out like Fords. These films on the rear guard also adapted to public taste in the late teens and early twenties, but the channels were more corporate than artistic. Early producers wished to capitalize on the popularity of serialized novels, name recognition of famous benshi, and more "realistic," athletic displays of swordsmanship to give the tired worker his money's worth. These are indigenous, economic motivations that partly account for the crossover, if not colonization, into the Japanese popular imagination by Western action heroes.

As Sato concludes his introduction to the roots of *jidai geki* (period film), "Although *jidai-geki* has incorporated many influences, the essence of *jidai-geki* remains the 'hidden subconscious' of the Japanese masses."[69] His statement is cryptic, but it firmly establishes the connection between samurai films and the masses, rather than an elite provenance issuing from ruling-class media prescriptions. This connection could not easily persist in a time of militarist imperialism, when all minds must bend to a national ambition. In the mid to late 1930s, of course, things change. At this time we see close state monitoring of the film industry, kokusaku eiga (national policy films), and the monumental style.

Japanese efforts to gain world recognition as national cinema were unsuccessful in the 1920s. The earthquake of 1923 devastated the film industry in the Tokyo area. By the time it recovered, production was centered in Kyoto and Kansai, where new styles were being imagined and articulated (see chapters 3 and 4). After the devastation of the Pacific War, however, efforts to export Japanese cinema were spectacular. This was due mostly to the unexpected momentum generated by Kurosawa's *Rashomon*, which took top honors at Venice and around the world in 1951–1952. The Japanese press speculated endlessly about the ingredients that had made *Rashomon* such an international hit. After *Rashomon* critics took international festivals very seriously (some even comparing them to the Olympics), and delegations returning from festivals without a prize apologized publically as if they had personally failed the nation.[70]

Again at Venice Mizoguchi won a Silver Lion in 1953 for *Ugetsu Monogatari*. Meanwhile Kinugasa Teinosuke was making his color epic *Jigokumon* (*Gate of Hell*), winner of the Grand Prize at Cannes and an Academy Award in 1954 (see chapter 8). These circumstances were not simply fortuitous, but were the result of persistent campaigns by trade associations and sponsored film festivals abroad, advised by offices in the Foreign Ministry and the Ministry of International Trade and Industry.[71] Nineteen fifty-three saw the establishment of offices in Los Angeles by Toho and Shochiku, with the latter opening one in London as well.[72] Studio presidents Kido Shiro (Shochiku) and Nagata Masaichi (Daiei) went on world promotional junkets, with stars in tow for publicity, in 1955. The government, especially MITI (Ministry of International Trade and Industry) was an active promoter of Japanese film culture abroad, with money, trade organizations, festivals, and diplomatic prestige. By 1960 Toho bought two of its own theaters in America, one in Los Angeles and the other in New York. It shared a theater in Honolulu with Shochiku, although Toei had had an exclusive arrangement with the locally owned Consolidated chain since 1957.[73] There were also several first-run Japanese theatres in Sao Paulo. The plan was to be ready for another *Rashomon*, to have a showcase for periodic festivals of Japanese movies, as well as permanent screens for genre pictures shown to Japanese-speaking residents in those cities. But the New York Toho, which sold 60 percent of its tickets to non-Japanese, operated for only twenty-eight months, closing permanently in 1965.[74] The Toho La Brea lasted well into the 1970s, and the Japanese Honolulu theaters into the 1980s.

The birth of "Japanese cinema" for the reformers of the Pure Film Movement was possible only by forsaking its roots in indigenous popular forms and appealing to both actual and metaphorical foreigners, mimicking American and European models. This is patently contradictory, but exemplary of the constitution of specularized subjects along intersecting lines of gender, race, class, and national difference: "Paradoxically, Japanese silent cinema could construct itself as wholly Japanese only as long as it was fundamentally split—*not* homogenous—only as long as it contained within its fractured body those contradictions which, as the object of efforts to solve them, formed the basis of the creation of Japanese cinema."[75]

Ozu's *I Was Born But . . .* (1932) is a belated embodiment of these contradictions. The long comic scene of the boss's home movie night is a tissue of incompatible forms of spectatorship. The importation of home movies signifies "class," and pretensions to it. It is a brilliant device for teasing apart

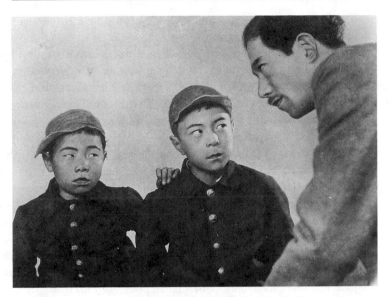

I Was Born But . . . (1932). Museum of Modern Art Film Stills Archive.

the institution of cinema within the Japanese home. At first the obstreper-
ous boys embarrass their father, played by the obsequious Saito Tatsuo,
who is trying to curry favor with his boss (Sakamoto Takeshi). He is surprised and unhappy to see his two sons grinning at him from the back
room, and once the film starts is mortified to hear them make off-color
remarks about zoo animals and loudly fight about whether the zebra's
stripes are white on black or black on white. This is not behavior that will
endear him or his family to the boss. But then the boys are subjected to the
second reel, in which they see their father clowning and mugging for the
camera to the delight of the boss and his cohorts. As the general hilarity
mounts, the boys become more ashamed. They are not used to seeing
Father play the fool and leave in disgust. Father's onscreen antics, moreover, are welcome diversion from the material showing the boss flirting
with geisha, to the great irritation of his wife and other women in the audience. Saito's obsequious clowning, so devastating to his authority as father,
actually heads off any questioning of his boss's authority as husband and
salvages the boss's domestic consensus—at the expense of his own. Ozu's
use of home movies as polarizer of spectatorial responses, splitting audiences according to their class, gender, and generation, is a beautiful illustration of the volatile, unpredictable effects of film. Just when it appears
that the scene will unfold as a patronizing gag on the gullibility of prepu-

bescent boys, the hypocrisy and fawning of middle-class respectability is unceremoniously displayed.

Although most histories of Japanese cinema, in English and in Japanese, are framed in a biological narrative striving toward some authentic national cinematic identity, the evolution of Japanese film form, like that of the West, really unfolds as a process of commodification. To be accepted as a universally consumable commodity, cinema had to become respectable, and what better road to respectability than official sanction by the national? Someone had to turn cinema from a toy into a real product.[76] Instead of some inchoate struggle for national expression, producers and critics like the Pure Film Movement consciously articulated a vision of nationality as a selling point, at home and abroad. Not to do so fixated Japanese, and other national cinemas, at a point of arrested development unable to compete in a rapidly developing international market increasingly dominated by Hollywood. Yet the fixation of Japaneseness on cinematic scaffolding appears as a quixotic pursuit when an achievement of the national is at once its negation. In Japanese period films from the 1930s, the resolution of that picture is as sharp as it could be.

3

Approaching the
Monumental Style

People define their national identities through *identification* with these symbols. If this proposition is correct, a comprehensive investigation of the national identity of a given nation-state should encompass not merely the categories by which inhabitants differentiate themselves but the nature and meaning of the symbol system with which they identify.

       —Lowell Dittmer and Samuel S. Kim, *China's Quest for National Identity*

The so-called Pacific Century is already with us, despite its official coming out at the turn of the millennium. In spite of fifty years of consistent methodical expansion, Japan's steady growth is stubbornly regarded as an "economic miracle," unless we pause to give credit to MacArthur and the Marshall plan. World War II is without question the watershed event in U.S.-Japan relations, yet its prominence often obscures the importance of the preceding years. If we bracket for a moment the overweening status of the war and closely scrutinize the 1920s and 1930s, Japan's postwar phoenix comes to appear more like a foregone conclusion than a miracle. The ways in which the Japanese managed to integrate alien entities, actual and metaphorical, into their inimitable native structures is reminiscent of a vaccine, which protects the organism by introducing a dose of foreign substance. If this is a pattern consistently manifested in both prewar and postwar periods, then Japan's "Pacific Century" encompasses the twentieth as well.

A rigorous study of Japanese language, culture, and history is well underway in the United States. In addition to examining the official Japan, however, it behooves us to explore its popular culture. Japanese popular culture allows us glimpses of Japanese society from the "inside," because it often represents more directly than high culture what ordinary people consume. We can also look to the popular culture of the past to help determine the route through which the Japanese negotiated contradictions of modernization, industrialization, and Westernization.

The prewar cinema of Japan was an important milestone on this route because it shows how the Japanese completely mastered a Western technology—talking pictures—in service to a national cause undertaken against that same Western adversary. In the 1930s a complex, bewildering dialectic was unfolding between East and West, tradition and modernity, art and propaganda, peace and war.

As a technology capable of influencing the minds of millions, sound cinema was at the cutting edge. On the one hand, the movies were a tool, like the internal combustion engine or the assembly line, that was adapted from abroad for native purposes. Initially, these purposes were not so different from those of the West: profit through entertainment of the masses. On the other hand, when cinema was used to mobilize support for the war in China, it appealed to an indigenous Japanese spirit unsullied by Western influences and attempted to galvanize a unique national identity in service to a policy of foreign military expansionism. Here the native purposes of Japanese cinema are not the same as those of the West, even though the West also used cinema for propaganda purposes. A Western technology was employed to disseminate images of Japaneseness that eschewed Western technique and ideology. Homage was paid to a Western propaganda medium even while the message of that propaganda exhorted a self-reliant freedom from Western impurities.

My subject concerns innovations in prewar cinema that articulate a national identity. An obvious place to look for this is in propaganda, whether in overt or more insinuating forms couched in entertainment. In America serious study of (foreign) national cinemas began with wartime analysis of propaganda by respected scholars like Siegfried Kracauer ("Propaganda and the Nazi War Film") and Ruth Benedict ("Race and Cultural Relations: America's Answer to the Myth of a Master Race," *The Chrysanthemum and the Sword*).[1] In such work there was a pressing need to uncover the psychology of fascism, to crack the code of ultranationalism in order to arrest a genocidal course. The unsparing racism of "Know Your Enemy,"

Frank Capra's propaganda documentary series on the Axis adversaries, amplifies the urgency of the wartime mandate because it ruthlessly justifies its means (picturing the enemy as subhuman) in terms of the end (obliteration of fascism and the triumph of liberty). Japanese propaganda was never this inflammatory, yet it was highly effective, in part because it generally avoided the fanaticism attributed to Japanese militarism by Capra and his employers and in part because it was artful, appealing, and relatively sensitive. The ways and means of Japanese propaganda have been much discussed elsewhere,[2] and it is instructive to remember that Capra was reportedly astounded by its sophistication, saying, "We can't beat this kind of thing. We can make films like these maybe once in a decade."[3] Thanks to Capra and the requirements of the Office of War Information, the "art" of propaganda has yet to be untangled from its association with simplistic, means-ends indoctrination, with accompanying social science tools and historiographies. In his discussion of Aryan rites in National Socialism, George Mosse voices a similar lament about the liabilities of the term *propaganda*, "for it denotes something artificially created, attempting to capture the minds of men by means of deliberate 'selling' techniques."[4]

For this reason I will set propaganda aside, in its most conventional, generic sense, because I am concerned with a more subtle and compelling instance of cinematic Japaneseness: films that exemplify the monumental style of the late thirties and early forties. These historical period films glorify Japanese tradition through a canonization of the past, a celebration of traditional aesthetics, and an exaltation of hierarchic family structures, particularly the patriarchal formations of *bushido*, the way of the warrior. Characteristic of the style is a series of techniques employing a slow, implacable narrative, an epic sweep in story and spectacle, and a reverential, even hieratic gravity that lends majestic connotations to its subjects and themes. The monumental style is more than a little like Greek or Shakespearean tragedy. It also exemplifies a peculiarly Japanese dialectic between medium and message because, although it is the most powerful and prestigious instance of Japanese nativism ever seen in the mass media, its stylistic innovations sometimes obstruct the transmission of its messages. Monumental style roughens the smooth "selling techniques" of propaganda in the name of a more authentic presentation of Japanese aesthetics on the movie screen. This is evidence of a dialectical modernism, as explained below.

Historically, the monumental style is sandwiched between the frantic Westernization of the early thirties and back-to-Japan cultural policies dictated by the militarists in the Pacific War. Stylistically, it starkly represents a collision between the artistic momentum aroused by a Western technology and the traditional aesthetics incorporated into its fabrication by militarist

mandate. The monumental style's relation to its historical context is therefore a divided one: stylistic experimentation was jockeying for prominence
with the demand for a clear, uncomplicated celebration of an indigenous
Japanese spirit. Monumental style is therefore a site of intersecting determinations and consequences—historical, political, cultural, and cinematic.

The monumental style emerged from a multiple collision of influences.
The interwar period was a time of unprecedented cultural experimentation
and exuberance in the big cities. From the end of World War I to the beginning of the Showa era in 1926, there was an intense consciousness of
modernity subsequently known as "Taisho liberalism." These were formative years for Japanese cinema, whereas the film industry in America was
firmly established in its industrial, social, and aesthetic practices. Not surprisingly, Japanese studio bosses, stars, and technicians looked to Hollywood in this period for lessons on capturing the public imagination (and

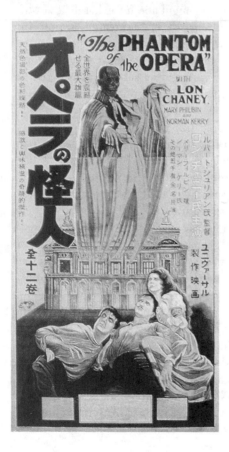

Universal's *Phantom of the
Opera* (1925) with Lon
Chaney.
Private collection.

pocketbook).[5] There were many lessons learned and compromises struck with traditional theatrical and narrative practices, and by 1920 a lively, innovative national style emerged from a Japanese-Western filmic syncretism (see chapter 2).

But this took time. After the Great Kanto Earthquake of 1923, Japanese film art and industry struck a balance between genres (corresponding to the bifocal production centers in Tokyo and Kyoto), technical mastery, and artistic ambitiousness, with a satisfactory division of labor and lucrative market. By the end of the decade, however, the political climate had changed. The worldwide depression of 1929 hit Japan especially hard and has much to do with the authoritarian, militarist turn of the 1930s. Throughout the early 1930s Japanese films continued to exhibit the exuberant, cosmopolitan escapism that had been a staple in postearthquake urban culture. But as reaction, militarism, and war loomed, changes in the film industry were inevitable. Authorities now decried the cheap sensationalism of Japanese film and called for its regulation. An elaborate (self-) censorship mechanism was instituted. The studios, eager to ensure their product's distribution and artistic legitimacy, cooperated in encouraging a return to more "authentic" Japanese stories, themes, and techniques. A new emphasis was apparent when *rekishi eiga* (historical films) were produced in the mid-to-late 1930s. Instead of using a Tokugawa feudal backdrop for criminal intrigue and spectacular swordplay, these films emphasized the specifics of Japanese heroes and folklore, liberally accompanied by didactic themes meant to inspire. Monumental films, closely related to the *rekishi eiga*, came on the scene around 1938. These films were an attempt to sanctify the feudal heritage that was a permanent historical backdrop for the jidai geki, or period drama. To the education and military officials who now oversaw the film industry, the austere traditionalism of the monumental style was a welcome change from the potboilers that had survived a more cosmopolitan, exuberant, and "decadent" Japanese culture.

Toward a Definition

It should be emphasized that monumental style is a retrospective designation highlighting the extreme concentration of Japanese nationality in these films. As far as I know, monumental style was not a term used in contemporary discussions of Japanese film in the 1930s, even though its turn toward the didactic, the ritual, and the sacred was duly (and tactfully) noted. Monumental style is a "strong" style in that there are only a handful of fully monumental films (perhaps no more than a dozen before the

Pacific War started). Its potency comes from its stylistic rigor, its intensity, and its religious fervor, having more in common with Dreyer's *Day of Wrath* or Eisenstein's *Ivan the Terrible* than with the hooks of popular propaganda. There is little in common between the monumental style and genuinely popular cinema, Japanese or otherwise, but because Japanese popular culture was thought to be excessively Occidental (i.e., frivolous) in the early 1930s, there came policies and possibilities that resulted in the monumental style. Monumentalism was something that was visible in other films as well, though not in such concentrated form, and could be discerned in songs, buildings, food, and clothing—the very fabric of daily life in the 1930s. The group of films discussed here as the monumental style, then, is really only the most striking and powerful instance of an aesthetic of totalitarianism permeating the Japanese empire.

A similar aesthetic can be seen in other contemporary totalitarian regimes, in Germany, Italy, or the former Soviet Union. Although I cannot elaborate here, this points toward the fruitfulness of the monumental concept. What makes it striking and initially plausible is what appears to be its international validity. What is it about monumental style that makes it so fitting, so inevitable as an aesthetic of official civic religion? Whether that "religion" is Nazi, Italian fascist, Soviet socialist realist, revolutionary ornamental Maoism, or Japanese imperialism, why do similar tropes, figures, and rhetorical appeals keep recurring? Or are they only superficially similar, and show resemblance only because they draw on similar nineteenth-century Romantic wellsprings of the sublime to which totalizing and totalitarian regimes obsessively return?

In Japan the cultural circumstance of the monumental style is late 1930s imperialist nationalism. The efficient causes of the monumental style, however, are the directors, talent, technicians, and studio bosses laboring in a heavily charged political climate. It is not just the politics of the monumental style that are important, but its institutional setting, its pertinent generic, stylistic, and narrative norms, and, finally, its textual features. Most important are the tensions and negotiations between these multiple determinations. A key determination in the monumental style is the generic and stylistic norms of jidai geki film traditions. Nowhere is this more evident than in Mizoguchi's *Genroku Chushingura*, the finest example of the monumental style.

Genroku Chushingura (*The Forty-Seven Ronin of the Genroku Era*, 1941–1942), has an ascetic gravity that contrasts markedly with scores of earlier versions of this most celebrated of Japanese morality tales. Earlier renditions, which emphasize the physical action in the Chushingura tale, differ radically from Mizoguchi's concentration on the static, hieratic quality of Japanese court life. Other examples of the monumental style include Mizoguchi's *Zangiku Monogatari* (*Story of the Last Chrysanthemum*, 1939), Kumagai's *Abe Ichizoku* (*The Abe Clan*, 1938), Kinugasa's *Kawanakajima Kassen* (*The Battle of Kawanakajima*, 1940), and Makino's *Iemitsu to Hikozaemon* (*Shogun Iemitsu and His Mentor Hikozaemon*, 1940). Though classic examples of the monumental style in its initial phase are rare, the legacy of monumentalism in its broadest outlines continues to flourish in Japanese films even today. In chapter 8 I will analyze postwar and contemporary period films: Kinugasa's *Jigoku Mon* (*Gate of Hell*, 1953), Kurosawa's *Kagemusha* (*The Shadow Warrior*, 1980), *Ran* (1986), and Teshigahara's *Rikyu* (1990) for vestigial developments of the monumental style.

The first step toward defining the monumental style is to ask, is it unified? Films in the monumental style share a characteristic action or gesture that marks their apparent manner of creation: a gesture of appropriation.[6] Appropriation must have an object and a purpose, and films in the monumental style appropriate the pre-Meiji Japanese cultural heritage for a sacramental purpose. The sacramentalizing of the Japanese cultural heritage, further, has the goal of consolidating a national identity in service to the war effort mounted in the late 1930s. The monumental style, therefore, exhibits a basic strategy of appropriation, a broad base of material encompassing a classic cultural heritage (which it shares with other jidai geki period drama), and a sacramental objective in the context of late 1930s nationalism.

The gesture of appropriation mobilizes Japanese tradition through a canonization of the past, an exaltation of native aesthetics, and a celebration of feudal social structures. But nearly any jidai geki will do this to some extent in order to provide period authenticity, a sense of atmosphere, or simply to retell traditional legends and tales. The monumental style is distinguished by the dominance of the indigenous tradition. It is appropriated not for some other purpose within the film, but rather for its own sake as an intrinsically valuable heritage to be regarded with pride and even awe. The average jidai geki employs samurai heroes and villains who converse, plot, and fight in Japanese houses and palaces and courtyards. Most will use characters who have some standing, as chapter heading or footnote, in Tokugawa history. These aspects of the film are necessary vehicles for the primary purpose of putting some twist on a popular yarn or generic convention. They are part of the dramatic furniture, so to speak, of mounting a proper period film.

But the monumental style rehabilitates these indigenous elements, this furniture that makes jidai geki what it is, and makes them the real center of interest. The monumental style turns the dramatic spotlight on Japanese period design, behavior, and ethics and renders them, as much as the characters and situations based upon them, objects of reverence and respect. This is done primarily through style. Paradoxically, the appropriation of Japanese tradition to be celebrated "for its own sake" more readily serves extracinematic purposes (namely, nationalistic ones) than does more instrumental appropriations of Japanese tradition in other jidai geki. Where the primary motivation is a brisk narrative and explosive action in ordinary jidai geki, the period setting is formulaic to the point of invisibility.

The connection between the gesture of appropriation and the articulation of a national identity is made by an appeal to the sacred. In the monumental style a strong mythologizing impulse operates not only on the traditional forms appropriated from the cultural heritage but also on the film techniques—narrative, stylistic, thematic—that constitute the form of the individual film. The aura of traditional forms permeates the films and gives them their epic scale, hieratic gravity, stately camera movements, and long takes. The appeal to the sacred is the work that films in the monumental style perform on the traditional forms they appropriate from the past and is also the quality that gives them a strong pull toward the mythic, the nativist, and the ultranationalistic.

There is nothing unique about Japanese archaic appropriations for a sacramental purpose, but it was done in a prototypical way, sufficient to serve as a model for other national mythologies. Lowell Dittmer and Samuel S. Kim make the point that the Japanese amalgamated the national and the sacred in the nineteenth-century term *kokutai* ("national essence"), which the Chinese derived from the Japanese and translated as *guocui*:

> This "essence" might consist of a canon of sacred texts. Thus the Jews are bound together by the Talmud, the Christians by the Bible, the Americans by their Constitution and Declaration of Independence, the English by the Magna Charta; the prewar Japanese were likewise bound by the Imperial Rescript. Beyond that, it might also include an oral tradition of myths and rituals—flags, holidays, national ceremonies of commemoration, inauguration, or even mourning; tales of national heroes, villains, battles, a foundation myth, and so forth.[7]

Nationalism in the monumental style implies some period limits. Monumentalism involves a gesture of appropriation and mythologizing of the cultural heritage, but also has the quasi-religious purpose of articulating a uniquely Japanese identity. The films set forth an ideal Japanese role for the spectator to play by identifying with exemplary characters and with a uniquely Japanese style of presentation. If it is unique (or perceived as such), then only Japanese people will be able to recognize and identify with its solicitations. Japanese identity, however, fluctuates according to the representations that construct it in response to historical circumstances.[8] The contents and consistency of Japaneseness during the Meiji era, the prewar period, postwar reconstruction, and the "economic miracle" of the 1960s and 1970s vary dramatically. The monumental style in cinema helps articulate a national identity in the immediate prewar period (1936–1941). On the one hand, it reacts to the cosmopolitanism of the Taisho and early Showa years by pushing a back-to-Japan movement; on the other, it presages Japan's total involvement and eventual defeat in the Pacific War, when the Bomb and MacArthur's "democratization" campaign ineradicably imposed a new kind of Japaneseness. Within the prewar period, moreover, constructions of Japaneseness similar to those in the monumental style were being discussed and promoted in the arts, media, and culture generally.

The techniques typical of the style, like the long shot and long take, moving camera, and spectacular locations and costumes, cannot serve as exclusive stylistic markers. Nor can typical themes, such as the concern with *bushido* and the sacredness of Japanese aesthetics. The peculiar manner in which these features are appropriated, combined, and put to a particular purpose distinguishes the monumental style from other similar films and styles.

A provisional definition of the monumental style is as follows: it is a prewar cinema permeated by a hieratic, sacramental appropriation of a classical heritage in order to promote an apotheosis of Japanese national identity. No doubt this is cumbersome and overly abstract. Moreover, it fails to identify specific aesthetic features that constitute the appropriative and sacramental functions of the style. But, for the moment, an ostensive definition that delineates the family resemblances, or prototypes, of the monumental style is sufficient. The characteristic appropriation, sacredness of tradition, and contemporary nationalistic mission pragmatically outlines these resemblances.

To these qualities may be added another, more subtle one: the syncretism of the monumental style. The self-consciousness of their nativism marks films in this style as dialectical or contradictory texts, because of the technology's dogged pull toward Western modes of representation. As Tanizaki recognized, it was wrenching for Japanese performance and narrative to undergo projection onto an alien screen in the 1910s and 1920s. The 1930s saw the movie screen take on the didactic function of awakening cosmopolitan Japanese to the glories of their own culture. This is a self-conscious gesture, yet symptomatic of a second, unexamined Japaneseness that only reached the screen in subsequent decades, after the war. The sacramental qualities of the monumental style are clues to the spirituality with which many Japanese associate their nationality, making clear the quasi-religious aspects of membership in the Japanese "cult."

In any case, this is a connotation of the monumental style that defies containment in a laconic formal definition. As a whole, this book is actually a progressive redefinition of the monumental style in its various aspects, forms, and manifestations. But a common thread throughout my scrutiny of the monumental style is its dialectical modernism: how the construction of *Japaneseness* is accomplished out of that most Western of materials, cinema. The form and meaning of Japaneseness will vary according to the themes, styles, and historical contexts in which it is cinematically constructed. Despite its seeming implacability, one should recall the contingency and pluralism of the monumental style. Its purposes and goals will vary according to the social, political, or aesthetic contexts in which it is analyzed. Eventually, these aspects are ultimately tied together in the following hypothesis: in its quest for ways to represent a pure Japanese spirit, the monumental style inadvertently reveals the growing cosmopolitanization of Japanese popular culture. The fundamentalist conversion back to pure Japaneseness is also a sophisticated step "forward" in the integration of tradition, technology, and mass indoctrination. The fact that a general idea of Japaneseness as well as the concrete forms of an idealized, classical Japaneseness are appealed to in prewar Japanese cinema betrays the distance traveled since the days of Japan's hermetic isolation. The fact that a prominent group of works in the most modernized of urban media extolled an ethic of self-reliance from Western contamination shows how much Western culture had already been assimilated. We now turn to those things Japanese urban audiences had assimilated by the mid-1930s.

How does the monumental style address the contemporary Japanese spectator? Drawing a picture of a Japanese spectator in the 1930s is largely a matter of constructing a composite cultural history of urban Japan, with special attention to the film and entertainment industry. We can expect Japanese spectators to be familiar with traditional references and allusions on which the monumental style so heavily relies. In addition, we can assume that by the mid-thirties the urban Japanese audience was well schooled in the genres and styles of Hollywood cinema, for it was largely Hollywood-style popular images of extravagance and individualism that militarists and conservatives ranted against. In many ways the monumental style encourages a "conversion experience" back to Japan from the prodigal waywardness of an excessively Westernized urban culture.

Urban Culture: *"The East Wind in a Horse's Ear"*

There is always color, or noise, or both together to be found in the
harbingers of modern culture. Posters, the telegraph, radio, billboards,
necklaces, fads, clothing, electric lights, automobiles, rotary presses,
motors, airplanes, et cetera . . . We cannot imagine modern culture
without the color and the sounds of these things.
   —Chiba Kamei, "Shinkankakuron" (The new consciousness, 1925)[9]

A good part of the picture we have of urban popular culture in the 1930s
must be outlined through the discourses that fulminated against it.
Because the exuberant Westernization of city life by 1930 was a popular,
grassroots force that impressed ruling elites mostly for its potential harm
(as in the old saw "injurious to public morals"), there is little direct record
of its impact and development. These cosmopolitan crosscurrents flowed
freely through people's consciousness, like "the east wind in a horse's ear,"
to use a Japanese expression meaning "in one ear, out the other." My picture of popular urban Japan in the 1930s is based largely on the testimony
of those who were sufficiently important to have made it into the "official"
historical record made up of English-language newspapers (especially the
Japan Times) and books;[10] that record is generally pejorative and disap-
proving of mass culture in the cities, so it is necessary to use it as a
palimpsest that traces a negative image of its antagonisms—which is our
primary interest.

   The disjunction between official ideology and popular consciousness is
nicely described by Harris Martin:

> With the upheavals in urban life following the Meiji revolution
> and a new cosmopolitanism after the Russo-Japanese War and
> World War I, there developed a self-conscious sophistication in
> the urban Japanese mind which was distinctly different from the
> national consciousness so carefully and deliberately nurtured by
> the Meiji government. This new sophistication does not always
> seem to have pleased the Japanese ruling class as it over-spilled
> the elite ranks to inform the urban masses. As it spread it made
> its own demands on the producers of entertainment, often to
> the distress of the arbiters of good taste.[11]

Since ideology is not just wrongheadedness, official or otherwise, but
rather "a plural and dynamic field of ideas and practices," contemporary
discussion of rampant "sophistication" of the 1930s can be used to outline

horizons of urban experience that lie outside the realm of healthy civic-
mindedness prescribed by the official commentators:

> This threatening faintness they expressed in a revealing vocab-
> ulary of ideological failure, lamenting the indifference to their
> words, which . . . like "the east wind in a horse's ear" (*baji tofu*)
> hardly grazed the people's consciousness. Because these com-
> mentators then went on to identify in colorfully censorious
> detail the baleful influences to which the people were not indif-
> ferent, they offer indirect evidence of other currents of late
> Meiji social, economic, and political life that competed with
> the ideologists for popular attention.[12]

The "baleful influences" to which people paid attention are the things
that distract them from their proper disposition as dutiful subjects. These
are the influences accounting for the reaction against the decadent and the
foreign, a reaction of which the monumental style was a part. Ordinary
Japanese found themselves in the middle of an irresistible cultural eclecti-
cism, much like Weimar Germany, in which new technological and social
innovations threw time-honored ways into relief and opened them to question.[13] This process was not new; since the mid-nineteenth century the
Japanese had parried threats and promises of the outside world with enviable agility, and there had always followed periods of traditional reaction.
Postquake urban Japan, however, was different, in that new technologies of
mass communication in the publishing, broadcasting, and film industries
allowed strange winds to blow through the windows of the average person.
The very accessibility of foreign, dissenting, unwholesome, marginal, and
outright bizarre modes of behavior and cultural practices made many in the
establishment very nervous.

In a time of economic crisis and preparation for war with China, the
penetration of the bureaucracy into every aspect of private life became all-
pervasive. Gregory Kasza writes of the moral highmindedness of the early
Showa administrators:

> They were concerned not only with revolutionary politics or
> pornography narrowly understood, but also with the family,
> religion, education, and economic life. Bureaucrats did not rec-
> ognize a clear boundary between legitimate state interests and
> an inviolable sphere of civil activity. This reflects a highly
> paternalistic attitude, an underlying belief that officials were
> not merely a political elite but a moral elite qualified to oversee
> every aspect of social life. Administrators did not distinguish

sharply between political and moral subject matter. In their view, politics and manners and morals were inextricably related and were to be considered in tandem. Censors discussed eroticism in the same terms (and often in the same sentence) they used to complain of socialist films. The hazy boundary between politics and manners and morals paralleled the absence of clear demarcation between the public and private spheres.[14]

The monumental style, as one of the most stark representations of Japanese nativism in the mass media, is a radical prescription against the "baleful influences" in manners and morals that engulfed Japanese cities through the 1930s.

According to Fujitake Akira, "The development of material civilization in the early 1930s as symbolized by the rapid progress of the technology of communication media, aroused an inordinately gay atmosphere amid a succession of raging depressions. The atmosphere of the times has been described as *ero, guro, nansensu*, namely, erotic, grotesque, and nonsensical."[15] Nothing could articulate a mood more antithetical to the monumental style than "erotic, grotesque, and nonsensical," especially when combined in a perverse conglomeration of urban practices and attitudes. *Ero, guro, nansensu* is a cultural complex that forms the clearest image of popular urban culture against which the monumental style reacts in the late 1930s. This image should not be confused with the more sweeping *modan* (modern) phase of Showa urbanity, whose vestiges lingered through Pearl Harbor and beyond, but it is prototypical, setting the stage for further attenuation and reaction.[16]

It is too summary to describe such a complex and often bizarre phenomenon simply as Westernization or modernization, because it involved such extravagant bundles of intertwined cultural trends. With these trends marched not only Westernization and modernization but also massive urbanization, marginalization of the provinces, maturation of monopoly capitalism, emergence of mass culture, and, finally, the militarism and fascism of the middle 1930s. All these elements jostled one another in a riot of complexity and contradiction, a time both progressive and regressive, divided against itself. Small wonder that the Tokyo struggling to balance such disparate trends came to be known as "grotesque" and "nonsensical." Moreover, these were forms of modernity actively opposed by groups who otherwise favored modernization: women's suffragists, Christian social reformers, health professionals.[17]

Ero-guro-nansensu was a combined literary, theatrical, and graphic trend that found its sharpest expression in the explosion of magazines, poster art, and satirical comic strips that grew out of the so-called Kodansha culture of the 1920s, which came originally from a plethora of youth-oriented magazines in the years around World War I. The magazines had titles like *Katsudo Gaho* (Pictorial news of the movies), *Ze Supiido* (Speed), *Kinema Gaho* (Pictorial cinema), *Opera* (Opera), *Pairotto* (Pilot), *Katsudo Sekai* (World of motion pictures), and *San-esu* (The three S's: screen, speed, sex). These publications ushered in a period of intense mass marketing, when publishing companies realized that their most lucrative strategy was to adopt a lowest common denominator policy. This was carried out most dramatically by the Kodansha company in the fanfare surrounding the inauguration of *Kingu* (King) magazine in 1925. *Kingu* exemplifies the domination of mass Kodansha culture over the more intellectual Iwanami culture purveyed by its onetime rival. *Kingu's* high-concept approach is revealed in its advertising hype: "The most interesting in Japan, the most instructive in Japan, the most inexpensive in Japan, the largest circulation in Japan."[18] Its combination of instruction and entertainment assuaged any qualms readers may have felt about reading a publication that "teemed with vulgar morality stories stimulating human interest."[19] And its massive sales campaign, using direct mailings (1,835,000 postcards), newspaper ads, posters, handbills, signboards, balloons, and even those uniquely Japanese *chin-don-ya* and *kamishibai*, gainsaid any chance that city dwellers or villagers would miss the advent of this event.[20]

Ero-guro-nansensu arrived on the scene after this, when mass consumerism became more frantic and more difficult with the economic crises of the late 1920s. *Tokyo Puck* is a good example of a satirical magazine that takes aim at the degradation of life in the city. The corrupt politician, the greedy capitalist, the cynical taxi dancer and *mobo* ("modern boy") dandy— all these are fodder for *Puck's* playful but devastating sketches, both visual and literary. The emphasis on the underside of city life, not only its criminal underworld but its institutionalized corruption as well, brings to mind the grotesque satires of George Grosz and John Heartfield.[21] The nonsensical comedy of these magazines, comics, revues, and movies comes out of Chaplin and Lloyd's physical pratfalls, but its spirit is more wry and often deliberately incomprehensible.

Ozu's earliest surviving work, *Days of Youth* (*Wakaki hi*, 1929), is a procession of Western props, gags, and smutty situations. "The film constitutes a good instance of ero-guro-nansensu filmmaking," writes David Bordwell, "with the *ero* supplied by Watanabe's patting of Chieko's rear end, the *guro* by his scratching a doll's hindquarters and jamming gum in a statuette's eye, and the nansensu by the outrageous gag of the runaway ski and by such lines as a student admitting after an exam: 'I didn't memorize anything because I hate

Ero-guro-nansensu: Ozu's *Days of Youth* (*Wakaki hi*, 1929).
Kawakita Memorial Film Archives.

to forget things.' "[22] The ero-guro-nansensu trend culminating in the early
1930s was both documentation and parody of the permeation of *modan* into
Japanese urban life. To the young officers who wished to restore the original
promise of the Meiji restoration, the mass culture of the city must have
appeared debauched—"nothing other than an orgy," as one writer put it.[23]

One author of a 1930 work called "The New Korea" found traditional
family customs sorely lacking in Japan, where "young Japanese couples in
the new Japanese family in the interior attend jazz concerts and the cinema,
at a time when sports events take place in a Japanese jazz-music atmosphere,
as part of the fundamental addiction to Euro-American culture."[24]

Intellectuals and writers such as Watsuji Tetsuro, Yanagida Kunio,
Tanizaki Jun'ichiro, and Hayashi Fusao were concerned about the corrosive
effects of "Americanism": "crass, hedonistic materialism" embraced by
affected youth caught up in the consuming frenzy promoted by mass production and marketing of cheap thrills, gadgets, and instant gratification.[25]
"American movies, especially, had spread the cult of 'fast living' (*supiido*-
speed) and 'eroticism,' seducing young Japanese minds and leading them
away from their cultural roots."[26]

"Kawabata said that two subjects monopolized the media in those days,
depression and eroticism," writes Edward Seidensticker, and as for eroticism, the most popular attractions in the entertainment quarters of the

cities were the movie houses.[27] It is testament to the hold movies had over Japanese that in the early 1930s, as in America, there was great concern over the movies' effects on public morals. Foreign films were firmly established as major drawing cards for entertainment combines like Shochiku, and their newfound voices, sound effects, and jazz music added an exotic and erotic barrage to the already flamboyant city streets. In the months around the turn of the decade, hardly a week went by without some breathless newspaper report on the movements of Mary Pickford and Douglas Fairbanks, who visited Japan in December of 1929.[28] In the spring of 1932, Charlie Chaplin arrived. Though it is hard to accuse Pickford, Fairbanks, and Chaplin of eroticism, their popularity was seen by some as a symptom of cultural debilitation, an encourgagement of indifference to traditional ways.

A letter in the *Japan Times* blames American films for the degeneration of Tokyo youth. In a remarkable diatribe called "The Movies and Public Taste," the writer finds Hollywood a harbinger of doom in all cultural spheres: "Westernism is creeping in upon us with a horrible persistency, and it seems to be eating up all our good sense and to have destroyed all our better taste."[29] He blames Hollywood movies for the "hideous monstrosities" that fill our public museums,

> picture after picture of nude figures unlike anything God ever made, out of shape, overcolored, loathsome to see, and really so bad that they merely succeed in being ridiculous. Tokyo is full of young artists who wear greatsy [sic] long hair, dress like tramps, and who earn their living in fashioning these daubs for artless judges and the ridiculous public.

The outrage of modern art is nothing compared to the abomination of Hollywood, however: "The modern 'talkie' or 'movie' consists almost always of leg-shows, crime, wild parties, cocktail drinking, and vulgarity." The writer laments the disappearance of the "healthy and amusing" Chaplin and observes that the slavish consumption of American movies "does not reflect wisely or flatteringly upon our taste." He decries the hegemony of American movies when there were so many worthwhile French, German, and English films available, comparing the French *Joan of Arc* with the recent Fox release *Red Wine*, which he calls "stupid and vulgar."

American movies "seduce young people, crazy for anything new, or anything they think is really Western. . . . They are gulled into believing that they are looking at Western civilization and they go away satisfied and hungry for more. It awakes [sic] their young sexual appetites, and what more can we desire?" Concerned lest his readers dismiss him as a cantankerous killjoy, the writer insists he is not a prude, "nor does it shock me to see people making pigs and asses of themselves, but it bores me and disturbs me to think that as a people we Japanese can put up with so much of it."

As important as the salaciousness of American films was their indifference to traditional customs, such as the institution of arranged marriage and carefully orchestrated courtship rituals. American movies were especially culpable, many Japanese felt, in the popularization of the "modern girl," or *moga*.

The *moga* was a fashionably liberated symbol of women's rebellion against a stifling patriarchal order. With her bobbed hair, tight skirt, makeup, and insouciant cigarette, the moga was both a fictional and historical emblem of women's liberation in the 1920s and 1930s. Greta Garbo, Clara Bow, and Louise Brooks were the models for moga. She was a favorite character in literature, as in Tanizaki's *Naomi* (*Chijin no ai*, 1925), and the movies, as in Ozu's *Dragnet Girl* (*Hijosen no onna*, 1933) and Mizoguchi's *Naniwa Elegy* (1936). In magazine stories and on film, she embodied a new femininity that both challenged traditional patriarchy and popularized new vogues of conspicuous consumption. She was also a hotly disputed figure on the streets of Tokyo, as a frank embodiment of feminine sexuality.

Ad for Sapporo beer,
with likeness of
Crown Prince Hirohito, 1924

Ad for Sapporo beer, 1934.

In the Japanese context she signified the "advances" of Westernization to old Japan.[30]

The Japanese woman was an important stake in the early Showa struggle between cosmopolitanism and nativist reaction. Insofar as screen images of women both reflected and shaped emerging expressions of femininity, movies themselves were embroiled in the struggle too. First, women's suffrage was a more contested issue in the early 1930s than at any time until its achievement in the postwar period. Second, the legality of court-mandated marriage and reproductive decisions made without women's consent understandably outraged many women and strengthened the women's movement. These struggles and concerns became crystallized in the figure of the moga, who came to function as a controversial figure around which to rally for the causes of women's, especially young single women's, rights. As an inspiring, iconoclastic figure on the screen and on the street, moga were a strike against interlocking puritanical impulses toward moral rectitude and conservative cultural impulses to preserve the status quo. This dual concern about the moral and cultural effects of the movies distinguishes it from singularly sexual worries of American reformers, and accounts for the controversial figure cut by the moga.

One commentator seizes on the ambivalence the moga holds for traditional Japanese morals. In her insistence on *jiyu kekkon* ("free marriage"), she

Ozu's *Dragnet Girl* (*Hijosen no Onna*, 1933). Kawakita Memorial Film Archives.

provokes debates over whether she is an example of progress toward Western-style enlightenment or a precursor of the Japanese family system's
demise.[31] As an urban phenomenon she threatens provincial values of the
country, and as an aggressive, outgoing character (in dress if not always in
demeanor), she threatens men, at least those men in a position to benefit
most by her indenture within the family system. The aggressive urbanity of
moga, moreover, is given a poignant urgency when we remember that "a
flood of girls poured in upon the city from the poor northeastern provinces
in the mid-thirties. Rural poverty and the depression were the general causes,
and crop failures the immediate ones. . . . The poor girls added to the indignation, even as they made work easier for the purveyors of *ero* and *guro*."[32]

But the threatening aspects of the moga are a blind, insists one writer at
the time. The moga herself does not necessarily espouse the statements
connoted by her dress and behavior, because an achievement of the liberation she seeks would make her an unnecessary, antiquated figure.[33] She
requires the background of an authoritative patriarchal order to make her
statements. Paradoxically, the moga's very existence testifies to the possibility of her own cultural obsolescence.

Clearly the moga was a cultural fixture of the 1930s justly deserved by
an oppressive patriarchal family system. News of the struggle for women's
rights was pervasive, with reports on the progress of women in religion,
such as the first ordination of a woman in the Jodo sect of Buddhism,[34] in
the law, in the arts, and in education: "Our country has been far behind the

Mizoguchi's *Naniwa Elegy* (1936). Kawakita Memorial Film Archives.

Mizutani Yaeko in *Kyukancho*
(*Myna Bird*, 1928).
Private collection.

Western nations in the matter of women's education," says the Japanese language *Kokumin*.[35] The moga was a constellation of heterogeneous cultural influences, including the foreign, the passionate, the extravagant, and the individualistic, all of which militated against the hegemony of traditional social mores. Her representation in the movies, magazines, and in popular songs served to broaden the base of her notoriety and appeal.

While she was less than wholesome, the moga nevertheless helped popularize a "modern" and "cultured" lifestyle that incorporated all that was new and in vogue. The words *modan* and *bunka* ("cultural") were used as prefixes for things that were supposed to exemplify an ethic of convenience and taste: *bunka seikatsu* (living), *bunka jutaku* (dwelling), *bunka kamisori* (razor), *bunka nabe* (casserole), and of course *mobo* and *moga* all signify a faster, more stylish consumer commodification of city life. Along with the wildfire popularity of American jazz and other popular music, these buzzwords of the early 1930s capture a strain of urban culture that, while convenient, was still "deprecated as decadent 'modern disease.' "[36] " 'Modern life' was pronounced *modan raifu* as often as *kindai seikatsu*," writes Henry D. Smith, "and critics were quick to point out the pervasive Western—particularly American—cultural influence."[37] The American flapper was a similar popular icon of women's liberation that called forth similar controversies. But the flapper and her cousin, the vamp, crossed cultural boundaries less than ones of gender and propriety. Moga had the cachet of sexual adventurism, but, as noted above, was less likely to actually consummate the temptations she embodied. She had the added attraction of foreign exoticism, which, when displayed in the figure of a Japanese girl, represented a kind of cultural miscegenation as shocking as it was alluring.[38] Similarly, American movies themselves functioned as a siren urging a relaxation of the vigilance required to maintain the purity of Japanese virtues.

But Japanese movies were also regarded as culprits in the deterioration of youthful morals. In the *Japan Times* there appears an extended article on "The Three Dangerous S's: Sports, Screen and Sex."[39] The title of the story says it all, yet in addition to the platitudes about precocious youngsters imitating gangsters and claims that cheap American films are not conducive to "proper healthy mental or spiritual training [and] cater to the lower tastes," there is a remark about so-called *chan-bara*: "Often we hear of five or six-year boys [sic] hunting or even killing each other with tiny swords after imitating the samurai in the movie stories."

It is a significant concession that films with traditionally Japanese subject matter can also "cater to the lower tastes" and incite little boys to violence. This raises an important issue, namely, the attempt to winnow healthy from corrupting influences of Western practices is not as simple as

one might suppose, when Western technologies have already been assimilated into "traditional" culture. For instance, perhaps it is a certain tone or
style of motion picture, regardless of its subject matter, that is injurious to
public morals, especially to youth. It follows that the motion picture is not
an inherently "foreign," and therefore corrupting, apparatus. Consequently
the door opens for motion pictures to uphold traditional values and expressions of Japanese culture, not only to subvert them.

It is much the same with sports, the first dangerous "S." By 1930 baseball
had become a national mania, and was the most popular national sport in
Japan. Japanese society could not afford to lose its best and brightest to a
debilitating obsession with baseball, according to "The Three Dangerous
S's." The writer concedes that this is a social problem. But the answer is not
to throw out baseball, especially since baseball and other sports are blessed
with the enthusiasm of the emperor. Regardless of its American provenance,
baseball must be turned to purposes that fulfill the traditional goals and
virtues of Japanese society. The Japanese minister of education, Itta Kobashi,
favors the use of athletics as a way to check the spread of "dangerous or radical ideas" among the students. The pursuit of physical excellence can therefore serve as an inoculation against the threat of ideological contamination.

The next Saturday, November 30, 1929, the headlines blared "Education
Minister Quits; Suspected in Rail Scandal, He Resigns to Save Cabinet;
Premier Reported to Have Accepted Offer of Mr. Itta Kobashi." Not surprisingly, the early 1930s were as full of egregious political corruption as
they were of ultranationalist assassinations. According to the *Kokumin*
newspaper, "The people will probably not place much confidence in the
words and doings of these older-type politicians now that these unpleasant
scandals have been [uncovered]."[40]

The scepticism about the trustworthiness of elected officials was evident
in the rise of "dangerous thoughts" (*kiken shiso*), or radicalism, tainted usually with a Marxist revolutionary purpose. A review of the year lists the
mass arrests of 825 young communists in March and April as one of the key
events of 1929. According to Richard Mitchell, March 1928 saw the arrest
of 1600 communist and fellow traveler suspects.[41] Many of these young
communists were undergraduates and women for whom it was deplorable
to be associated with a movement that professes "disloyalty to the Throne,
than which there is no greater crime in the eyes of the nation."[42] While the
Asahi applauded the general elections in 1928 under the 1925 Universal
Suffrage Act, the *Japan Times* applauded the mass incarceration of young
communists under the Peace Preservation Law passed that same year.

The 1925 Peace Preservation Law extended the ability of the government to regulate political discourse and gave the power to suppress dan-

gerous thoughts to the police, thereby effectively prohibiting the formation of any organization that wished to change the form of government. This was passed in the name of safeguarding the Constitution; what it really amounted to was a mandate of complete police discretion in the regulation of public discourse:

> The police have actual control over the wording of speeches or printed matter used by the candidate, as well as power to permit or forbid the use of places for canvassing by any candidate. Whenever the police recognize "the nature" or "the contents" of a speech as being likely to disturb public peace and order, they can stop it and dissolve the audience, or they can prohibit the distribution of a pamphlet on a similar ground.[43]

The author concludes with the comment that it is completely up to the police how much a political candidate, particularly a proletarian candidate, will be handicapped. The police also had total discretion over the labor movement. An article in the *Yorozu* paper reported that the number of crimes in the capital were up four times what they were in 1929, from 128 in the first five months of 1929 to 430 in 1930. The article admonishes the police to ease its persecution of labor unions and begin to protect ordinary citizens: "As it is, the police force is used in controlling labor troubles and only a small part of it is employed for the purpose of protection of the masses. Thus, the police force has been used for the sake of capitalism rather than the public."[44]

Throughout the end of 1930 the police were constantly at war with labor unions, not only breaking strikes but scattering private meetings, intimidating labor leaders, imprisoning and beating suspected agitators, and generally forcing labor underground. There were 1,519 cases of labor-related violence registered through October of 1930, according to the Home Office.[45] This was 510 more cases than for the comparable period in 1929 and involved 136,539 people. A sharp rise in disputes over "output curtailments" like more holidays, cutbacks in hours and layoffs, as well as direct reduction of benefits (especially employers who reneged on discharge allowances, accounting for 660 cases alone) is attributed to the prevailing business depression. In 1929 alone there were over a thousand strikes and nearly 2,500 labor-related work stoppages.[46] The film industry was also consumed by labor strikes and other disputes.[47]

As the depression grew more acute, the Hamaguchi Ministry, especially the office of Home Affairs, grew more nervous about reports on the economic and financial condition of the country. Greater discretion was granted to the police to suppress dissent, not only in radical areas of labor strikes and student revolts but in the mainstream press as well. The economic and social crises of the early 1930s bred a paranoia that fed on any tolerance to deviation from strict norms, and consequently what was seen as dangerous thought grew along with it. The so-called thought movement was part and parcel of contemporary economic difficulties and an infatuation with Western customs and ideologies. The crudest evidence of this was revealed in 1923, when an imperial edict was issued expressing displeasure at the upsurge in "abnormal alien thought" and simply ordered everyone to stop thinking radical thoughts.[48]

In the cultural sphere there was an "overwhelming intellectual fashion for Marxism in the late 1920s."[49] The plight of the proletarian became a preoccupation of novelists, playwrights, and filmmakers. At the same time, one must also allow that the proletarian arts movement was also another manifestation of Japanese infatuation with the West. In any case, a review of the year 1929 cited the growth in demand for proletarian literature and the death of Osanai Kaoru—a pioneer in "tendency," or agitational, drama and film—as the two most important events of the year. But there was also a concurrent proliferation of escapist, not proletarian literature: "Readers in general seemed to want only cheap or ephemeral literature. The one-yen volume has established itself and rules the roost as aggressively as for the past few years."[50] The *Yomiuri*, moreover, called the authors of proletarian literature "selfish proletarians" who make fortunes selling their stories and enjoying lavish lifestyles while the plight of their farm and factory subjects remained wretched.[51]

The mere fact that commercial movie producers clambered onto the proletarian bandwagon is evidence of the economic rewards of the genre. Suzuki Shigeyoshi's *What Made Her Do It* (*Nani ga kanojo o saseta ka*, 1930) was a tendency film that, with its rousing denunciations of capitalism, provoked rioting in Asakusa and became the highest grossing picture in Japanese silent film history.[52] Written by a famous proletarian writer, Fujimori Seikichi, it was cleverly camouflaged for the benefit of the censors and was scheduled to run in the Soviet Union. Contemporary observers wryly commented on the appearance of "capitalist-leftist photoplays," whose accusations of capitalism and sympathy with the proletariat were belied by their eye on the marketplace.[53] Nevertheless, the headlines proclaim, "Japanese Turn To Serious Photoplays; Producers Derive Inspirations From Labor-Capital Conflicts."[54] The writer makes a point of contrasting the escapism of American talkies with the ideological drama in Japanese tendency pictures, in which social clashes represent the transformations of urban modernization. Many of the films ran afoul of censors.

Kataoka Teppei, a popular proletarian writer, turned to screenplays with his *Living Puppet* (*Ikiru ningyo*, dir. Uchida Tomu, 1929), the story of a man who starts to fight the capitalist establishment but ends up playing into their hands. The film was slashed by the censor but was still successful at the box office. He also wrote *Metropolitan Symphony* (Tokai kokyogaku), a film directed by Mizoguchi in 1929 that uses "dynamic montage" borrowed from the Soviets and "modern" heroines with "short hair, Western clothes, rouge, and lipstick."[55] Shochiku came out with *City in Turmoil, Bullets, The First Fire,* and *The Challenge* for its entries in the tendency film movement; Makino made *People Who Dance on the Line of Fate;* Kawai made *Women;* there were many others.

In such times of economic and political uncertainty, the tendency film movement was short-lived. When censorship pressure brought it to a quick conclusion, ero-guro-nansensu pictures stepped in to provide irreverent titillation, a sublimation of the social frustrations that had been represented explicitly by the tendency films.[56] New styles of jidai geki, too, manifested the social protest inherent in tendency pictures, though they were slower to meet the censor's blade due to their subject matter.

Chambara films made in the late 1920s clearly presage the leftist sensibilities of the more topical tendency films. Ito Daisuke, known as the father of chambara, began to make films with more social and political references at this time. His 1927 *Servant* (*Gero*) is said to be "a direct forerunner" of the tendency film, and his subsequent *Chuji Travel Diary* (*Chuji tabi nikki*) and *Ooka's Trial* (*Ooka seidan,* both 1928) continued his interest in a "sentimental nihilism" whose heroes "neither defended nor ignored the social system, but were instead in full revolt against it."[57] Makino Masahiro, Inagaki Hiroshi, and even Kinugasa followed this critical turn taken by chambara.[58]

By 1930 the tendency film movement, whose brief social protest was an excuse for the crackdown that tolerated ero-guro-nansensu, also developed issues treated earlier and more obliquely by the nihilistic chambara. In the early and middle 1930s chambara absorbed the comic side of the earlier chambara "nihilism" (the side most fully developed by ero-guro-nansensu) and this levity was what the monumental style rectified. The period setting of chambara, then, allowed greater leeway in both social criticism and stylistic experimentation. This leeway was later perceived as aberrant and steered back toward the true north of historical authenticity and monumentalism. From that more sober time, in 1937, one critic reflects on these nihilistic chambara: "While depending upon the historical past for their stories, they were all unfeignedly expressions of a most modern psychological type."[59]

It is important to see that the monumental style was a belated reaction against media representations whose social and political wellsprings are to be found in the 1920s. While the political situation turned toward authoritarian imperialism by the time of the Manchurian incident (1931), popular culture lagged from the era of Taisho liberalism. Literary critic Okuno Takeo writes, "The years 1933 through 1935 . . . marked the very height but simultaneously the finale of capitalism and liberalism in Japan after the First World War."[60] Urban life was clearly out of step with the increasing authoritarianism of the state, because vestiges of Taisho liberalism are plainly visible in popular culture long after the advent of Showa militarism in the early 1930s. During these same years the Army and the Home Ministry saw the need for tighter controls on popular information and entertainment. References to decadent Western influences in the censorship materials of the late 1930s bears out this historical tenacity. By the end of the decade the institutional mechanisms for censoring and enabling productions reflecting official preferences were in place. A brief description of their central features follows.

Self-Censorship: Prophylaxis of Dangerous Thoughts

At this very moment Japan stands at one of the great turning points in its history and, in carrying out its mission of rebuilding Asia, she must thrust aside all opposition. We Japanese have the blood of our ancestors throbbing in our veins. It is unthinkable that we should ever allow our splendid Japaneseness to fall into ruin. On the contrary, this love for things Japanese is destined to well up within (the creative artists among us), taking on marvelous new forms. Seen from this vantage point, the way forward for Japanese cinema is the bringing to real life of that unique beauty which is native to Japan. It is this which we must carry with us as we march out into the world.[61]
        —Otsuka Kyoichi, "Japanese Film at the Crossroads"

The critic Otsuka Kyoichi wrote this in 1939, the year in which the battle of Nomonhan was fought and the year in which Mizoguchi's *Story of the Last Chrysanthemum* was released. At Nomonhan the Kwantung Army pushed outward toward Mongolia and clashed with the Soviets. Over seventeen thousand Japanese soldiers were killed, after being exhorted by their officers to show their Japanese fighting spirit (*seishinshugi*), a spirit supposedly invincible to material force. They crashed like human waves against superior Soviet weapons and tactics, an ignominious defeat that was thoroughly suppressed from the Japanese people by Army censors. Though the idea of a superior, invincible Japanese spirit was a fiction, the Army continued to promote it within the ranks and on the homefront well before its more

notorious manifestations in the Pacific War.[62] *Seishinshugi*, and more generally *kokutai* ideology, was crucial to sustaining the war effort not only within
the military but among the civilian population as a whole. The censorship
of films and the regulation of the industry followed suit, in a mass indoctrination with kokutai ideology. This was done through the production of
kokusaku, or national policy, films. Their appearance was the culmination
of a gradual consolidation of state control over the production and content
of Japanese films.[63] Two aspects of prewar censorship especially set off the
textual features of the monumental style. The monumental style represents
first an imaginary Japaneseness defined in opposition to a threat perceived
as alien; a sort of Occidentalism, to borrow Said's famous term. According
to Miriam Silverberg, "The powerful draw of American culture as late as
1937 is evident even from a reading of *Kokutai no hongi*, the 1937 document
exhorting the Japanese people to acknowledge their singularity."[64] In order
to clarify the essence of their own culture, policy makers constructed a
Western "other" and this "required that it be portrayed as the mirror image
of the indigenous culture . . . usually imagined as a collective threat to
Japan's national independence and cultural autonomy."[65] The control over
the media that resulted in the monumental style was a reaction formation
against what Carol Gluck calls "metaphorical foreigners in whose alien
reflection the silhouette of patriotism emerged that much more clearly."[66]

Second, the mechanisms of censorship—the power structures and procedures used to secure consent—were continuous with time-honored
strategies of compliance gaining inherited from the Tokugawa era. Despite
the upheavals of the restoration, industrialization, and modernization, the
same avenues for compliance to state demands were available to the
authorities to exact cooperation from Japanese subjects.[67] Foremost among
the parallels between the imperial and Tokugawa censors was the absolute
authority of the state and the lack of any redress against that authority.[68]
Despite the Meiji constitution and the establishment of an ostensibly independent judiciary, the ensuing years saw an intensification of official vigilance against dangerous thoughts, whether Marxist, Christian, libertine, or
other dissenting varieties. The inoculation against dangerous thoughts
appealed to the two main creeds of kokutai orthodoxy, the unbroken lineage of Japan's imperial heritage and the organic unity of the body politic
figured by the emperor. For the sake of the nation-family, competing ideologies were systematically stamped out. Japanese historians have esti-
mated the number of books that were banned in the Meiji era to be 659 (in
forty-three years), in Taisho 651 (fourteen years), and in early Showa
through 1944 3,195 (eighteen years).[69]

But the numbers tell an abbreviated story. It was not the heaviness of the

censor's hand but its reach into the most private recesses of human activity—the mind—that transformed censorship into thought control. The
distinction between a properly public realm and a realm of private conviction off-limits to official intrusion was totally undermined. It was not just
the contents of particular thoughts that made them dangerous but the very
idea of thinking outside the pale of official scrutiny. A system of internal
self-censorship was foisted upon artists, authors, and entertainers. One side
of the coin was formal stipulations on the circulation of information, the
other was the expectation that the people censor each other and themselves. According to Mitchell,

> As the war crisis deepened after 1937, writers, journalists,
> broadcasters, and movie makers were faced with one choice:
> accept the rules of the onerous censorship system or withdraw
> from professional life. Confronted by strict government cen-
> sorship, on the one hand, and by what Maruyama Masao terms
> an "all pervasive psychological coercion," on the other hand,
> most people went along with the trend of the times.[70]

Censorship in the late 1930s is one important connection between the
monumental style's textual features and its social functions. The imposition
of specific guidelines in style and content on the one hand and the regulation of the film industry on the other is the institutional mediation between
the look of monumental films and the political purposes they serve.
Another connection is expressive: how technique and performance
expresses a sacramental version of Japanese nationalism. We usually think
of censorship as a form of constraint, but it can also be thought of as an
enabler, a compensation for the artificial guidance imposed upon artistic
creation. If censorship suppresses certain ideas or images, it also encourages and even demands others. So it is appropriate to analyze the monumental style in light of an internal preproduction code that governs the
patriotic implications of story and style.[71]

In addition to the carnage caused by seishinshugi fanaticism, 1939 also
saw the implementation of a new comprehensive censorship law, the *Eiga
Ho* No. 66. The 1939 Film Law was a codification of ordinances that had
sporadically governed film exhibition since 1917. Its purpose was to ensure
the steady production and exhibition of kokutai ideology on Japanese
screens; the product coming out of Japanese studios had to help raise a
specifically Japanese consciousness so that the war would be won. "Art
must be mobilized, said the Minister, for the sake of the nation."[72]

Oddly enough, the Film Law was one of the few in the late 1930s not justified as a war emergency measure. The law's first article declared its purpose to be the "healthy development of the film industry and the elevation of film quality."[73] The bill was sponsored by politicians who called it Japan's first "cultural law," but it shook the film industry to its roots by a complete restructuring of its relationship to the state.[74] In the name of cultural amelioration, then, the film industry was mobilized as a cog in the vast government propaganda machine.

The "healthy elevation" of Japanese film culture is a clue to the official disavowal of wartime emergency measures. Consistent with seishinshugi and kokutai ideology, there seemed to be a silent consensus that the people did not need to be persuaded of the propriety of the war in China so much as they needed reminding of the glories of their unique heritage. With the success of this cultural prompting, political support for the war would naturally follow.

Why, moreover, did Japanese film culture require a "healthy elevation"? Why was it felt that a film law was needed? By the late 1930s it was officially held that traditional Japanese values were widely in decline, and nowhere was this more in evidence than in the movies. In July 1938 a five-hour consultation between film writers and Home Ministry censors resulted in the following consensus.

First, they decided there was a need to eradicate the individualism fostered by foreign movies: "Avoid scenes of corruption and excessive merriment. Eliminate tendencies toward individualism as expressed in American and European pictures." Second, it was necessary to discourage frivolous language and behavior, especially that of young "modern" girls enamored of Western fashions and customs: "Because young men and women, especially modern women, are being Occidentalized, reeducate the people through films toward true Japanese emotions." Third, there was a need to elevate the Japanese spirit by encouraging admiration for the family system and the virtue of public sacrifice: "Develop the Japanese national philosophy, especially the beauty of the peculiarly indigenous family system and the spirit of complete sacrifice for the nation." And finally, Japanese moviegoers needed to be reeducated on the virtues of filial piety and respect for fathers, elder brothers, and other superiors; in other words, to re-Confucianize the Japanese people: "Banish insincere thoughts and words from the screen; deepen the respect toward fathers and elder brothers."[75]

These recommendations show a presumption that Japanese moviegoers had somehow lost their moorings and consequently required a reeducation in the fundamentals of their Japanese heritage. This was explicitly shown in the 1937 educational pamphlet, *Kokutai no Hongi* (The fundamentals of our national essence), that was issued for use in all public schools by the

Ministry of Education. Like the efforts made by those who championed the kokutai, state Shinto, the neighborhood associations (*tonarigumi*), and recitation of the Imperial Rescript every morning in the schools, discussion leading to the film law rested on a recovery of true Japaneseness through the resacralization of an indigenous heritage. The recommendations also show that "the distinction between political concerns and questions of manners and morals, fuzzy at best in earlier years, all but disappeared after 1937, with the growing aversion to foreign social customs."[76]

Less than a year later the Film Law was enacted and put into effect. Its provisions covered all phases of the industry, with regulations dealing with personnel, with pre- and postproduction censorship, and with exhibition. The Home Ministry and the Army tried to get the industry to internalize official standards of civic morality and taste; this entailed accepting the dissolution of the boundary between public propriety and private morality. For instance, everyone working in the industry, including producers, directors, actors, technicians, and distributors, had to have a state license. To work without a license was to earn a penalty of six months in prison and revocation of the right to work.[77] To get a license, actors and technicians had to pass competency tests that examined not only their professional skills but their politics as well. For example, in 1941 and 1942, prospective film workers were asked,

> What is the purpose of the Imperial Rule Assistance Movement?
> Why was it necessary to launch the "New Order" movement?
> Our country has an exalted national polity unmatched through-
> out the world. Why? Since the eruption of the Great East Asia
> War, the imperial armed forces have won consecutive victories,
> and now America and Britain are absolutely incapable of laying
> a hand on the Far East. However, it is said that "the real battle
> remains for the future." Why?[78]

These tests were not administered directly by the censorship arm of the state but by the Greater Japan Film Association (*Dai Nihon Eiga Kyokai*), a trade organization formed in 1933 for the purpose of consolidating the industry and performing official tasks. This gave the appearance of an industry dutifully regulating itself by ensuring the ideological correctness of its employees. The use of competency tests and the like also gave the impression that the government considered the film industry important enough to establish formal means to prevent any subversive influences from finding their way onto Japanese screens. It is also worth noting that in 1940 the head of the Cabinet Film Committee, the government liaison for the Greater Japan Film Association, was none other than Mizoguchi Kenji.[79]

As for the censorship of film content, the Film Law maintained strict supervision over all phases of the creative process: "Scripts will be censored before production and will be rewritten until they fully satisfy the Censorship Office of the Home Ministry."[80] Every time the ministry inspected a script or a film, a fee was charged to the studio. Inspections were also made after a film was completed, and censors could choose to ban, cut, or require reshooting of a film before it could be shown. The censors were concerned that films uphold national standards of patriotism and decency in two broad areas: "public safety," involving questions of ideology, patriotism, and other political matters; and "manners and morals," centering on questions of "proper" Japanese behavior.[81] Under the category of public safety censors were on the watch for breaches in the following areas: imperial family, nation, constitution, social organs, class conflict, national ethos, foreign affairs, group conflict, crime, and public business. Under manners and morals: religion, cruelty/ugliness, sex-related, work ethic, education, and family. Kazsa reprints a Home Ministry chart listing the amount of film cut under the inspection regulations of the Film Law between 1937 and 1942: an ultranationalist "dirty laundry" list on the cutting room floor.[82]

Since the orthodoxy sought by censors applied equally to politics, morality, and behavior, the rules imposed on Japanese films were not subject to any restraints on their proper sphere of influence. Film censorship therefore amounted to a near total discretionary power over what was considered acceptable thought and behavior, both in public and in private. For the sake of the nation the Film Law could categorically state that "Slice-of-life films (*shomin-geki*), films describing individual happiness, films treating the lives of the rich, scenes of women smoking, drinking in cafes, etc., the use of foreign words, and films dealing with sexual frivolity are all prohibited. Films showing industrial and food production, particularly the life in farming villages, should be presented."[83]

The Film Law also enabled the Home Ministry and Army to control exhibition. They could compel theaters to show nonfiction educational films consisting of newsreels and shorts.[84] These so-called culture films (*bunka eiga*) were explicitly modeled after the Nazi *Kulturfilm* promoted in Germany by Joseph Goebbels, and they were an economic boon for the struggling film industry, partly because they were exempt from the inspection fees imposed on entertainment films and could find an easy release. The last three months of 1939 saw the release of 985 culture films and in 1940 4,460.[85] Shochiku Studios' Kido Shiro claimed that it was his idea to adapt the *Kulturfilm* from Germany, although the Film Law as a whole was patterned after the Nazi *Spitzenorganization der Filmwirtschaft* and "even contained an anomalous warning against 'Jewish influences' within the nation's cinema."[86] Kido's reminiscence about his contribution to article 15, which provided for mandatory showings of newsreels and culture films, shows a startling ingenuousness about the benevolence of the government's involvement:

> It is the one thing from that era which even today I am really proud of having accomplished. I got the idea when I was visiting Germany and I saw how they stimulated the development of their own culture films by eliminating admissions taxes for theatres that showed them. It never once occurred to me that the Law would be used as a means of drawing cinema into the web of the new totalitarian regime.[87]

What Kido saw in the Film Law was product rationalization and marketing predictability, the twin grails of any businessman, especially those in the volatile film industry. Industry leaders applauded the elevation of their prestige in the passage of a law—long overdue—that specifically regulated film as an important medium in its own right. In return, studio bosses were only too happy to ally their companies with the government in the interest of ensuring the completion and distribution of their films. The Film Law, especially the first article, which mandated prior inspection of scripts, "not only allowed the authorities to participate 'positively' in the inception of a film—which put them in a fostering or nurturing position—the filmmaker was given a certain amount of assurance that his work would not be bureaucratically ambushed further down the line."[88] Censorship as it arrived in the Film Law, then, was welcomed as a way to minimize the risk inherent in the film industry by guaranteeing a market share for the right films through the intervention of the authorities. The Film Law not only gave the censors the legal right to dictate the content and style of Japanese film, it gave the industry an economic motive for upholding the censor's standards.

The Film Law also enabled the Ministry of Education to recommend feature films that upheld the national mission, thereby enhancing their visibility to a wide paying audience. An annual "Education Minister's Prize" was established to honor the best films of the year; it is testament to the jury's taste that the inaugural prize was awarded to Mizoguchi's *Story of the Last Chrysanthemum*, although some historians have speculated that the ministry nevertheless disliked the film for its portrayal of kabuki family authoritarianism.[89]

Kokusaku films were given special treatment for their ability to contribute to "the cultural advancement of the nation," to use the language in article 10. In the very late 1930s and early 1940s there was a lively debate over the future of kokusaku and culture films. This was partly a result of the Film Law and partly because of a general admission in the industry that Japanese film, especially chambara programmers, was in a precipitous decline. Some historians insist this was a "false consensus" that allowed the industry an easy rationale for starting a cozy relationship with the government.[90] Kokusaku films were usually overtly propagandistic, often taking inspiration from contemporary accounts of battlefield heroism like the "Three Human Bomb Patriots."[91] Influenced by newsreel techniques, kokusaku films grew more subtle in the late 1930s with the release of pictures like Tasaka's Tomotaka's *Five Scouts* (*Gonin no sekkohei*) and *Mud and Soldiers* (*Tsuchi to heitai*, both 1939). Nevertheless, kokusaku films were still regarded as the proper bearers of seishinshugi, that invincible spirit of Japanese fortitude.

A subgenre of kokusaku films that was more explicit than newsreel-influenced battle films in its expressions of seishinshugi was the rekishi eiga or historical film. These spectacular period pieces set in the Tokugawa era were developed around 1938. They were beloved by the authories for their tireless promotion of the glories of the Japanese feudal heritage, unlike the often irreverent, sceptical samurai in earlier jidai geki pictures. One of the earliest instances of rekishi eiga is *The Abe Clan* (*Abe Ichizoku*, 1938, directed by Kumagai Hisatora; see chapter 7). The former director of tendency films, Uchida Tomu, made *History* (*Rekishi*, 1940) a projected epic trilogy, but only the first installment was completed.[92] The best example of rekishi eiga is of course Mizoguchi's 1941 *Genroku Chushingura* (see chapter 6). Rekishi eiga was first envisioned by the critic Hasegawa Nyozekan, who called for a uniquely Japanese film aesthetic/ethic: "The *rekishi-eiga* must dedicate itself to the preservation of the Japanese past by building it into a new art form. The *rekishi-eiga* will then serve the function of training the people in that Culture of Feeling which is our special heritage."[93]

The rekishi eiga, then, became the province of that "Culture of Feeling" evoked by seishinshugi ideology. As the most explicit articulation of nationalism in the cinema, rekishi eiga is the most proximate generic norm from which the monumental style takes shape. Through a surprisingly labyrinthine course of concerns about the quality of Japanese film, economic motivations, patriotic fervor, industrial organization, and outright censorship, the monumental style came about. The monumental style is a product of the nationalist fervor manifested in the film industry of the late 1930s, though its technical features are not a simple reflection of nationalist propaganda. The rich complexity of the monumental style exactly suggests this hesitation and occasional ambivalence about its nationalist scaffolding. The mediations between its official sponsoring ideology and its formal textures are just as important as its patent nationalism. One suspects that the filmgoing experience in the late 1930s was a good deal more unpredictable and entertaining than the written historical record might suggest. A typical program to be seen in a Tokyo movie theater in 1940 might be imagined as follows.

Suppose a family hears rumors about developments on the Manchurian front. An elder son is serving in the Kwantung Army, so Mother and two younger children rush to the movie theater to see the latest newsreel. It is Wednesday, and the family is surprised to find that the Home Ministry has declared every Wednesday to be Home Front Day, on which immediate families of soldiers at the front are granted free admission.[94] The program begins with patriotic songs and slogans; then, before the anxiously awaited newsreel, one minute of silent meditation for the destinies of Japan's fighting sons.[95] With a fanfare of brassy trumpets, the newsreel, produced by an Army-sponsored combine of news services, comes on. Despite the cold, the soldiers are in high spirits as they march, scout, and camp on the frozen steppes. Footage of the front is distant, flat, and rather undramatic, and there is no reason to question the confident narrator's prediction that the front is steadily advancing with minimal casualties. The family relaxes and settles down to watch a short culture film about the Kitano Tenjin shrine to the legendary scholar-hero Sugawara Michizane. The film also covers the *matsuri*, or festival, held to commemorate the deification of Sugawara.

Finally comes the feature of the day, called *Heiroku Yume no Monogatari* (Heiroku dream stories), a children's musical fantasy released by Toho studios. Before the opening credits a statement informs the audience that the film has been inspected by the Motion Picture division, Cabinet Information Bureau of the Home Ministry. The film is a beautifully shot parable of a young runt of a samurai (played by the usually irreverent nansensu comedian, Enoken) who prevails over the goblins tormenting him by listening to his inner voice—which turns out to be the voice of his mother! The film has a light, even whimsical touch and the orchestral music is beautifully arranged and recorded. It is a profoundly reassuring film, and, when it is over, Mother is touched to see her two young children have dozed off in a pleasant slumber. As she gently shakes them awake the closing credits roll, followed by a message reiterating the inspection and registration of the film with the Home Ministry and an exhortation to join and contribute to the local neighborhood war relief committee. Mother makes a mental note to do that, alongside her silent recitation of things to pick up from the market on her way home.

In the background of this scenario a myriad of industrial, policy, and ideological factors work together, not without considerable friction, to encourage the development of the monumental style. There are, of course, the aesthetic and personal concerns of directors, writers, producers, and actors. During this period the inclinations of creative personnel cannot be dismissed as capitulation or even passive resistance to the demands of the state, as some critics are tempted to do.[96] The fact that a film was produced under the patronage of a repressive regime does not automatically negate its aesthetic stature. *Birth of a Nation* and *Triumph of the Will* are examples of films whose fascination and notoriety, if not their aesthetic stature, is enhanced because of their ideological monstrosities. A similar case can be made for *Story of the Last Chrysanthemum* and *Genroku Chushingura*, two films that fixate on nationalist visions but nonetheless are masterpieces. It is unacceptable to simply subordinate the films to the immediate cause of kokusaku national policy censorship, just as it is wrong to make Mizoguchi's, Kinugasa's, or Kurosawa's autonomy from censorship pressure a condition of their films' value. There is much evidence for Mizoguchi's collaboration with the militarists, like his travels to China to shoot "patriotic potboilers."[97] But Mizoguchi was such a headstrong, imperious character that it is more likely his personal and stylistic preoccupations developed parallel to, but independent from, the direction in which state policies were taking Japanese cinema.

In any event, Mizoguchi's personal concerns overlapped with state film policy in his contributions to policy directives as head of the Cabinet Film Committee in 1940. Mizoguchi's accountability to censorship regulations was minimized precisely because he was a member of the film establishment that propagated the regulations. Donald Kirihara maintains a parallel, but not necessarily a causal, link between film policy and Mizoguchi's film style:

> The government's increasingly hard line coincided with a move by Mizoguchi away from contemporary dramas and toward films with period settings. . . . The historical themes of Mizoguchi's late 1930s-early 1940s films were not simply films set in pre-modern periods. A "neo-historical" genre of films developed in the Japanese films of the late 1930s, centering around actual historical events and personages in situations of contemporary relevance. . . . Furthermore, these 1939–1944 films were not unattractive projects, in part because of the heightened popular emphasis on loyalty in the arts of the late 1930s.[98]

The monumental style, despite its intimacy with late 1930s Japanese nationalism, has a wide variety of purposes and functions: social, political, aesthetic, and religious. Its cultural significance is to be found in the multiplicity and even inconsistency of its cultural appropriations, not just its nationalist pedigree. My approach to the monumental style maintains as much as possible a balance between the dialectics of art and mass media, form and function, East and West. There are many ways to seek out these influences on the films, but I will be concentrating on features of style. Perhaps style is a more reliable, because it is a more discreet, indication of cultural changes than overt topical references to themes and events. Despite its fixation on Japaneseness, monumental style represents a distinct challenge in its crossing of so many cultural and historical borders. We will have done it justice if we can analyze it in depth and still maintain the fertility of its provenance and legacy.

4

Two Cultures and the
Japanese Period Film

Everyone is familiar with the way to turn earnest family parables like *Father Knows Best* or *The Brady Bunch* into high camp through historical and contextual displacement. The reason such dramas appear comic in the 1990s is not because the writers secretly larded the work with tidbits of subversive ridicule, but because of the changes rung in society and the family. The same storytelling conventions can be construed in modes that are heroic, realistic, or comic, depending on the norms of the society that produces and consumes the story. Changes in social norms determine the predominance of one fictional mode over others and moreover, regulate shifts from one mode to another.[1] The contemporary appearance of bygone family morality tales and Hollywood melodramas reveals a shift "downward" into comic and ironic modes from more earnest, elevated melodramatic and romantic modes of fiction.

I propose that around 1930, an opposite movement took place in Japanese storytelling. Not only is there a clear difference in the social and political norms of mid-1920s Taisho liberalism and mid-1930s Showa militarism but there is also a shift in the mode of fiction from a primarily comic to a primarily melodramatic mode. This shift loosely corresponds to the evolution of a second culture that radically departs from the cosmopolitan mood of Taisho liberalism. In literature there is a movement away from Western literary inspirations in the post-World War I period to a form of Japanese "culturalism": "The search for value led first to an examination of Western culture, which invariably sent the seekers to a 'return' to the 'native place of the spirit' (*Nibon kaiki*). After less than a decade, Japanese writers and intellectuals abandoned the cosmopolitan civilization for the familiarity of traditional culture."[2]

Tendencies in the Jidai Geki

The jidai geki genre of film also shows clear evidence of a shift "upward" from a primarily comic mode to a primarily melodramatic mode.[3] This shift clarifies the narrative and style of monumental films according to their jidai geki predecessors. In the early 1930s, when Japanese samurai films were still silent, chambara potboilers were at their most rambunctious: flashy, violent, and excessive. This was the time when chambara took on the fierce energy of the erstwhile nihilistic samurai movies and the freewheeling comedy of nansensu pictures (see chapter 3). Of this felicitous combination of "nihilistic nonsense," Peter B. High contends that it derives from the "Americanization" of samurai films, which attended the reorganization of the film industry after the Great Kanto Earthquake of 1923.[4] But by the late 1930s jidai geki had become more sedate, as if the conventions that earlier were just an excuse for acrobatic swordplay were now taken at face value.

The shift upward from comedy into melodrama was part of a more general redirection of cultural policy away from "crass Americanism," and, accordingly, the film industry came under increasingly close scrutiny by the censorship wing of the Home Ministry and the Army. The official view was that movies were a means to exercise control over popular perceptions of military-industrial activities on the Continent.[5] Jidai geki films up to Pearl Harbor can be classified, then, within two broad modes, the earlier comic mode (through ca. 1933) and the later melodramatic mode (through ca. 1941). Within these are complementary tendencies: the comic vs. the parodic tendencies within the comic mode and the melodramatic vs. the monumental tendencies within the melodramatic mode. We can diagram these tendencies as follows:

Mode	Tendency
Comic Mode (ca. 1924–1933)	Comic..............Parodic
Melodramatic Mode: (ca. 1933–1941)	Melodramatic.........Monumental

These are tendencies, not watertight categories. A film within the earlier comic mode is a more-or-less "ordinary" jidai geki: its hero is physical, volatile, and outside mainstream society, yet he prevails over antagonists that threaten social stability and functions as an affirmative, reassuring figure. An ordinary jidai geki in the later melodramatic mode, however, primarily functions on a level of sentiment and spirit rather than in the chambara realm of physical bluster. Not only the political climate but also the fact that the melodramatic mode comes into its own in the mid-1930s talkie era is an important factor in the shift from the comic to the melodramatic mode. A film showing a given tendency can be seen differentially in two ways: it can be situated on a continuum within a given mode, as an ordinary or distended example of its mode, or it can be seen historically, in contrast to a different mode altogether.

This classification of samurai movies is not meant to be a taxonomy of jidai geki but rather a tool for distinguishing eccentric from more ordinary films. Generally, the melodramatic mode is more narrative- and character-centered than the comic mode, which is somewhat surprising considering the movement toward nativist, anti-Hollywood expressions in the late 1930s. The parodic and monumental tendencies within the modes show a greater concern with style than comic and melodramatic tendencies, because they depend upon the codification established in the earlier tendency.

There is a rough homology between the two jidai geki modes. The monumental style is to melodramatic jidai geki as the parodic is to the ordinary comic jidai geki. Melodramatic jidai geki has in common with the monumental style a didactic purpose, but while the former teaches a fairly straightforward lesson, the latter seeks to inspire, to exhort, to awe. Melodramatic jidai geki bear some resemblance to socialist realist films: glorification of the folk hero, frequent use of a collective protagonist (especially important for *Genroku Chushingura* and *The Abe Clan*), a strongly didactic objective, clear differentiations between good and evil, a larger-than-life parable that illustrates a moral lesson. This resemblance marks the step taken away from the primarily comic orientation of jidai geki before 1933 into the officially preferred melodramatic mode.

The melodramatic mode, that is, aims to teach a lesson by means of attention-getting stories. But the monumental style goes further than this. Films in the monumental style don't just illustrate the glory of Japanese tradition, they embody it. I will elaborate in my discussion of the "perceptual" techniques of *Genroku Chushingura* in chapter 6. The monumental style differs considerably from melodramatic jidai geki in its technical repertoire, even though the two share a primary teaching function. While melodramatic jidai geki uses basically the same materials as the monumental style, its principles of narrative economy, stylistic utility, and ideological predictability put it in the same family as the "American-style" chambara films of the 1920s and early 1930s. The chambara films employ a combination of stabilizing and disorienting techniques: clear establishing shots, orientational matching, rapid cutting, occasional swish-pans, and an overall furious pace. With the melodramatic mode, a new kind of film practice has taken over from the comic jidai geki, but classical Hollywood techniques are still de rigueur, as in the case of the straightforward propaganda of *Miyamoto Musashi* (Inagaki Hiroshi, 1940). The monumental style tries hard to break out of this evolutionary tendency. It resists classical Hollywood technique at the level of form for the crucial wartime purpose of renewing the audience's perception of the Japanese cultural heritage. People would perhaps thereby see their country and its traditions with the veneration it deserved and make draconian sacrifices for its survival and glory. Melodramatic jidai geki are supposed to do this, but the monumental style is a more radical challenge to its audience and its genre. In his capacity as head of the Cabinet Film Committee, Mizoguchi proclaimed the necessity "for film practice to change with the times, to express current political reality with the proper 'expressive gesture.' That gesture, he believed, could be found by adopting the spirit of Japan's noble past."[6]

The more prewar jidai geki one watches, the more reasonable becomes the idea that jidai geki are basically comic.[7] Excepting pre-World War I jidai geki that are kabuki adaptations, the comic mode is the oldest and most influential kind of jidai geki. In other words, jidai geki are essentially comic, this being the "default" from which others take their defining features. Not only are jidai geki from the 1920s and early 1930s generally humorous, with plenty of wit, pratfalls, and outrageous situations, but they also often evoke a sense of healthy irreverence. A good example is the *Tange Sazen* series made throughout the 1930s: Tange Sazen is a tough, cynical ronin whose nihilism is more endearing than threatening. The films do not hesitate to probe his more human vulnerabilities, as in the 1940 *Tange Sazen: Lovesick* (Nakagawa Nobuo).

Tange Sazen prewar
souvenir program.
Private collection.

Okochi Denjiro as Tange Sazen in Yamanaka Sadao's *Pot Worth a Million
Ryo* (*Hyakuman Ryo no Tsubo*, 1935). Kawakita Memorial Film Archives.

A more typical example is a two-part Nikkatsu chambara film made in 1932, *Mito Komon* (Tsuji Kichiro), a Japanese Robin Hood film that employs physical "low comedy" (pratfalls, pantomime, mugging the camera, etc.). Much of the film's humor comes from Okochi Denjiro's deadpan smirk; his truculent pout makes him look like a perpetually disgruntled yakuza. A scene in which the protagonist and his cook exchange glares over a domestic tiff plays off the tough guy reputation of chambara samurai; samurai and cook stand at loggerheads, daring each other to back down. Another gag in a chase scene employs the traditional design of 90 degree Japanese corridors with the camera stationed at empty intersections; the hero and his pursuers appear and disappear from unexpected directions. The scene has the hero escape by jumping up on the roof and pelting his tormentors with tiles, not even giving them the dignity of a real sword fight. Mito Komon's cook practices his *nagauta* singing technique, intercut with shots of a howling dog. Much of the plot revolves around Mito Komon's ability to outwit his antagonists by eavesdropping on their plans—hiding in the belfry and in other undignified places.

The ordinary comic jidai geki usually has a happy ending; the hero cuts down a few dozen of his enemies, spurns the affections of the girl he has saved, and jauntily sets off in search of new adventures. The integration of the hero into the community through marriage, the usual mark of the Western comic hero, is almost nonexistent in jidai geki. Instead, the comic jidai geki stresses the hero's fallibility and humanity. He will prevail over his antagonists, but not without committing some error of judgment or enduring some excruciating humiliation, as in the 1937 black comedy *Hitohada Kannon* (The mercy goddess of Hitohada Shrine, Kinugasa Teinosuke). The same year, Kinugasa embarked on a more monumental course with *Summer Battle of Osaka* and, later, *Battle of Kawanakajima* (1940).

In the 1932 *Kaigara Ippei* (Nikkatsu, Kiyose Eijin), the eponymous hero is napping as the prisoner he is supposed to be guarding slips away. As a stand-in for the escaping prisoner, a cat creeps stealthily along the edges of the corridor. The cat turns out to belong to Kaigara; however, when he grabs it he attracts the attention and the wrath of the boss who discovers his prisoner is gone. Kaigara's humiliation is compounded when he and his little cat take refuge in the skirts of a friendly priest who stands between the enraged boss and the cowering Kaigara. He later redeems himself with the help of a crafty water juggler (cf. Mizoguchi's 1933 *Taki no Shiraito*), but it is a long road back from such an undignified initiation.

In silent jidai geki the hero's trials and triumphs are very predictable, both in plot and style. This is why an ordinary jidai geki lends itself to parody so easily; its conventions are so schematic that they virtually beg for some kind of twist. Most comic jidai geki have elements of self-parody in them, and it is often difficult to clearly sift out parodic from ordinary comic

A simple thief outwits a samurai in *Hitohada Kannon*
(*The Mercy Goddess of Hitohada Shrine*, Kinugasa Teinosuke, 1937).
Kawakita Memorial Film Archives.

jidai geki. Nevertheless, jidai parodies tend to take a slightly jaundiced distance on the protagonist, making him the butt of jokes and humiliations no less than his antagonists. This gives the jidai parody a darker side, revealing not only an ambivalent representation of the comic world but also a reflexive awareness of representational conventions. The willingness to lampoon beloved conventions of the standard jidai geki shows not only the extent to which the conventions are codified but also the different kinds of comic satisfaction to be taken in the objectification, scrutiny, and ridicule of established forms. This is another aspect of the "nihilism" held over from the earlier politically progressive jidai geki: the films do not necessarily take their own formula elements very seriously.

A good example of a jidai parody within the comic mode is the well-known 1931 Nikkatsu silent, *Beni Komori* (*Red Bat*, Tanaka Tsuruhiko). This flashy picture takes the debunking implicit in *Mito Komon* and *Kaigara Ippei* over the top. The hero is obviously lower class: vulgar, uninhibited, full of bile and gags. The drinking scene, an indispensable element of jidai geki, is used as an opportunity for technical tricks like animated sake bottles appearing out of nowhere, faces, objects, and titles going out of focus, dissolves, and a shaky, hand-held camera. What makes the scene exceptional, though, is the attempt to render subjectively, through perceptual point-of-view structures, the sensations of drunkenness. This shows how the conventionality of formula elements can often encourage attempts to experi-

Jidai geki parody: *Beni komori* (*The Red Bat*, Tanaka Tsuruhiko, 1931).
Kawakita Memorial Film Archives.

ment with what would otherwise be overfamiliar. Stylistically or narrative-
ly, the more entrenched a formula element is, the more likely it becomes a
target for rehabilitation or defamiliarization.

Nowhere is this more apparent than in chambara fight scenes, and *Beni
Komori* again takes its fights to wild, experimental extremes.[8] The opening
scene begins with an Eisensteinian montage of canted angles and fragmented shots of carts, wagon wheels, and tools flying through the air.
Every technique imaginable is used here to show the hero's swashbuckling
strength. Split-screen, upside-down, warped, and out-of-focus images are
furiously intercut together, adding up to "attractions" worthy of *Strike*. The
acting style, moreover, recalls Kuleshev's experiments with biomechanics.
The hero, laughing uproariously at the consternation he causes the townspeople, swaggers along in a highly stylized, exaggerated burlesque. He
starts to mimic the lumbering movements of a sumo wrestler as he seizes an
antagonist's haunches; he rocks back and forth in mock exertion, and the
crowd rocks back and forth with him. Tiring of this pantomime, the Red
Bat flings the other man far out of the area, flattening the gaping crowd.
Then he turns, looks directly into the camera, and laughs maniacally.

Although this differs from the more serious culminating sword fight, it
does show, first, that the conventionality of a jidai geki episode is grounds
for innovation and parody, second, that the conventions comprising the
"normal" comic jidai geki—the ordinary hero, the gags and humor, the

happy ending—can easily be burlesqued and transformed into satirical, even grotesque extremes. The *Enoken* (Enomoto Ken'ichi) samurai burlesques are exemplary, possessing an outrageousness comparable to Monty Python send-ups of genre conventions. This will change in the late 1930s when the center of gravity in jidai geki shifts "upward," from a comic to a melodramatic mode. But within the melodramatic mode the same dialectic between the ordinary jidai geki and its complement still holds. The complement of the melodramatic jidai geki is the monumental style.

In the mid-1930s jidai geki evolved out of the comic mode and became more earnest and didactic. They avoid the irreverence that is a feature of the comic jidai tradition, especially the physical sight gags and slapstick that populates comic jidai geki. They rely more on drama and characterization where the standard comic jidai geki centers on situation and spectacle. Melodramatic jidai geki from the late 1930s are the source of what we usually think of as "samurai films": impassive swordsmen à la Mifune/Eastwood who despite their better judgment, step into a flawed society to right some injustice or exact some vengeance. In the melodramatic mode more is at stake than in the comic: the evil perpetrated against the innocent is more threatening; the hero is wise, not just clever; the community is restored with a greater sense of urgency. These heroes are more dignified, more implacable and mythical, and are less likely than samurai heroes from

Enomoto Ken'ichi (Enoken) burlesquing Kondo Isamu (*Enoken no Kondo Isamu*, 1935). Kawakita Memorial Film Archives.

the early 1930s to suffer chastisement. Melodramatic jidai geki are "serious" historical dramas that are usually just as hidebound as the chambara potboilers that preceded them, but they set their sights higher, aiming to tell an entertaining story and, along with it, to deliver an instructive theme. A good example of a melodramatic jidai geki is *Edo no Taka*.

The 1938 *Edo no Taka* (Falcon of Edo, Konoe Sushiro) is set in very late Tokugawa Japan and champions education as the key to redirecting samurai energies in changing times. It is unusually sophisticated in its use of cutaways and ellipses that skip over sword fight scenes, traditionally the bedrock of jidai geki entertainment. Although some samurai films confiscated by the Occupation had their sword fight scenes clipped for propaganda and research purposes, the internal structure of *Edo no Taka* confirms its elliptical style by emphasizing the brandishing of knowledge rather than the *katana*, long sword. Since the film deals with the transformation of samurai from martial artists to civil bureaucrats, its evocative, metaphoric cutaways from fight scenes to freshly sliced reeds is consistent with the thematic material of the film.

Comic jidai geki consist largely of standard situations (street confrontations, drinking scenes, festivals, planning attacks, and of course the culminating sword fight), which work as scaffolding for spectacle and do not primarily function to carry narrative or thematic meaning. In the comic jidai geki, sword fights are a whirling choreography of flashing blades and spinning bodies, inviting a kinetic experience of abandonment to a playful, vertiginous chaos. Melodramatic jidai geki like *Edo no Taka* are more dignified, with sword fights punctuated by moments of extreme tension signifying the imminence of death. A seriousness of purpose (bordering on the pretentious) chiefly distinguishes the melodramatic from the comic jidai geki.

An illustration of the melodramatic tendency is Inagaki Hiroshi's 1940 version of *Miyamoto Musashi* (Nikkatsu, not to be confused with Inagaki's samurai trilogy from the mid-1950s with Mifune Toshiro). To this day, Musashi has the legendary reputation in Japan as a sword-saint, but this alone does not account for the solemnity with which he is presented in Inagaki's film. There were, after all, many legendary swordsmen—Benkei the rogue monk, Yasubei, hero of Takadanobaba, Iwami Jutaro the strong man, and the one-eyed Tange Sazen—who were heroized, and then humanized, in the earlier comic mode. The original novel *Musashi* by Yoshikawa Eiji also emphasized the fallibility of its eponymous hero. The snail's pace and solemn tone of *Miyamoto Musashi* is a deliberate effort to mythologize Musashi, even in his abject, tormented moments when he begs his implacable abbot to show him the way to enlightenment. The historical Musashi is known to have been caught between inclinations toward the life of a warrior and that of a contemplative Zen monk.[9] Postwar renditions of the

Musashi story often dwell on this schizophrenic pull between action and contemplation: "how to reconcile self-effacement and Zen with self-aggrandizement and the sword."[10] But Inagaki's 1940 version clearly shows Musashi coming to terms with his heroic destiny. The abject supplications and humiliations before his abbot-mentor are a trial Musashi must endure before reaching his spiritual apotheosis; this could be a remnant of the comic jidai geki convention of putting the hero through some humiliation to puncture his hubris. But here the humiliation is self-imposed and unlike the postwar schizophrenic Musashis, it is clearly resolved in favor of a higher spiritual attainment.[11]

It is nevertheless a rather masochistic film, not only because of Musashi's torment but also because of the tribulations undergone by Otsu, the young woman in search of Musashi. In a pouring rain she frees old Osugi, who knows Musashi's whereabouts but is trapped inside a cave. When Osugi emerges she savagely beats Otsu. The old crone accuses her of base motives in her act of kindness. When the three are finally united, they all ask each other's forgiveness for having failed one another. The relationship between Musashi and his mother-surrogate on the one hand and his mistress-surrogate on the other is obviously love, but it is sublimated into expressions of worship and protests of unworthiness. The film is very static in certain ways, full of declamatory speeches and histrionic soliloquys, but in others it is very cinematic,

A highly sublimated *Miyamoto Musashi* (Inagaki Hiroshi, 1940).
Kawakita Memorial Film Archives.

using beautiful outdoor locations to good advantage, with plenty of long shots and tracking movements.

The single most "mythological" touch in the film is an extremely long take of Musashi and Sasaki Kojiro, his archrival, squaring off in a final showdown on the Ganryu Island beach. If, as Burch says, chambara films' original raison d'être was a greater "realism" (i.e., violent spectacle) in their sword fights, it is easy to see how far melodramatic jidai geki has come from its low comedy chambara roots. One could imagine that samurai films had reached some kind of saturation by 1940 from the enormous buildup given to the showdown between Musashi and Kojiro—with hardly any violent payoff. In the earlier comic mode it is almost all payoff and very little buildup. The high angle, extreme long shot of Musashi and Kojiro crouched on the beach, swords ready, lasts well over a minute—with no movement in the frame at all, save the breaking of the waves at their feet and the ripple of their robes in the wind. Then an abrupt match-on-action to a close-up of Kojiro's lunging sword breaks the spell, and the fight is over. Kojiro's triumphant smile turns into a hideous leer as blood dribbles from his mouth and he falls on his face.

Though the scene is tremendously overblown, it is also electrifying compared to more conventional samurai fight scenes, which aim to milk the last drop of action from the dramatic situation. The scene suggests that the conflict between Musashi and Kojiro is not one of technique, but of will and spirit. The shot is held for so long that the suspense of who will win gradually drains away and we are left with an almost abstract tableau of pure confrontation. The interminable buildup to the climactic moment invites the viewer to "fill in" the dramatic suspension with something besides the diegetic material already provided. The near silent soundtrack (faint sound of ocean waves) enhances this process of detachment and abstraction from the diegetic situation. One is reminded of Tadao Sato's description of Japanese rhythm in dance and music based on *mie*, "fixations," "movement toward a fixed posture, a hesitation in perfect balance, and then the dropping away from this posture toward the achievement of a further and later fixation."[12] The particulars of the Musashi tale drop away and the ideology of the film, a stark epitome of the conflict of Self and Other, is laid bare.

We are here straying into territory of the monumental style, in which the displacement of physical action by technique counts as a primary feature. Yet *Miyamoto Musashi* does not quite reach the status of the monumental style, because the sacramental technique of the climax is untypical of the whole film; this is one reason why the climactic scene is so striking. The major portion of the film reveals it to be a standard Nikkatsu jidai geki picture. It has a gleeful action sequence at the beginning of the picture in which Otsu valiantly fights off a gang of bandits. The sequence in which Musashi's Zen mentor sets him on the course of enlightenment is shot with a patent studio slickness. The spotlights in the day-for-night woods illuminate a rather cheap-looking (and cheap-sounding) sound stage. Optical tricks like a montage of signs and split screens tell the time and place of the Ganryu Island duel. And an interesting use of "Q. and A." cutting can be found in a village scene in which everyone wonders where Musashi is just before the big confrontation. One man says, "Where could he be?" while someone in another part of town seems to reply, "I bet he's chickened out!" to which a woman in a tearoom says, "He wouldn't miss a chance to cut down Kojiro," etc. This synecdoche establishes the common people as background spectators and well-wishers of Musashi and assigns him the role of a people's folk hero. From the perspective of the monumental style, however, such techniques only call attention to themselves.

Miyamoto Musashi exhibits vestiges of the standard Nikkatsu jidai geki in the postquake film industry. Nikkatsu and Shochiku were the biggest players in the vertically integrated industry and their productions basically divided the market into the period genres dominated by Nikkatsu and the contemporary genres controlled by Shochiku. Because of Shochiku's success adapting Western styles for Japanese audiences, Nikkatsu found it profitable to experiment with the samurai formula, injecting doses of rapid-fire cutting, close-ups, and above all more realistic, physical swordplay (chambara). Along these lines Ito Daisuke, Makino Masahiro, and others, devised the modern nihilistic samurai hero, who presaged the more explicit social protest films in the late 1920s tendency genre. By the 1930s Nikkatsu was struggling. Labor disputes and creative differences among stars, directors, and studio bosses led to the formation of independent and subsidiary production companies, such as Dai-Ichi, P.C.L. (Photo Chemical Laboratories), and the J.O. company. Toho was formed from a merger of P.C.L. and J.O. in 1935 and was an important reconstitution of the jidai geki market. Its specialty was star-stealing, and the company's success at luring into its ranks such luminaries as Hasegawa Kazuo, Yamada Isuzu, Hara Setsuko, Irie Takako, and Takamine Hideko, as well as directors Kinugasa Teinosuke, Makino Masahiro, and Yamanaka Sadao, meant that its domination of jidai geki was assured.[13] At about the same time Shochiku bought out Nikkatsu, its former rival, in 1936. Toho recognized that national policy pictures could be profitable and concentrated on military pictures and big period film extravaganzas. Eventually these were given official approval under the rubric of rekishi eiga (history films). These long didactic period pieces were the least economical way for the strapped film industry to spend its limited war

Yamanaka Sadao's bitter *Humanity and Paper Balloons* (*Ninjo Kamifusen*, 1937)
Private collection.

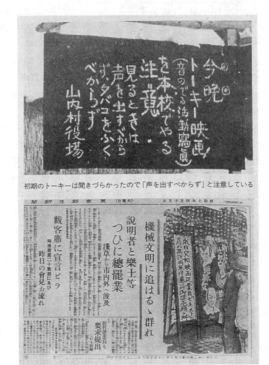

初期のトーキーは聞きづらかったので「声を出すべからず」と注意している

A warning not to talk
or smoke during
talking picture shows
(early 1930s).
Private collection.

resources, but they functioned as a vehicle for suitably elevated exhortations to dutiful Japanese deportment (i.e., obedience) as well as departing from the frivolity of standard Nikkatsu chambara. Toho therefore did enormously well up through the end of the war.

I have already suggested one central feature of the monumental style: the displacement of physical action by technique in a genre whose defining trait is the celebration of physical violence. Other stylistic complexes of the monumental style include the glorification of Tokugawa ethics and deportment, graphic representations of collective spectatorship, concentration on the aesthetics of period detail and design, and a valorization of familial and clan structures, especially when they require self-immolation. The number of films in the monumental style is limited because their entertainment value is limited. If melodramatic jidai geki are deliberate in their pace and dignified in their tone, monumental films by comparison are ponderous and magisterial. The monumental style does not compromise the integrity of its pace, narrative design, or period authenticity. It is limited in its use of expository devices, cause and effect, and individuation of character, which, in melodramatic jidai geki, carries along our interest as well as edifying us. Such techniques seem adulterations in a representation whose primary concern is the hieratic preservation of classical forms. Compared with the lightness of the standard comic jidai geki and the earnest clarity of the melodramatic films, the monumental style seems rather opaque. But no one expects a sacrament to be easy. Rather than list other features of the monumental style in the abstract, consider now a film in the monumental style for an inductive display.

Shogun and Mentor

Iemitsu to Hikozaemon (Shogun Iemitsu and His Mentor Hikozaemon) was made by Makino Masahiro for Toho Studios in 1940, and released in March of 1941. It tells of the lessons learned by the famous "barbarian-quelling generalissimo" in his youth. His mentor Hikozaemon, a crafty old Falstaff to Iemitsu's Prince Hal, teaches him the tricks of diplomacy and character judgment, only to fall prey to young Iemitsu's decision to retire him—a decision made on the basis of his lessons with Hikoza (his informal name). The faithful old retainer is sent to Nikko in retirement/exile because as official mentor of the shogun he cannot participate in affairs of state. But Hikoza performs a final service for his young master. He aborts a coup attempted by a sinister adviser—the same one Hikoza outmaneuvered in the power struggle for Iemitsu's protectorate. Hikoza's craftiness and penchant for eavesdropping allows him to see through the evil adviser's scheme and help the shogun escape the sealed-off castle, which was planted with a bomb. They escape in the nick of time.

The film concludes with a long section on the death of Hikoza: a lively crosscut scene between Hikoza on his deathbed and the young shogun rushing to his side, the sorrowful parting, and obligatory obeisance to the emperor (a revisionist fillip considering the real shogun's primary concern was to keep the emperor in check). The narrative of *Shogun and Mentor* is basically about a surrogate filial relationship which explores the mutual regard and interdependency between Iemitsu and Hikoza.

Stylistically, the film is a period court drama detailing the machinations of interpersonal politics in the royal (shogunal) family. Although it begins with a battle scene, this is merely background material and most of the drama takes place in the opulent halls of the shogunal residence. The bulk of the film consists of meetings, consultations, and formal audiences between various samurai officials, high-ranking priests, and the shogun himself. These take place in lavish period tearooms, gardens, and verandas. The film emphasizes the beauty and simplicity of Japanese design and constantly employs ink paintings, pottery, and flower arrangements as important parts of the set. There are several dance performances in the film, one of which is the famous lion dance (*shishi mai*), a noh-inspired kabuki favorite performed by the villain before he dies. The other dances are not very traditional; they are performed by courtesans and serve a special function in the narrative. The film is very ceremonial, dwelling not only on the physical aesthetics of the mise-en-scène but also on the behavioral protocols of life at court, the polite speech, the deep bows, the arrangements of officials and samurai assembled in formal congregations, performing formal duties.

Into this environment old Hikoza is introduced as a foil. In one sequence a group of young officials, including Iemitsu, is busily writing documents while the bumbling old man wanders aimlessly about, unsuccessfully awaiting their attention. The scene continues in a series of discontinuous shots of the old man in different parts of the stateroom, shuffling along, muttering to himself, and adjusting his heavy spectacles as the young officials obliviously continue their work. The spatial discontinuity of the individual shots suggests temporal ellipsis—we don't exactly know how much time has elapsed between shots—but the real intent might be to show off the opulent screens, *fusuma* sliding doors, carved roof supports, and tokonoma alcove of the surrounding space. The sequence also reveals Hikoza to be a nuisance and a deadweight in the eyes of the shogun and his colleagues, and they obviously do not bother to conceal this from Hikoza. As with Prince Hal and Falstaff, it is a classic conflict of generational perspectives: decorum vs. decrepitude, detachment vs. demonstrativeness.

The young Shogun Iemitsu does not have a monopoly on courtly protocols, however. The first scene in which old Hikoza outwits the dour Takechi for the protectorate of the boy shogun is a model of monumental formality. The scene is set by an establishing shot of the shogun's castle at Edo. Instead of a direct transition to the imminent showdown of wits, a series of close-ups show us a ball being kicked around the formal garden by the boy shogun and his companion, Izu. They are looked after by a watchful wet nurse, and these shots establish the stakes in the upcoming contest.

Cut to a prototypical monumental setup: a large group of samurai assembled in a meeting hall and perfectly centered by a low-lying camera positioned at the back of the hall in the center aisle. The samurai bow in unison as the official in charge enters from frame right. The scene establishes a theatrical and pictorial space through the prosceniumlike geometry of the congregation. The salience of pictorial composition is emphasized by the extreme formality of the configuration. Another important aspect of this setup is the fact that it is not the camera but the authority figure at the furthest remove from the camera that justifies this congregational arrangement. The scene is hypercentered, but not around the viewpoint of the observer/spectator; it is rather more like the centeredness of a cathedral nave than that of a Renaissance perspectival painting, Other-centered rather than ego-centered.

When the action begins a series of shots and reverse-shots is initiated that is typical of virtually all "serious" jidai geki. A medium close-up of a retainer in the front row is shown over the shoulder of the presiding official as the lead retainer begins his request. The shots ritualistically shift back and forth between the official and congregational fields of view as the audience continues. In the present case these shots smoothly alternate in medium shot between the officious Takechi and the suavely condescending shogunal regent who discharges responsibility for the boy shogun's training. Takechi requests permission to take the boy into his custody for the purpose of inducting him into the political and ceremonial protocols in which he, Takechi, is so adept.

A brief insert of the two boys, Iemitsu and Izu-dono, punctuates the scene in the meeting hall. Back in the hall, the samurai perform another deep bow, but are interrupted by the wheezing Hikozaemon ambling into the room. He manifests outrageous, atrocious behavior, and even the unflappable regent is appalled. Hikoza casually makes his case to the regent for custody of the boy and casts sly aspersions on Takechi's appropriateness for the position.

Takechi takes offense, and when the regent denies Hikoza his petition the old man plays his trump card, saying he has no choice but to kill himself then and there. Hikoza was a favorite of the late shogun and in fact carries him to safety in the battle scene that opens the film. Though the regent allows Hikoza to get far enough into his seppuku preparations to show that he is not merely bluffing, the regent relents and awards the young shogun's guardianship to Hikoza. Both regent and Hikoza know that once the new shogun took power he would be ruthless with those who allowed the beloved Hikoza to take his own life. The camera then returns to its "sacramental center" six inches off the tatami aisle. The scene ends with the boy cavorting with his beloved *jii* (grandpa) Hikoza as tears well up in the old man's eyes.

The entire sequence outlines a salient monumental technique, which I call objectified spectatorship. A scene is constructed around a compositional principle that centers not on the camera/empirical spectator but on a collective spectatorship implicit in the configuration of the group. This is clearest in the "sacramental center" of the opening and closing shots, but there are other moments when it comes forward, e.g., the interruption of the samurai's bow when Hikoza first comes shuffling in. A collective configuration is outlined by the ceremonial ritual, and Hikoza's disruption sets it off in clearer relief. As mentioned before, Hikoza tends to be defined in opposition to the monumentalism that prevails in the film, both stylistically and in the mood of courtly decorum. Although he is a heroic character (after a fashion), his inability to negotiate the graces required of court life makes him an anomalous, comic, and often pathetic figure.

This is emphasized again when Hikoza and Shogun Iemitsu, now a young man, confront each other on the question of Hikoza's future. The old man wants to remain with his beloved shogun when he travels to Kumamoto to investigate a potential disturbance. Shogun Iemitsu refuses, insisting that Hikoza is too old to make the trip and that his desire to accompany him is really a death wish. Hikoza refuses to accept this and keeps pushing the shogun until Iemitsu finally breaks down in exasperation, sobbing "Baka! Baka!" ("Stupid!") on Hikoza's shoulder and ineffectually beating him on the head. Here the shogun reverts to a childhood tantrum, which, as Hikoza knows, indicates the degree of Shogun Iemitsu's dependence on his mentor. Stylistically, the scene is as unmonumental as can be, shot in intimate close-up as the young shogun totally loses his composure, to Hikoza's secret satisfaction. It is as if Iemitsu is drawn to a monumental deportment by virtue of his position while Hikoza holds him back in a state of infantile dependency.

Considering the accomplishments of the historical Iemitsu, this is a plain whitewash of the shogun's character. Far from a soft, compassionate general motivated by emotional concerns, Iemitsu is known as a brilliant and ruthless consolidator of the shogunate. He is known for programs that stripped provincial daimyo of their power of assembly, such as the *sankin kotai* system of forced residency in Edo, programs of taxation and land reform that allowed the shogunate to keep constant tabs on their activities, and severe sumptuary laws that regulated the lifestyle of daimyo. Iemitsu is even known to have forced his own brother to commit suicide when it seemed apparent that he and his supporters were plotting to take over the shogunal title.[14] A short coda to the scene has Iemitsu silently pondering this state of affairs, musing in extreme close-up on the fate of his beloved mentor.

A resolution of the emotional deadlock between Iemitsu and Hikoza is suggested in the following scene. The shogun is having a farewell celebration and calls forth his stable of dancers. Performed by geisha, the sequence is distinctly un-Japanese. It is accompanied by nondiegetic music played on Western instruments and shot from a long high angle that emphasizes the choreography of the dance. The music and dance are light, sentimental, even a bit tawdry—more like the Takarazuka Revue than the *shishi mai* (the classical lion dance)—and Hikoza doesn't like it at all. (Toho Studios was in the habit of featuring its in-house dance troupe, the *Toho buyo tai*, regardless of its appropriateness to the plot of the film.)[15]

To make things worse, the shogun chooses a woman, joins in the dance, and insists that Hikoza dance too. It is a bizarre spectacle: an effeminate "matinee shogun" (played by Hasegawa Kazuo) dances a Western bowdlerizing of classical Japanese forms while his mentor Hikoza disrupts the performance and insists that his behavior is not proper. Hikoza's bumbling protests, shot from an extreme low angle, are gradually integrated into the dance when the camera pulls back to show him crazily bouncing from one geisha to another, confused, dazed, but also curiously happy that his master seems to be enjoying himself. The two end up in each other's arms by the end and regard each other with plain filial, perhaps homoerotic affection.

The dance clearly is a turning point in shogun and mentor's relationship. It seems to be something manufactured by Iemitsu to distance himself from Hikoza's clutching interference. If Iemitsu can convince Hikoza that his only improprieties are hedonistic ones, then perhaps Hikoza will be content to play the role of royal nursemaid and stop meddling in affairs of state. If Iemitsu cannot persuade Hikoza to leave him alone in his role as shogun, perhaps he can control Hikoza by allowing him the illusion of playing the avuncular mentor's role. In any case, it is clear that the shogun shows some initiative and independence by means of a spectacle that is both effeminate and meretricious.

It is important that the same style of pseudoclassical dance is underway when the Kumamoto Castle is sealed off and ultimatums are made under a bomb threat. Hikoza is here too, but this time he is not hoodwinked and laughs contemptuously at the spy Kawamura's "performance" (*shibai*). The geisha dance, this time with a singer, is interrupted when armed guards abruptly stride into the hall and order the building secured, the lights off, the show stopped. Interestingly, on both occasions when the geisha dancers are entertaining there is some important deception going on behind the scenes: the first time, Shogun Iemitsu has decided on a way to deal with Hikoza (to send him into retirement at Nikko); the second, Kawamura uses the dancers to lure Shogun Iemitsu and his advisers into an exploding building. The shogun and his followers escape, thanks to Hikoza's intervention; the old man knows something about Kawamura's collaboration with one of Iemitsu's quisling attendants that brings Kawamura's ultimatum to nought. They escape without so much as a scuffle, while Kawamura, gyrating in the harsh spears of light, performs a beautiful, macabre, and authentic lion dance as the building falls into the light shafts that surround, then overwhelm him.

This sequence, too, illustrates a key trope in the monumental style: the dignified death. Since the monumental style makes a sacrament of sacrifice, to die well is to be redeemed, even if one is on the "wrong" side. Shogun and mentor both call out their farewells to the stricken Kawamura as he continues his dance of death. The spectacle of a samurai bravely continuing his dance in the half-light of a castle falling down around him is, after all, a tragic vision that is the highlight of the film, which otherwise is totally devoid of physical conflict. It is *shibai*, not competence or accomplishment, that redeems samurai whose martial skills have been traded for martial arts in a time of enforced peace. Ultimately, there are no villains in *Shogun and Mentor* because they are forgiven by the bushido code for which they sacrifice themselves. The film concludes with the willing submission to the hierarchal bonds of lord and retainer.

The canonization of the traditional Japanese heritage, the displacement of physical action by technique, the collective configurations of objectified spectatorship, the lingering on the aesthetics of period detail, the importance of a dutiful discharge of familial obligations, and the noble death— these are some stylistic complexes of the monumental style that are present in *Shogun Iemitsu and His Mentor Hikozaemon*. This film is not the best example of the style, but the ingredients are sufficiently present to classify it within the monumental family. Specifically, technical aspects of the monumental style—the long take and long shot, the graceful camera movements, and the ascetic repose of blocking and design—are honored in the breach as in the observance.

But this does not make it a comic or even melodramatic film. It is clear that this film reinforces the stylistic norms of monumentalism even if, in the interest of "mere" characterization or visceral impact, it sometimes ignores those norms. For instance, Hikoza's interruption of the meeting with the regent starkly sets off the protocols of courtly behavior precisely because he violates them. The violation of proper behavior makes it all the more noticeable. Another clear case is the shogun's childish tantrum. This is presented as so egregious that it is as interesting for what it ignores, or reacts against, as for what it positively represents. In *Shogun and Mentor* this "scene" of infantile indulgence is almost titillating in its explicit representation of a behavior, and a technique, that is the antithesis of the monumental style. Like the official spokesmen who fulminated against Japanese urban life, and thereby sketch a bas-relief of the waywardness they deplore, the abrupt departure from a properly monumental deportment of the shogun also betrays an important symptom of how the monumental style functions.

Another example of the monumental style is Kinugasa's *Kawanakajima Kassen* (*The Battle of Kawanakajima*). This film makes an interesting comparison with *Shogun and Mentor* because it combines the domestic and the martial in opposite proportions to that of Makino's film. And in an opposite way it sets into relief the salience of the monumental style. *Shogun and Mentor* contains a short prologue of war footage showing Hikozaemon rescuing the former shogun from the battlefield; the rest of the film deals with the domestic consequences of this bonding within the political and emotional spheres. But *Kawanakajima* is a war film in a period setting, even if its presentation of the battle is disproportionally naturalized and domesticated. Like *Shogun and Mentor*, the film is not a prototypical instance of the monumental style because it lacks the sacramental invocation of traditional aesthetics. Still, its beauty and gravity surpasses its commitment to the didacticism of melodramatic jidai geki, and its spiritualization of nature and history places it definitively in the monumental style. Curiously, this is precisely the aspect of the film that lends itself to an "internationalization" of the monumental style in the postwar period, with the Academy Award-winning *Gate of Hell* (chapter 8). This aspect reveals the dialectical quality of the monumental style in its interdependence on foreign, and specifically American, ghosts in the Japanese machine.

The Battle of Kawanakajima (1940)

Kawanakajima Kassen (Toho, Kinugasa Teinosuke) is unusual because it mobilizes nature in the glorification of martial spirit. The monumental style generally emphasizes the cultural achievements of native traditions. Techniques and themes of the monumental style target the arts, family loyalty, and religion, but seldom invoke the landscape itself as a metonymic signifier of war spectacle. On the other hand, the battle of Kawanakajima is a famous skirmish between two daimyo in the Sengoku period (Warring States, 1467–1568), and the film's appropriation of nature as historical glorification places it within the monumental style.

In fact, the five engagements in the battles of Kawanakajima are less important historically than for their commemoration in the popular literature of the succeeding Edo period.[16] The battles between Takeda Shingen and Uesugi Kenshin were inconclusive in themselves, but they were analyzed by subsequent Edo treatises and chronicles of "military science," such as the *Koyo Gunkan*, a paean to the exploits of Takeda in which "the ruthless warlords Kenshin and Shingen are romanticized as chivalrous heroes, and the Battles of Kawanakajima are transformed from haphazard forays into epic encounters."[17] Kinugasa Teinosuke performs a similar romanticizing in his film, relying especially on the sacramental connotations invested in the surrounding landscape. War itself is situated in the film as a force of nature, which both beautifies it and renders it inevitable. In this, as in its concentration on behind-the-scenes preparations and personal relationships of the battle, *Kawanakajima* uses strategies typical of contemporary war films like *Five Scouts* (1938) and *Tank Commander Nishizumi* (1940).

All but two of the thirteen reels of this film explore the preparations for and aftermath of the battle. Strictly speaking, *Kawanakajima* is less a war film than a homefront film that takes place at the front. The bulk of the narrative concerns the experience of a common foot soldier getting ready for battle, particularly his close relationship with his squadron leader and a budding romance with a local peasant girl. The squadron leader in turn takes orders from the infantry captain, who likewise looks after his men with fatherly concern. The father-son motif is generalized further by paralleling the surrogate filial relationships within the infantry with the presence of the infantry captain's son, who is a young officer in the cavalry. He tries to stay in touch with his father, the infantry captain. While anxiously awaiting news of his father's movements on the field, the young officer also serves directly under the commander and so struggles to fulfil a second filial obligation to *his* surrogate father, Uesugi Kenshin. The film thereby consolidates themes detailing the filial relations between fathers and sons,

Wartime leaders now . . .
Tank Commander Nishizumi
(*Nishizumi Senshachoden*,
Yoshimura Kimisaburo,
1940)

and then: *The Battle of
Kawanakajima* (*Kawanakajima
Kassen*, Kinugasa Teinosuke,
1940). Kawakita Memorial
Film Archives.

officers and soldiers, and strategically makes little distinction between the two ties.

Uesugi Kenshin's army is portrayed as one enormous happy family; the soldiers live a spartan life on the move, but together with their superiors they eat, wash, march, and even sing in unison. The film is nearly over before the fighting breaks out, and when the characters we have come to know so well are killed off, the impression left by the film is a wistful regret for the breaking of familial bonds, not any outrage for the lives that are so abruptly cut short.

This resigned, wistful attitude toward war is perpetuated in the character of Neya, a young peasant woman played by Tanaka Kinuyo. She becomes part of the structure of wartime paternalism by accepting the kindness of the foot soldier protagonist. As a member of the local community invaded by the Uesugi army, she represents the penetration of the war ethos into the community. Far from being victimized by the soldiers, Neya and her friends fraternize freely with the soldiers by helping with the washing and feeding and even joining the soldiers in their impromptu folk dances around the fire. They also accept the kindness of the soldiers in the offers of food and, in Neya's case, medical attention given to an injured leg. The identification of the local folk with the military extends the family harmony between fathers and sons, officers and soldiers, to the relation between military and village. This one-for-all (*issho kenmei*, "all together") solidarity, which blurs class and status distinctions, is consistent with the official military picture of an army that champions traditional peasantry and associated values of the land.[18]

Again, this conceit recurs constantly in contemporary war films, in which "the master discourse . . . is that of a *gemeinschaft*: a seamless continuity links individual to nation, civilian to the fighting man, peace to war and, indeed, life to death."[19] The peasant and military, moreover, are portrayed as natural allies bound together by ties of mutual interest, because the peasantry reduced to subsistence-level tenant farming was seen by the right as victims of "Western" capitalist practices of exploitation and avarice. This thinking is expressed most clearly by the radical agrarian "fundamentalist" Tachibana Kosaburo, who "promised resolution through a reidentification of people with land as the source of the necessary spiritual regeneration that would culminate in a patriotic reordering of the nation itself."[20] Wrote Tachibana, "There can be no people who are separated from the land. There can be no national society separated from the people."[21]

Hence the tendency in *Kawanakajima* to beautify and sanctify the land. This is a crucial link in a mythological structure that unites the land with the people and the people with the emperor, using the military, not constitutional representation, as the intermediary. Richard Smethurst clearly identifies this merging of interests and identities:

> Prewar rural Japanese had superimposed national identity and affiliations over their hamlet orientations. But superimposed is the wrong word to use here. We might better conclude that national villagers believed that the goals of the two were identical. When one served the hamlet, he served the emperor and nation, and when one served the emperor and nation, he served the hamlet—either way, he became a "national villager."[22]

Why is it so crucial for a period war film like *Kawanakajima* to forge such tight quasi-familial relationships between its primary characters? One might expect the classical war film, whether contemporary or period piece, to highlight the conflict and the causes that inevitably draw the conflict to a climax. But this is a minor part of *Kawanakajima*, a mere pretext for dwelling on more personal stories that take place against a military backdrop. So why does the film so obsessively draw parallels and equivalences between military, family, and peasants? "Why, in the final analysis, was this overpowering mystique of the 'family state' necessary?" asks John Dower. "Because the authoritarian and militarist state had destroyed the nuclear family."[23]

The absence of the nuclear family is pervasive in *Kawanakajima*. Neya is first introduced as a panic-striken mother who later loses her baby. The foot soldier who befriends her is shown floundering in a forest pond and is affectionately fished out by his gruff squadron leader. Later, the infantry captain fondly draws a blanket over the sleeping form of one of his men. Neya later scrubs the clothes of the soldiers as they all take baths in steaming hot springs. The soldiers and villagers make merry in a complicated, densely choreographed sequence of folk dancing and music; the officers join in from their separate quarters. Aside from intermittent reports on the progress of troop movements, most of the film deals with quotidian concerns of displaced domesticity: the work involved in keeping a massive army fed, clothed, and properly equipped, as well as the important psychic demands of filial intimacy and even romantic designs. These are needs usually fulfilled by the nuclear family, and in the attention lavished on the surrogate fulfillment of these needs the film reveals its ideological objectives.

The beginning and end of the film bear this out. The exposition introduces the Uesugi army making its way into the village as an invasion of a previously sleeping community. The first shot of the film shows the silent

Anticipating Kurosawa: Kinugasa's *The Battle of Kawanakajima* (1940)
Kawakita Memorial Film Archives.

village street crisscrossed by yelping dogs; lights come on and people come
out of their houses, scurrying about wondering where to hide from the
approaching soldiers. Throughout, the steady pounding of horses' hooves
grows louder. A few scouts run into the village to check for spies or snipers.
The sequence emphasizes the disturbance created in the village by the
approaching army, before finally cutting to exterior location shots of the
massive horde descending upon the little village. The series of extreme
long shots are held for a very long time to emphasize the vastness of the
Ucsugi army; it takes almost five minutes of screen time showing the passage of the army before the first dramatic incident takes place: a wagon gets
hung up on a steep shoulder and the foot soldier in charge of unsticking it
is our protagonist. Shots of such scale and duration are not used again until
late in the film, when the battle finally begins. The battle footage alternates
between majestic panning shots of the cavalry and tighter shots of the
Uesugi foot soldiers cut down by unseen snipers hiding in the tall reeds. In
the meantime medium shots predominate of the soldiers and villagers
going about their duties in the dense richness of the Northern forest.

The end of the film similarly revolves around the village's point of view
through Neya. In her slow, shell-shocked meanderings around the charred
battlefield, Neya plays a role comparable to that of the maid Osaki in *The
Abe Clan* (chapter 7). An outsider, innocent of the ways of war, simply tries
to register the extent of the destruction. The shot sizes through which

Neya wanders are enormous, and she is dwarfed by the huge plains and hillocks holding a vast array of smoking, overturned cannons, oxcarts, and bodies. The scale of these shots is such that the eye is forced to scan the frame in order to keep sight of Neya. The frame is layered with sky, mountains, hills, overturned carts, and scattered bodies occupying succeeding depth planes. As in the beginning, shot scale and duration bring out the enormity of the Kawanakajima battles with their consequent resistance to human comprehension and imperviousness to emotion. Aside from Neya's survey of the battlefield carnage, the last verbal assessment of the battle is made by an old villager who keeps marveling that it was the biggest and fiercest battle he had ever seen. When impatiently prompted by his younger listeners about the outcome of the contest, he makes a pithy pronouncement: "It's not a matter of this army or that army winning; it's a matter of bullets over arrows—which ones fly better?" The issues of "naturalization" of war and the scale of destruction as a function of technology are the very ones Kurosawa takes up forty years later.

It is appropriate for the film to end on a remark that compares old and new technologies of killing because *Kawanakajima* in many ways replicates strategies typical of the modern war film. One such strategy for mobilizing family sentiment in the war effort is the "militarist mother" figure seeing her son off to war. The Japanese militarist mother will outdo her son in patriotic fervor so as to encourage him in his resolve; at the same time her son would be dying on the battlefield, crying out the beloved imperial name, *Tenno Heika Banzai!* Both mother and son's patriotic fanaticism are plainly displacements of the anguish of subjecting the closest of familial bonds to the abstract and abject loyalty to the emperor-state. Evidently Japanese soldiers on the field would actually cry out for their mothers rather than for *Tenno*, as they invariably do in the movies; "this [displacement] served to emphasize the subsumption of the role of the parent into that of the Emperor."[24]

At the same time, though, the militarist mother has antecedents in feudal Japanese stories. *The Abe Clan* begins with an episode in which a young samurai about to commit *junshi* (ritual suicide) is awakened and refreshed by his smiling, toothless mother. She sends him off to die with the cheerful concern of one seeing him depart for the office. Gosuke the dog-handler also is encouraged by his mother; she reminds him to keep his pride and stick to his suicidal resolve in the face of samurai condescension. And Chikamatsu's *Goban Taiheiki*, the oldest surviving play about the Chushingura vendetta, has an important scene in which Yuranosuke's wife and mother slit their throats to help him in his resolve to avenge his master's death.[25]

The most famous militarist mother on the Japanese screen is the mother played by Kinuyo Tanaka in Kinoshita Keisuke's *Rikugun* (*Army*, 1944). Until the last scene the mother has been bravely trying to deny her feelings of abandonment on learning her son is about to be shipped off to war. She tries to persuade herself that he is already dead. Then on the spur of the moment, she runs out to try to find her son in a passing military parade in hopes of getting a last look. A long tracking shot follows her every move as she pushes through the crowded street craning her neck and peeking over the shoulders of bystanders. The camera takes her optical point of view, which scans and backtracks along the line of unfamiliar faces. She finally finds her son marching in the procession and shows a look of utter relief and joy that lights up her hitherto dead features. The scene is also an animation of the film's technique, which up to this point is generally confined to closely cut medium close shots of family members cooped up in tiny, underlit flats. The complexity and duration of *Army*'s final scene gives it a liberating, joyful quality out of keeping with the patriotic sacrifice it apparently encourages, therefore earning it some notoriety as a war film that condemns war.[26]

A similar scene in *Kawanakajima* has Kinuyo Tanaka again playing the mother figure, but this time it is a departure from the timid, dependent waif she plays earlier in the film. The foot soldier with whom she is involved gives her his most personal effects to watch over while he is in battle. Then he moves off down the road with his oxcart full of weapons. The shot is framed from behind Neya, and as he moves deeper into the frame, he is obstructed by horses, soldiers, and other carts moving back and forth in other planes of the picture. As his figure recedes and intermittently appears and disappears, Neya responds in the foreground by standing on tiptoe and craning her neck to get a last glimpse of her man. As he is about to disappear for good, he stops and waves back. She jumps up and excitedly returns his farewell. An oxcart in the distance comes between them, and when it passes, her young soldier is gone.

The narrative and thematic significance of this segment is congruent with that of *Army*, though the latter is more pessimistic in its assumption that the son will never return to his mother. There is also a technical parallel between these scenes depicting the militarist mother in that both episodes are structured around the mother's searching gaze. However, in *Army* the scene is drawn out in space and time using an elaborate tracking technique incorporating both the mother and the object of her frantic search. The scene in *Kawanakajima* is less elaborate, but even more eloquent in that both camera and Neya are stationary, yet a similar searching and sifting of the frame for the departing "son" is undertaken by both Neya and the spectator. We are restricted to her view of the departing soldier but still privy to her reactions, even though we cannot see her face. In a very off-hand way this subtle, elegant use of depth planes and duration involves the spectator in the visual and emotional dynamic of the scene. The episode is structured as a visual eavesdropping rather than an emotional intensification of the moment from the "inside" through crosscutting or tracking.

Kinugasa uses an elaborate play with depth planes in his battle footage as well. One memorable shot of a hillside shows four separate horizontal lines of soldiers and horses moving laterally across the frame in opposite directions. The nearest line of soldiers is running screen left; above that, an infantry line is hauling cannons to the right; a third line of horses picks its way to the left; and silhouetted against the sky is a fourth line of galloping horses. As if all this compositional complexity weren't enough, the shot is framed so that the sky takes up the top half of the frame, squeezing the rest into a small, but clearly articulated frame; moreover, a grove of trees fragments the spectacle with intermittently obstructing leaves and boughs in the near foreground.

Such complex decoupage within the frame overwhelms the eye not with confusion but with amazement at the apparent beauty and orderliness of battle. Kinugasa stages battle scenes with the stylized detachment of Heike-Genji battle scrolls. There is almost no attempt to convey a sense of progress in the course of battle. We know that Takeda Shingen appears to be winning because characters introduced as part of the Uesugi camp are cut down, one by one, by invisible snipers. But despite the emphasis on the mass movement of troops and equipment, there are few orientational cues that help the viewer make sense of the battle's progress. The real significance of the battle sequences in *Kawanakajima* is simpler: an encouragement of an appreciation (and perhaps acceptance) of war as spectacle. In *Kawanakajima* this is best seen in the naturalization of the forces of war. The causes and even the outcome of the Kawanakajima battles are relatively unimportant compared to the anticipation of war preparations, on the one hand, and the overwhelming vertiginousness of battle, on the other. In either case, a consideration of why the war was fought is conspicuously absent.

The majesty of war is conveyed in a series of eight shots, silent but for the clopping of horseshoes. These shots initiate the battle proper and, like the sequence that begins the film, depict the arrival of the Uesugi army at Kawanakajima plain. Extreme long take-long shots show thousands of soldiers and horsemen moving first through fields, woods, meadows. They are integrated into the landscape: a high angle shot of a squadron of soldiers with lances trudging through a deep sun-dappled forest has shafts of light spearing and bouncing from trees and lances. (This is a full ten years before

Miyagawa Kazuo's celebrated forest shot in *Rashomon*.) Again, the shot is held for such duration that the sheer size of the army is emphasized, but also the abstract patterning of the sunlight playing through trees and spears aestheticizes the representation qualitatively as well as in scale.

A long crane shot shows thousands of horsemen crossing a wide, sunny river. The shot begins from a low height that mostly catches the horses' flanks, then pulls back and swivels up along the riverbank to show the full extent of the cavalry. From here the shot continues to track along the river-bank with the army as the horses splash through shallow, sun-dappled water. Here, as in the forest, the spectacle of a huge army's approach is made to look majestic; more than that, the composition and scale is orga-nized around features of the landscape, into which the army is integrated and with which it is identified.

Such spectacular scale and visual effects is surprising, considering the straitened circumstances of the wartime film industry. *Kawanakajima* fully holds up to comparisons with modern-day historical epics for spectacle and polish. Other Japanese historical war epics, such as *Ahen senso* (*The Opium War*, 1943, Makino Masahiro) and *Genghis Khan* (1936, Ushihara Kiyohiko), are preoccupied with their propaganda functions and, as a result, scenes that pretend to be spectacular only intensify the wooden, declamatory hollowness of the films' ideological zeal. *Kawanakajima*, by contrast, does not crown its efforts with a civics lesson. Instead, the lesson is there to be drawn on the surface of the film, in the texture of the images, in the naturalization and consequent acceptance of war. In its refusal to superordinate its propaganda functions, *Kawanakajima* distinguishes itself as a monumental film as opposed to the canonical strategies of these other propaganda films. *Kawanakajima* is more along the lines of Griffith's *Intoler-ance* and Eisenstein's *Alexander Nevsky*—films whose didactic intentions are plain but not simple, because their didacticism does not enjoy pride of place at the expense of narrative and, especially, style. More recently, Kurosawa's war epics *Kagemusha* and *Ran* have much in common with the emphasis on spectacle found in *Kawanakajima*.

A final aspect of *Kawanakajima* that distinguishes it from classical instances of the monumental style is its domestication of war, an appropri-ate corollary to its naturalization process. In the hieratic contours of the monumental world, the domestic sphere is a complication added to samu-rais' primary predicament with daimyo or shogun. We have already seen how *Kawanakajima* dwells on the representation of surrogate family relation-ships in a wartime context, similar to contemporary "humanist" war films like Kinoshita's *Army*. Another way in which the film domesticates the front is by means of performances and rituals that 1. humanize soldiers and officers alike, 2. sanctify the imminent death of the men, and 3. dignify not only the battle itself but also the associated preparation for battle by employing the same techniques for the representation of these "peripheral" activities.

Something as humble as a community outdoor bath in hot springs can be rendered monumentally by staging and shooting the scene in a complex, visually stunning manner. Early in the film a rapport is established between the Uesugi army and the village near the encampment. Neya is shown washing clothes in the river and a sound bridge has a voice calling, "Hey, the *onsen* (hot springs) is open!" Cut to a medium long shot of the hot springs, partially obscured by wisps of steam; naked men plunge in from all sides of the frame, including the foreground, which contains some trees behind which men jump into the steaming pool, and background, which is partially blocked by a cliff. Around the edge of the cliff more men come running. There is so much "business" in all parts of the frame that it is difficult to keep visual track of it all. It is further testament to Kinugasa's (or perhaps his editor's) skill and delicacy that he succeeds in staging a large nude sequence without revealing any anatomical details.

The *onsen* scene is followed by a raucous soldier-civilian song and dance in which close-ups of dancing feet are intercut with longer setups that show dancers happily twirling and bouncing in all parts of the frame; it's hard to say just what the shot scale is because the frame is so full, yet at the same time it is organized and appealing, like the spectacular complexity of the battlefield footage. In domestic as in battle footage Kinugasa is a consummate organizer of chaos.

The party continues offscreen as the scene shifts to the woods in which the infantry captain sits writing poetry. He stops his writing and smiles at the sound of the merrymaking. Then he begins to dance, slowly at first, then increasing his pace until he is doing a lively, comic jig. Suddenly some grinning faces appear in the background behind the captain. He continues his jig, oblivious to the mirth of his soldiers. When he finally turns and sees them, he jumps up with surprise, then sits down on his stump and pouts.

Here we see again the bonding of the tastes and destinies of villagers and soldiers, soldiers and officers. But it doesn't stop here. A little way away at field headquarters, Uesugi and his commanders are questioning a woman from Zenkoji, a strategic village further along where it is thought that Takeda Shingen may have spies. Neya earlier told her foot soldier that she is from Zenkoji, thinking to impress the Uesugi soldiers, but she is lying. Meanwhile, Uesugi finds out what he can from the Zenkoji woman and promises to look out for her life and family. All this time the merrymaking continues offscreen. Uesugi listens for a moment, and mutters something about singing being good for morale.

A parallel situation occurs later on. The night before the battle, Uesugi performs a short, austere noh dance and sings a plaintive song accompanied by samisen. Cut to the infantry in the woods, who stop their preparations for a moment to listen to the old man's mournful song about the beauty of the moon in the water. Cut to a shot of the moon, then its reflection in a pond strewn with lily pads. The lyricism of these shots is shattered, however, when the head of a Takeda spy suddenly surfaces from under the water. He listens, marking the position of Uesugi headquarters.

These impromptu performances add a significant wrinkle to the plot. But for Uesugi's song, Takeda intelligence would not have as precise a mark on his position. But mostly their function is ceremonial and sacramental. This is nowhere more obvious than in the semiobligatory sake libation sequences in which soldiers perform their last testament to their squadron and officer in charge. What is interesting about *Kawanakajima*, moreover, is the cross-class unification that the sake libation affirms. As the ritual progresses the scene shifts from the infantry squadron to the archery division to the cavalry and also to the commanders. These components from lowest to highest are unified in their performance of the farewell cup of sake. The sake ritual seems to be the most obvious reference to the modern soldier fighting in China, but in all fairness similar rituals abound in other monumental films from this period.

Kawanakajima Kassen naturalizes, domesticates, and humanizes the civil war battlefied. This is a peculiar strategy for the monumental style, which in other films emphasizes the unique majesty of Japanese history. *Genroku Chushingura*, for instance, presents an ascetic, even otherworldly picture of the Japanese warrior so as to celebrate his purity. But the fact that the warriors of Kawanakajima are portrayed in familial, intimate terms does not detract from the majesty of the landscape surrounding them and their integration within it. If *Kawanakajima Kassen* beautifies the landscape, it also beautifies the warriors—contemporary and historical—who fight and die on its plains, rivers, and hills.

From this point on I will be closely analyzing individual films in the monumental style. The following films—*Zangiku Monogatari*, *Genroku Chushingura*, *Abe Ichizoku*, *Jigoku Mon*, *Kagemusha*, *Ran* and *Rikyu*—offer a strong case for the usefulness of monumentalism as a stylistic category precisely because there are so many fruitful tensions between single films and the family resemblances that tie them together. The analyses should also show the artistic superiority of these films as well as their distinguished legacy, which continues to the present day.[27] Up to this point I have tried to sketch out the historical and cinematic background to the monumental style.

Mud and Soldiers: on location in China. Production still,
Kawakita Memorial Film Archives.

From here on I will foreground the monumental style itself as it is manifested in the films, and in the stylistic extension of monumentalism in films
and film history.

The analysis that follows concentrates on technique, style, and form.
Rather than trying to explain stylistic developments through historical references, I prefer an intrinsic analysis because it is a more oblique, and thus
more discreet, indication of cultural and historical conditions than overt
references to themes and events. I have argued already that style functions
as a marker of how a work *appears* to have been made (not how it actually
was made—see n. 6, chapter 3); the work therefore manifests an affinity
with the conditions of its production, independent of authorial intentions.
Style can express things authors and artists never intended, or even
noticed, but it cannot escape the historical horizons of its genesis. While it
is impossible to trace all stylistic features back to the real calculations of
artistic production, it is always enlightening to compare the expressions of
style with the expressions of a specific culture and see where they are congruent and where they diverge.

It is time now to analyze a classic instance of the monumental style,
Mizoguchi's *Story of the Last Chrysanthemum*, in search of ways in which film
style articulates a sacramental ideal. The film's greatness (and it may be
Mizoguchi's greatest) lies in its integration of spiritual redemption with rigorous stylistic experimentation.

5

Story of the Last Chrysanthemum (1939): A "Riptide of Reaction"

Story of the Last Chrysanthemum (*Zangiku Monogatari*) is not only one of Mizoguchi's greatest films; it is also a parable, a moral lesson in much the same spirit as the tale of the prodigal son. But whereas the parable of the prodigal son illustrates the long-suffering patience of the father, *Chrysanthemum* emphasizes the son's struggle upward into grace. There is redemption in Mizoguchi's film, but it is bought at great cost: with exile from the comfortable but false reassurances of family, with years of toil and neglect on the road, and with the death of an innocent woman at the moment of greatest personal triumph. In its insistence on the ransom of Kikunosuke's artistic birthright by Otoku's sacrifice, the film actually illustrates the Christian doctrine of redemption better than the New Testament parable. Still, the return to the fold and the reunion with kin marks a fundamental similarity in the structure and intent of these stories.

Chrysanthemum functions as an admonition to the Japanese people to return to their rightful place in the imperial lineage. It is a conservative call in its definition of the empire/family along purer, straighter lines of the ancien régime. *Chrysanthemum* is a strange, wonderful amalgam of moral tract and aesthetic rigor.

The film is a sacralization of Japanese identity by means of an exacting artistic heritage and its accompanying family hierarchy, and this is its most salient contribution to the monumental style. Its spirituality appears in its indigenous artforms as counterweight to the "secular" urban culture of the 1920s and 1930s.

As related in chapter 3, the Education Ministry awarded *Chrysanthemum* a special prize for its representation of the Japanese family system and traditional artistic pursuits. The treatment of these two realms, the family system and traditional arts, within the dramatic world of a kabuki family struggling to perpetuate its lineage, ensures that the behavioral norms of filial piety and obedience are well represented. For this the government was apparently well pleased, but that does not detract from the film's stature as possibly the best Mizoguchi ever made.

The film is based on a popular shimpa play that ran continuously through the mid-1930s. Mizoguchi was "addicted" to shimpa for its embodiment of a "deeply ritualistic ethos" of Meiji-era domesticity and melodrama.[1] This bears repeating because the misconception remains that Mizoguchi "retreated" into Meiji-mono to avoid making crude propaganda films, as if he had no interest in the Meiji era otherwise. In fact, Mizoguchi made two more Meiji-mono (*Naniwa onna/Woman of Osaka*, 1940 and *Geido ichidai otoko/Life of an Artist*, 1941) to round out a trilogy on the world of Meiji theater before "retreating" still further into the Tokugawa era with *Genroku Chushingura*. Shimpa, originating in the Meiji period as a "modern" corrective to the "feudal" kabuki, was adapted for the screen and presented as a model of traditional Confucian values. This shows how once progressive forms could be recuperated as traditional, using still newer forms of reproduction. In the adaptation to film there was a relativization of the once progressive associations of shimpa, compared to kabuki, which favored an ambivalent play of historicized meanings. Early film adaptations of shingeki plays, like *Katusha* (1919), a theatrical recasting of Tolstoy's *Resurrection*, and Mizoguchi's own shimpa adaptation, *Taki no Shiraito* (*The Water Juggler*, 1933), emphasize the modernization implicit in shimpa drama. But in 1939 Mizoguchi's inclination and the mood of the times prescribed an explicitly conservative role for shimpa, and for *Chrysanthemum*.[2]

Since the play and the film deal with the travails of a kabuki family, a lively dynamic is struck up in the aesthetic modes within the film. This

Shingeki theater on film:
Tolstoy's *Katusha* (1919).
Private collection.

dynamic between film, shimpa, and kabuki devices will be described presently. For the moment it should be emphasized that the kabuki world, both onstage and off, lends itself to a form of Japaneseness whose traditional aspect, both artistic and familial, survives the challenge of individualism and modernization. Kabuki occupies a middle ground between shimpa, on the one hand, with its shifting balance of progressive and conservative associations, and noh, on the other, whose sacramental gravity remains inviolate. The Onoe family hallmark of strong performance and rigid apprentice system is seriously challenged by Kikunosuke's waywardness. But by the end of the film the conservative familial kabuki establishment prevails over the experimental wanderings of the prodigal kabuki troupe. The representation of kabuki in *Chrysanthemum* is consistent with the aristocratic associations of noh, *sumi-e* ink painting, Zen-inspired rock gardens, *shoin* (courtly) architecture, *chado* tea ceremony, and ikebana flower arranging. By the turn of the nineteenth century these arts had lost their contemporary currency with the dominance of popular mercantile culture. Thereafter, they entered the realm of antiquity because of their need for cultural preservation by an aesthetic elite. They acquired a cultural power associated with the ancien régime, a repository of "pure Japaneseness" untainted by contact with foreign arts and morals. The sacramentalization of these arts is both historical and canonical, due partly to their antiquity and partly to their classification as purely indigenous aesthetic forms. In the late 1930s traditional artistic expressions were given an explicitly religious cast in the practices encouraged by State Shinto and the policies promoted by the Home Ministry and the Army. These policies recommended a positive representation of indigenous art forms, performance, and behavior as a corrective to the corruption of Japaneseness in the urban culture of the 1920s and 1930s. *Chrysanthemum* is thus part of a call to arms to shore up the spiritual fortitude of the Japanese people. It is, to stretch a metaphor, an appeal to "muscular Confucianism."[3]

"Muscular Confucianism" is similar to "muscular Christianity," a semimartial idea of evangelical Christianity championed in Victorian England by Dr. Thomas Arnold (Matthew's father), among others.[4] If these allusions to Christianity seem contrived, it is notable that the sacramental aspect of the monumental style, recalling a "fundamentalist" repudiation of secular Western frivolity, is not simply an analogy. The nationalist ideology of "Japanism" (kokutai ideology, with monumental style as its most vivid image), has often been analyzed as a surrogate religion to compensate for the absence of a transcendental religious tradition in Japanese society.[5] Instead of owing ultimate allegiance to a spiritual father God, Japanese subjects were encouraged to put their faith in the earthly mother country. The deification of country was promulgated as an explicit ideology of the kokutai (national essence) in the late 1930s, especially through the "country as family" image maintained through the divine headship of the emperor. This idea was a civil reconstitution of the nineteenth century Neo-Confucianist concern with an "immanent ultimate instead of a transcendental deity," as Gregory Barrett puts it.[6]

An important means by which the abstract deities of Buddhism were brought down to earth was the deification of the parental role. In Neo-Confucianism filial piety was the sacrament through which one expressed devotion to God. Parents themselves were not worshipped, but rather parenthood, and especially ancestral lineage as it persists across many generations. As opposed to the mortality of individuals, the persistence of the extended clan acquires an affinity to timelessness, and from there takes on an ultimate aspect. "Since one's relation to the universe is mediated through the parents," writes Robert N. Bellah, "one's primary religious obligation is filial piety. It is thus that one expresses one's unity with the universe."[7]

Even today there is a strong sense of religiosity, or at least mysterious ineffability, that many Japanese associate with their nationality. In a chapter called "Prodigal Son, Forgiving Parent, Self-Sacrificing Sister," Gregory Barrett comments that "in place of a concern with a transcendental deity, there is among the Japanese a respectful idealization of a father image and a feeling of loving devotion to a mother who deserves eternal gratitude. Conversely, among Western Christians the concept of a transcendental deity deprived their parents of the sacred ultimacy of [Takeo] Doi's 'Parent' and the Forgiving Mother in *Sansho the Bailiff*."[8]

The ideology of Japanism cannot be completely identified with existing political institutions. Except for the Shinto authority vested in the emperor, there is no state church or "ministry of patriotism" charged with maintaining the religious trappings of civil authority. In the West the institutional church has always seen itself in relation to secular political authority as a check on the state's thirst for power. The idea that the church's role is a "prophetic" critical one that maintains a balance of power between secular and sacred realms allows for possible conflict between church and state. It also makes the church's collaboration with tyrannical regimes all the more deplorable. In Japan conflict between church and state had become virtually unknown since the 1637 Shimabara rebellion, in which some thirty-seven thousand Christians were massacred by the Tokugawa shogunate. It was understandably frightened by the thought of any allegiance to an authority beyond itself.[9] The shogunate therefore arrogated ultimate authority to itself, legitimating its rule, until it finally succumbed some two hundred years later to the divinity restored to the imperial family. "Muscular Confucianism," then, was a legitimation strategy exercised by the Tokugawa shogun and the imperial household alike.

During World War II Christians were again persecuted by the state. But this came after a long period of cooperation between Christian institutions established as early as the Meiji period (missions, schools, hospitals, orphanages, etc.) and civil authorities. Insofar as the latter saw modernization as overcoming backwardness, i.e., an inculcation of hygenic, frugal behavior that sought after the habits of "civilization," Japanese civil bureaucrats solicited the moral suasion masterfully wielded by Christian doctors, missionaries, and educators. From the turn of the century to the mid-1920s, the government subsidized Christian social agencies and deputized several prominent Japanese Protestant reformers. One of these Christians, Tomeoka Kosuke, even preached a "gospel" of Neo-Confucian thrift and diligence by popularizing the teachings of Ninomiya Sontoku, a Tokugawa agricultural reformer.[10]

Moreover, there is a real historical precedent for the Japanese adaptation of Christianity for its powers of ideological and spiritual suasion. In the early nineteenth century, well before the opening of Japan to the West, a scholar-samurai named Aizawa Seishisai published his *New Theses*, which advocated measures for the reinforcement of shogunal hegemony. One of the most important measures was the 1825 Expulsion Edict mandating the forceable removal of British, Russian, and American intruders from Japanese shores (known as *joi*, "expel the barbarians"). The reason for Aizawa's support of *joi* was not from a sense of paranoia toward the threat of Western naval power, because there was no threat posed by Western warships until 1853, with the arrival of Commodore Perry's black ships.[11] Instead, Aizawa's belligerent position derived from his extensive knowledge of Western society and politics. His insistence on continued national isolation (*sakoku*) was not an ostrich foreign policy of keeping Japan's head in the sand. On the contrary, *New Theses* recommends an *imitation* of Western means of nation-building through ideological suasion. For that, authorities had to keep volatile Western influences at bay long enough for them to devise a program of moral and national consolidation similar to one used with enviable success in the West: Christianity. Moreover, it turns out that the ideological power of Christianity was the inspiration for Aizawa's recasting of the concept of kokutai:

> Aizawa argued that the secret of Western strength lay in Christianity, a state cult that Western leaders propagated to cultivate voluntary allegiance both in their own peoples and in those they colonized overseas. Aizawa called the popular unity and allegiance so cultivated *kokutai*, "the essence of a nation" (and by extension, "what is essential to make a people into a nation").[12]

This "inoculation" process found its sharpest expression in the strategies of the Meiji restoration: "as the state religion of a new 'civilized' Japan," writes Tsurumi Shunsuke, "Shinto was given a role akin to that of Christianity in Western countries and an increasingly monotheistic character."[13]

Insofar as *Chrysanthemum* is a film in the monumental style that propagates kokutai ideology with its imperial family cult, it aims to coax its audience back to a national identity that was presumably lost. The recolonization of Japanese subjects, in turn, is a process that returns to the dawn of Japanese nation building: a strategy of inoculation against foreign contamination. The expulsion of the barbarians was a means to prevent a proliferation of gods. If Japanese subjects could be persuaded to attribute divinity to their own emperor, the result would be the birth of a nation, mandated by mass loyalty to their imperial throne, not to Rome, Paris, or London. In this way Japanese administrative elites deftly imitated the uses of Christianity by Western imperialists.[14]

The monumental style continues this legacy of nation building and subject creation through a kind of religious indoctrination. The central feature of the monumental style is its appeal to the sacred, particularly its tendency to foreground an imaginary Japanese identity that eschews the corrupting influences of the West. The monumental style calls for repentance from the tainted forms and expressions of Western ideology in favor of an uplifting, otherworldly transcendence that comes from the purity of the imperial house, the lifeblood of all Japanese. It is not stretching too far to consider the monumental style an altar call to jaded city dwellers saturated with the ennui of the modern and alienated by the meretricious promises of the West. "Muscular Confucianism," therefore, is a (re)flexing of the sinews and synapses of Japaneseness in opposition to urban foreign extravagance. The monumental style—and *Chrysanthemum* is exemplary—proposes a conversion experience that rediscovers in the ascetic regimens of Confucian morality a purity and serenity that every Japanese will presumably recognize. Films in the monumental style don't just preach the gospel of Japaneseness; they integrate kokutai—the body of the nation—into the technical design of the films to produce a work with a somatic, palpable flavor of Japan rather than a mere exhortation. In *Chrysanthemum* the prominent features of this process appear in the scaffolding that holds up the traditional family system, the redemption provided by artistic devotion, and the sanctifying effects of history through its Meiji period setting.

Splitting Force and Sense

A difference between the story of the prodigal son and *Chrysanthemum* is that the former characterizes the family as a place of contentment and plenitude. This in turn characterizes the prodigal son's decision to depart as vain, willful, and, well, prodigal. Mizoguchi's film is more evenhanded, blaming the family for its hypocritical arbitrariness as a motivation for Kiku's exile. In brief, here is a sketch of the key moments in the narrative.

As a coming-of-age story, *Chrysanthemum* portrays the vacillating and somewhat weak character of Kiku, the youngest member of the famous kabuki family of Onoe. At the outset, Kiku's acting is deplorable, but no one has the courage to bluntly tell him how bad he is. His onstage struggles are compounded by the fact that he is an adopted member of the family and so is in danger of being disowned unless he improves. The only person in the family who cares enough to honestly criticize Kiku is the nursemaid Otoku. Touched by her concern, Kiku spends time with her and soon falls in love. Kiku's parents discover the nascent affair and throw Otoku out. Defying his father, Kiku joins Otoku for a long stint on the road with a hack traveling company. Though their lives are squalid, Kiku's acting steadily improves. Years later the Onoe family agrees to give Kiku a second chance, but only on condition that Otoku leave him (unbeknownst to Kiku). Kiku gives a triumphant performance and is welcomed back into the limelight while Otoku languishes in a filthy garret and dies of consumption.

In his comprehensive study of four films by Mizoguchi, Donald Kirihara writes that "Kiku's departure and the dissolution of the clan . . . present the reunification of the family as a fundamental goal shared by all the major characters in the film."[15] Two other lines of action, Kiku's quest for artistic excellence and the romance between Kiku and Otoku, are woven into the primary fabric of the family's unification.

The opening problem is presented as a rift between Kiku and his family in that Kiku's need for criticism of his acting is deferred in favor of the family's need to maintain the appearance of harmony. This split between a fractious, intractable reality that belies an illusion of harmony is graphically prefigured in the opening kabuki sequence, which centers on a "quick change" figure of stage business called *toitagaeshi*.[16] The scene is from a famous kabuki play, *Tokaido Yotsuya Kaidan* (*Tokaido Ghost Story of Yotsuya*), which has a swinging door with dummy corpses tied to both sides and holes where the dummies' heads should be. The lead actor plays the part of one ghost, then in a moment appears in the part of the second ghost with a quick change of makeup that shows the versatility and virtuosity of the performer. After a pan away to Kiku's entrance, the entire stage is suddenly transformed into a new locale by dropping a new background curtain, the actors strike their poses, and the scene ends. But the crucial moment in the staging of the scene, the quick change itself, is elided when the camera pans to show Kiku's entrance. According to Kirihara, "Camera movement and editing direct our attention to him, and away from the spectacle of the performance. In this way the initial scene splits the viewer's attention between a colorful bit of stage trickery and curiosity surrounding this actor."[17]

The trickery really consists in the interplay of theatrical presentation and cinematic representation: filmic techniques are used to distract us from the central performance (by Kikugoro) to the mediocre posturings of a peripheral character (Kiku), without motivating the visual digression until the subsequent scene. Only then do we discover that it is Kiku's incompetence that was singled out by the camera movement and (retroactively) causes us to miss Kikugoro's quick change. Kikugoro's angry outbursts are directed at Kiku for his incompetence, but they might just as well chastise Kiku for his diversion of our attention away from him, the central actor, by

A schism between theatrical (kabuki) and cinematic representation in Mizoguchi's *Zangiku Monogatari* (1939). Kawakita Memorial Film Archives.

"luring" the camera away from the properly central stage business. Kiku-goro has been upstaged, so to speak, by what he excoriates as a miserably incompetent performance. And thanks to the hypocritical flattery of the attendants and family, Kiku does not even realize how bad he is. The schism within the kabuki family, then, is immediately foregrounded in the schism between theatrical presentation and cinematic representation. The illusion of a harmonious, venerable kabuki family is belied by the strife and recrimination caused by Kiku's questionable artistic reputation.

The kabuki story itself has an interesting relation to the jockeying of filmic and theatrical representation. *Tokaido Yotsuya Kaidan* is a revenge story of a lower-class samurai wife whose spirit hounds her husband after he has poisoned her to marry into a rich family. The wife suffers and dies from misplaced loyalty to her husband, and this parallels Otoku's death at the end of the film. Yet the kabuki yarn is premised on the wife's vengeance for her husband's treachery, while the shimpa story of *Chrysanthemum* is premised on Kiku's artistic triumph at the cost of his wife's sacrifice. Kiku does not kill Otoku, of course; on the contrary, he loves her and elopes with her in defiance of his kabuki family. Yet the shimpa convention of the weak *nimaime* heartthrob (see note 2) calls for the sacrifice of the loyal woman at the patriarchal altar of family welfare. It is ironic that *Yotsuya Kaidan*, the kabuki vehicle used to exhibit Kiku's artistic incompetence, contains an archetypal Vengeful Spirit whose quest for justice through revenge expresses a grudge against a society based on the disposability of women.[18] Moreover, the vengeful spirit whose most famous incarnation appears in *Yotsuya Kaidan* also represents a protective spirit. Once its grudge against an offending individual is satisfied, it is placated and becomes a patron spirit, as in the Japanese female dualism described by Ian Buruma as the "Demon Woman and the Eternal Mother."[19]

The original kabuki *Tokaido Yotsuya Kaidan* was first performed in 1821 on a double bill with *Kanadehon Chushingura*. Set in the same historical period, its male characters are either retainers of Lord Asano or Kira and it has been described as the flip side of *Chushingura*, because its avenging wife "illustrates the resentment which forms when a loyal wife is betrayed."[20] This wealth of intertextual allusions, condensations, and displacements is a function of *Chrysanthemum's* heterogenous combination of kabuki, shimpa, and cinematic elements. The scene contains a kabuki drama about a husband's treachery within a shimpa play about a wife's sacrifice and is filmed in a way that splits the viewer's apprehension of the scene between role, character, and actor.

In this way Mizoguchi finds a unique representational analogue for the modularity of kabuki presentation. Kabuki works simultaneously on separate registers, with different elements taking on different aesthetic roles. The diegetic (storytelling) function may be taken by the *joruri* chanter, while the actor may be taking a mimetic (showing) role that complements the story but serves mostly to exhibit some stage virtuosity, like a fancy flourish, a *mie* (freezing, or "fixing" an action), or *toitagaeshi*. Then the mimetic role might pass to some stagecraft, like a revolving set or trapdoor exit, while the diegetic function passes to an onstage character. Sometimes the music will take over the diegetic task while the performance onstage pauses to accompany with gesture or dance, or it simply stops and listens. This aesthetic independence of the separate elements adds up to an "absolute separation of action and telling" in which the medium is given a prominence equal to that of the message, resulting in total, but totally divided *"performances* in film."[21] Mizoguchi maintains a gap between the expressive functions of acting, camerawork, and music that concentrates and counterpoints these elements, arranging them to interact in a complex spectacle rather than in an organically unified representation. The most impressive thing about these performance sequences is the shifting between alternate modes of representation—filmic and shimpa as well as kabuki—as the performance moves along. In *Genroku Chushingura* Mizoguchi is able to assimilate noh performance technique into his decoupage as well. When Eisenstein expresses such admiration for the expressive possibilities of kabuki for film, Mizoguchi's staging and shooting of traditional Japanese performance is exemplary of what he sees.

"Excellent Family Customs"

The ideal of "excellent family customs" (*zenryo na katei no fushu*), a theme vigorously promoted by Home Ministry censors in the late 1930s, is set up from the beginning as a standard from which the Onoe clan has clearly lapsed.[22] Worse yet, the family does not acknowledge the rift between father's expectations and son's performance. When Kikugoro angrily calls Kiku into his dressing room to be chastised, a bevy of fawning relations interpose themselves between father and son, deflecting the imminent confrontation with false reassurances. Instead of attending to the accusations hurled at Kiku, these well-intentioned sycophants simply smooth Kikugoro's ruffled feathers and reassure Kiku that his acting is just fine.[23] In maintaining the illusion of family harmony by avoiding a confrontation at all costs, the family exacerbates the split between the "excellent family" ideal and the hypocritical reality, deferring an honest appraisal of the conflict until it is too late to mend.

The attempt to defer conflict by conciliatory interposition is shown most clearly in the major confrontation between Kiku and his father. By this time Kiku has flouted the family's attempt to dispose of Otoku and has secretly continued to see her. To the chagrin of his family, Kiku is not about to forget Otoku and carry on as before. This becomes painfully clear to Kiku's mother and elder brother as Kiku continues to parry his father's essentially class-based objections to Kiku's relations with Otoku. When things get heated, mother and brother physically seat themselves between them and try to conciliate. Kiku's elder brother especially makes things worse by saying that Kiku is naive about women, who "all are alike." This enrages Kiku, who insists on the purity of Otoku's motives.

Seeing that Kiku is becoming seriously intransigent, his mother and brother whisk him into the next room. The camera follows, but the glowering presence of Kikugoro remains just offscreen left, a volatile silence implacably awaiting Kiku's capitulation. His mother derisively echoes his father's objection: "They think you're in love with a wet nurse!" His elder brother gently but firmly stresses the importance of popularity to the kabuki actor. To this Kiku retorts that he doesn't want unearned popularity; he would rather make it on his own without the crutch of the Onoe family name. He blurts out that he will not sacrifice Otoku for his family (which is exactly what happens in the end), and father's offscreen silence explodes. Kikugoro rushes into the frame left and shouts, "Take your selfishness and get out!" then disappears offscreen again. Kiku's mother cringes

Over his family's objections . . .

Kiku insists on marrying Otoku, the maid.
Kawakita Memorial Film Archives.

and frantically beseeches him to go to his father and apologize. Kiku gets up, slowly walks into medium close-up, and addresses his father. Getting no response, he moves offscreen himself, and makes his request: instead of apologizing, he asks to marry Otoku! Onscreen, mother and brother wait with bated breath. The response (still offscreen): a choking refusal, a shout, and a muffled struggle as Kiku runs out, slamming the door behind him.

What are the functions of this spatial dislocation of the confrontation? One could perhaps speculate about a Japanese sense of *enryo*, or restraint, that withholds scenes of intense emotional conflict. It is also reasonable to see this as a generalization of the drama from an active, individual protagonist to a reactive collective protagonist consisting of the whole family and not just the combatants. Finally, one can see this as one of Mizoguchi's characteristic figures of style that explore the roles of observers and attendants.[24] Mizoguchi's long takes and fluid but restrained cinematography have been celebrated for their expressive sympathy. The plight of his characters seeps into the movement of camera and shot changes but their autonomy and that of the spectator is always respected through devices that block identification, like a more distant placement or an obstacle that partially screens an especially tormented moment. The displaced camera-work in this instance is less a shying away from an intensely unpleasant confrontation than it is an interrogation of the nature of observation, sympathy, and judgment. As such, this stylistic figure more completely explores this particular interaction, because it shows as great a concern with the reaction of the witnesses and, by implication, the spectators, as with the action of the participants. In fact the narrative importance of this scene is at odds with its expressive intensity, because while Kiku's confrontation with his father is the most arresting thing in the space, even though it occurs offscreen, Kiku's mother's reaction to the confrontation carries more narrative weight. As spectators, we already know that Kiku is irreparably alienated from his father. We share Kiku's mother's surprise to hear Kiku beg to marry Otoku, instead of begging for his father's forgiveness. But with Kiku's open rebellion the suspense for us is whether Kiku's mother will continue to play the intercessor and take his part before Kikugoro or capitulate to the patriarchal judgment and close ranks against her son. The story is here at a turning point. The displacement of the primary confrontation onto a key witness, Kiku's mother, fudges the distinction between actor and spectator, player and observer.

Another example of this reactive displacement is the sequence in which Kiku's mother chastises, then fires, Otoku. The technical handling of the scene rules out the idea that it expresses some diffident Japanese notion of *enryo*, because the camera returns to the most directly combative exchange *after* it has "wandered" away into a panning movement. The pan away from Otoku's trial reveals the presence of the other maids in the household, who discreetly listen to the mother's accusations. The camera does not return to the same angle from which it started, however; it crosses the line of action from a shot over Otoku's left shoulder, pans away past the open room with the eavesdropping nursemaids, traverses a grilled shoji screen window, and moves back to a two-shot of Kiku's mother and Otoku, now over her right shoulder so that their eyeline directions are reversed.

Again, we see the concentration on the role of the observers as a constitutive element in a dramatic exchange, even though Otoku and her mistress are apparently unaware of their presence. The maids belong to the same occupation as Otoku and might be expected to sympathize, but they are also the ones who inform Kiku's mother that Otoku was with Kiku the night of the fireworks. They are motivated by jealousy no less than Kiku's parents are motivated by social embarrassment. Both motivations are premised on a lie, as Otoku vainly protests. However, Kiku's mother points out that Otoku herself says she wants to perform the role of helpmate and encourager of Kiku's craft, which usurps her role as a mother. Thus Otoku's protests that her motives are pure only tightens the double bind in which she is trapped. For Otoku to defend herself against charges of opportunism, she must cast herself in the role of mother-surrogate, which, to Kiku's mother, is even worse.

Kiku's mother fires Otoku. Kawakita Memorial Film Archives.

Another technique implicates Otoku in the eyes of yet another set of witnesses: the empirical spectator. In Otoku's argument with her mistress, she is always framed over her shoulder and the back of her head so that we never get a clear view of her face. At best we get a three-quarter profile of her face as she tearfully defends herself. The face that dominates the screen is that of the angry mother. The fact that she continues to visually and emotionally dominate Otoku even after the pan away, which installs an expectation of reciprocity in the distribution of screen time, calls attention to the deliberate suppression of Otoku's onscreen presence. One could argue that the camera is taking Otoku's point of view (metonymically, not optically) and therefore privileges it, but there is no reverse angle in this scene to "anchor" the object of her look. The central presence here is that of the mother, who ruthlessly shoots down Otoku's feeble objections. We *know* that these accusations are unfair, but we *see* the irresistable force of the antagonists' arguments: it is their point of attack that controls the space and the screen. The weight of the representation is slyly lent to the characters who are clearly in the wrong; sadistically, the spectator is put in a position that discourages means with which to pity the victim, because her reaction is not given a full frontal representation. She is a cipher, utterly at the mercy of the antagonists and witnesses who dominate the screen.

Where is the empirical spectator here? At first, he or she is "with" Otoku in the expectation that the point-of-view setup will return to Otoku. The camera drifts away from the object of Otoku's gaze to show the maids in the next room, whom Otoku cannot see. At the same time the sound of the nursemaid's lullabye becomes louder as the camera follows the movement of the eavesdropping nursemaid. Conceivably this indicates a heightening of Otoku's auditory attention, but it is enough to point out the link between the nursemaid's song and what is happening to Otoku: she is fired from her job for doing just what the nursemaid/witness is doing in the next room. When we pan past the shoji screen, the option of regarding the camera movement as somehow representing Otoku's state of mind, let alone her perception, has run out. When the setup returns again to the mother, not Otoku, we see that we are cast in the role of yet another witness and, like the eavesdropping maids, not necessarily a sympathetic one. The sequence studiously avoids the bathos of pity, opting instead for an intensely interested, but mostly detached, examination of the whole situation, complete with eavesdroppers and inanimate spaces. The exploration of this social space is almost clinical in its curiosity.

The narrative line and the dialogue clearly favor Otoku as the one who deserves sympathy. But the way this sequence is shot places Otoku in a peculiar position. Even when she is answering the mother's charges, there is a steadfast refusal to grant her the full frontal close-up that Kiku's mother enjoys throughout. A close-up at this point would "lock in" our identification and sympathy with Otoku because the other elements in the drama so strongly encourage it. The consequence would be a corresponding indignation at the rest of the family for subjecting Otoku to such humiliation. Instead, we are divided between our intellectual understanding of the situation and the visual appeal of appearances so strongly embodied by the family. Otoku's protests fall on deaf ears (and eyes) because she appeals to the sense of facts and not the force of appearances. Otoku is a character who is acted upon; she is the scapegoat, and the stage on which tensions in the "excellent family customs" are played out. She is the ideal spectator, not us, because she is the victim in this theater of consensus. She objects, but not so strongly that she unravels the fabric of family roles and obligations. That is left to Kiku when he finds out about her dismissal.

Despite her suffering, Otoku is the object of desire in this film, and the role most worthy of emulation, because as an observer of both family customs and *ryofu bizoku* (good and beautiful customs) she is totally committed to the integrity of these venerable Japanese institutions. So committed is she to the artistic and personal triumph of Kiku that she happily overlooks the injustice of giving him up so that he can have a second chance at the limelight. In Otoku the conflict between artistic triumph and familial harmony is transcended. She willingly gives up her life so that Kiku can be reunited with his family and proudly take his rightful place in the artistic guild. What was once a rift between artistic excellence and familial traditions is healed, but only through Otoku's efforts, which in the end claim her life. Only she is able to reconcile the conflict, because she is totally selfless and has no interests of her own.

"Good and Beautiful Customs"

For the family to be reunited, the proper roles must be assigned and sincerely played. Specific roles govern everyday family life no less than the roles played by characters onstage. Theater and family in *Chrysanthemum* are mutually reinforcing metaphors. The theater is a metaphor for the role playing, intrigue, and face saving that are performed in the extended Japanese family. The family stands in for the lineage, training, and above all loyalty that is expected in the traditional Japanese artistic guild (or corporation). It has been argued that ritual role playing in Japan is a social strategy specifically devised to ensure the avoidance of conflict.[25] A structure of hierarchical roles substitutes for moral/religious abstractions internalized by individuals and used to adjudicate differences of opinion. In this view Japanese "proper place" replaces Western ideals of conflict resolution through "reasonable disputation." Proper discrimination of place, therefore, is crucial, and far from relinquishing moral judgment, implies an intimate and inextricable link between role playing and judgment. As we will see, discrimination in taste has ethical implications, but Mizoguchi's film inverts its public and private ramifications.

Chrysanthemum faithfully replicates the privileged role of the spectator, which in kabuki theater enjoys a prominence within the form of the drama that is unknown in popular Western theater. Because kabuki's provenance is in neighborhood street dances (*furyu odori*), and because its original participants were the urban middle and lower classes, the audience is an integral part of the performance.[26] Kabuki spectators, then, have an obligation to discriminate between authentic and meretricious performances, and to honestly communicate their judgments to the players. Mizoguchi's film does not hesitate to imply that the young girls who idolize Kiku are no better than the brazen hussies whose familiarity leave Kiku cold. And since kabuki runs on the hereditary guild system, judgments about individual performances reflect on the whole clan. Judgments on performance also reflect the tastes of the spectator, who in the prototypical theater was a participant in the street dances that gave birth to kabuki. According to Jacob Raz, Edo period painters and printmakers would take pains to include audiences in their genre pictures of kabuki theater because "the physical distinction between 'stage' and 'auditorium' was unclear. Thus there was no such thing as watching a 'clean' stage, a pure 'artistic' stage. Physically and conceptually, audiences were part of the scene and therefore when one attempted to describe the theater, the whole theater was a natural unit to depict."[27] These theatrical assumptions and allusions are an example of the *ryofu bizoku,* "good and beautiful customs," that are bound up closely with the "excellent family customs" the film explores and subtly promotes.

Kiku's rebellion and departure is a necessary step for a true appreciation of family values and artistic accomplishment. Kiku's status as adopted son of Kikugoro IV gives him intimate access to the charmed circles of the theatrical demimonde. But his ready access to prestige and privilege does not guarantee competence, either as performer or as heir. In the floating world of Meiji kabuki, Kiku's theatrical and filial roles merge, and his artistic incompetence is matched by his puerility as a son. The fact that these roles are thrust upon him by fawning admirers and conciliatory family only makes him spoiled. He takes these roles for granted rather than working at becoming worthy of them. Only when a lowly nursemaid has the effron-

Kiku is cajoled by his uncle . . .

and chastened by the nursemaid Otoku. Kawakita Memorial Film Archives.

tery to tell him how bad he is, breaking out of her role as hired help to offer brutally honest criticism, does Kiku see the need for redemption. Initially his determination to succeed artistically without familial support brings him into severe conflict with the clan and he is ostracized. But this brings an alignment of the two major goals of winning artistic recognition and achieving reconciliation with family. When Kiku's roadwork pays off, his family embraces him once more, and he is no longer the prodigal son. At precisely this point, however, he is separated from the relationship that provided the impetus for his quest: Otoku removes herself from him as a condition of his audition for the family. She is finally recognized as his wife when she is on her deathbed. A direct proportion is maintained, then, between private happiness and public role playing, including that of a dutiful son and member of the clan. Private fulfillment must be given up in service to artistic accomplishment and filial piety. Redemption is available through a disciplined course of artistic training, but at a very high cost.

Another aspect of the redemption attainable through art is the expression of "good and beautiful customs" through traditional architecture and design. Domestic and theatrical design is used as much to screen the action as to reveal it. When Otoku is being fired from her job by Kiku's mother, the intricate shoji window takes pride of place over Otoku's humiliation. Like an outsized hat that blocks our view of the movie screen, we cannot help but notice the details of the window because our attention strains to return to Otoku. This particular spatial digression also emphasizes the lay-out and materials of the Japanese room, which do not afford any privacy and lead to speculation about who else besides the maids could be over-hearing Otoku's chastisement.[28] The behavioral determinations of Japan-ese interior design are clearly brought out in this sequence, emphasizing the adaptability of behavior to situation and spatial context:

> With its open structure, the Japanese house is vulnerable to all kinds of intrusion, including dirt, dust, and insects. Noise and lack of privacy are another problem; screens and *shoji* (translu-cent paper-covered sliding panels) offer a measure of visual pri-vacy to the inhabitants, but for both of these situations, the Japanese have developed appropriate patterns of behavior rather than practical solutions.[29]

Linda Ehrlich has pointed out the expressive use of stairs in *Chrysanthe-mum*: she sees the association of stairs with moments of intense anguish and emotion, such as the humiliation of Kiku's ascent to his father's dressing room at the beginning of the film.[30] The stairs that lead to Otoku's garret also lead to the excruciating awareness that it is Otoku's sacrifice that makes Kiku's success and reconciliation possible. Stairs and theatrical wings also graphically express the splitting of force and sense, of appearance and sub-jectivity, that is so prominently established at the beginning of the film. Later on, Otoku is so concerned about Kiku's postexile debut that she retires downstairs to pray instead of remaining above to watch the end of his per-formance. Robert Cohen generalizes the significance of stairs by regarding them as emblematic of the vertical hierarchy of a venerable kabuki family.[31]

While making ingenious interpretations, both Ehrlich and Cohen leap to the expressive, metaphorical level too quickly. A more fruitful account of stairs and other design features is to regard them as facilitating activity and behavior peculiar to the Meiji milieu in which the drama takes place. This allows certain techniques of staging and shooting to take on distinctly Japanese and perhaps regional associations. The semidarkness and medium-long shot scale of the kitchen in which Kiku cuts watermelon for Otoku is an example of the intimacy with which a traditional kitchen can be invested. When Otoku asks, "You live here?" as she is first brought to Kiku's tiny Osaka garret, her question brings out the smallness and squalor of the place to which Kiku has fallen and where she will eventually die. A particular sense of place pervades the space of *Chrysanthemum*, which expresses first a strong Japanese flavor, of course, but more specifically a taste of Meiji-era Japaneseness in Tokyo, Osaka, and Nagoya. Mizoguchi frames particular spaces in the theater, the home, and public places in a way that maximizes their proxemic function, i.e., their expression of regional and local community, the particular territory of the "tribal" group.[32]

The distinctiveness, if not uniqueness, of Japanese design is its emphasis on the particularity of space, so that space is personalized and transformed into place. The Japanese idea of *ie* (home) is a functional, not a substantive, unit, and therefore domestic proxemic relationships can be transferred to other places (the workplace, say, or a city street) that might otherwise be impersonal.[33] For instance, consider the long tracking shot of Kiku and Otoku along the riverbank. The shot's trajectory is broken by a gentle rhythm of stops and starts, of soft, desultory conversation, a lullabye sung to the baby, and a purchase from the windchime man. The fundamental proxemic gesture that gives this space its intimacy is one of "bounding," of separation into units: it is a way of simplifying, to mark off areas of activity with rules and practices specific to each, thereby "making each of these manageable in its own frame."[34]

The separation of space into proxemic places grounds the oft-observed modularity of Japanese design and behavior. The Japanese insistence on bounding and articulating proxemic life not only conveys a strong sense of particular contexts but also an ability to accommodate differences that are relatively novel to Western habits of thought: the notion that self, reality, or God is not stable, unitary, and immutable.[35] This is a profound and ancient difference between Japanese and Western aesthetic principles, as shown in the radical separation of action and telling in the kabuki and the adjustment of *ma* (intervals) in traditional domestic architecture. Building a Japanese house is largely a matter of "adjusting *ma*, or relationships that already exist—a process that lies at the heart of traditional Japanese design. Once the structure is given, design is concerned with the realignment and alteration of already existing relationships. . . . Japanese walls are not defensive."[36] It is not just Mizoguchi's decoupage but its appropriation of Japanese design principles that personalizes space in his films, even that of public space.

The differences between the atmospheres of the grand Tokyo kabuki and the more modest Osaka theater is a major connotative axis in the film, as stated by one of Kiku's relatives: "It's all different from Tokyo." The Tokyo-Osaka difference is graphically expressed in an odd framing of the stairs in the Osaka garret. Mizoguchi uses a high angle that flattens the space looking down the stairs. Offscreen right, Kiku is celebrating his opportunity to show the family his improved technique. At the bottom of the stairs there is a commotion involving several workmen. The stairway is so small and narrow that it looks like little more than a hole in the floor, through which Otoku's face peers up. The workmen trying to negotiate their way up are told to stop because they will not be able to fit. Kiku comes into the shot and descends. Cut to the next sequence downstairs in which Kiku is admiring a dressing mirror bought for him by Otoku. It is a small piece, standard issue for a successful actor, but is nonetheless too big to be moved up into Kiku and Otoku's meager quarters. In narrative terms this brings out the reality of Kiku's straitened circumstances. The resemblance of Osaka stairways to trapdoors and upper-level rooms to attics also anchors the period detail and lifestyle, especially as distinguished from the comfortable surroundings of the Onoe family in Tokyo. The contrast between the opulent kabuki establishment in Tokyo and the unassuming proving ground of Osaka is clearly brought out in the crosscutting between Kiku's triumphant processional and Otoku's death in the final scene.

Mizoguchi also loves to pan past the wooden latticework of Meiji-era slotted windows, as if the camera were a casual eavesdropper on a typical Tokyo night in 1885. Ehrlich thematizes these constructions as emblems of both privacy and confinement, symbolizing the cozy yet claustrophobic paternalism of kabuki families.[37] A good example is the postperformance party at the beginning of the film, in which we cannot see so much as hear snippets of derisive commentary on Kiku's acting. The setup begins on a shot of upper-level slotted windows through which we hear gossip, then pans left as Kiku arrives and begins to ascend the stairs. The wooden grillwork, the camera movement, and the fragmented dialogue strongly conveys a sense of an inviolable boundary between the select denizens of the inner sanctum and everything that is outside, marginalized, and alone.

A "perceptual" explanation of this sequence is more direct and revealing than a thematic one. By training our attention on seemingly irrelevant details of furniture and design, and denying us the position of an ideal observer who has the best possible vantage point on the drama, these figures of style encourage an indirect approach to the action. Mizoguchi's style could be seen as "paradigmatic" in that we are compelled to attend to offscreen space and sound. Mizoguchi's technical choices make us aware of alternatives and hidden possibilities, and in this sense his style is paradigmatic. What we are shown is only metonymically related to the central dramatic action, viz., Kiku's ignorance of his artistic incompetence. When the expressive force of the work is divided between a variety of elements, "central dramatic action" is not always the primary value. When the expressive functions are distributed and modulated among separate units, aesthetic pleasure is distributed among different faculties. As we saw with Otoku's chastisement and the importance of the observer, the significance of action and utterance is not limited to the immediate participants. Mizoguchi's style involves the eavesdropper, the casual bystander, the inanimate design feature, and even the space next-door as constituent elements and potential agents of the dramatic situation. In this respect Mizoguchi's style is profoundly indiscriminate.

Barrie Greenbie, a professor of landscape architecture and urban design, interprets these aesthetic factors as clues to the holistic epistemology of the Japanese mind. While his ideas are extreme, relying partially on certain studies of neurolinguistics that are informed by *nihonjinron* ideology, they are extremely thought-provoking as well. Western rationalist epistemology elevates reason over feeling, says Greenbie, and this initiates a kind of mental schism that banishes affect from our concepts and abstractions. Since abstractions like money, prestige, and morality disregard particularities in favor of generalities, Western thinking evacuates feelings from our public life. But according to Greenbie,

> It seems that the Japanese do not abstract at the expense of feeling, at least not to the extent that modern Westerners do. The Japanese appear to acknowledge in their own behavior and in the arrangement of their habitat the contradictions inherent in [the divided] brain, whereas Westerners tend to deny those contradictions."[38]

With an acceptance of contradictions between affect and concept, particular and general, there is an opportunity to perceive, integrate, and express them in objects and behavior through the performance of an "imaginative unification/synthesis." This bridges the gap between the affective self and the potentially alien qualities of inanimate objects and concepts alike. These are humanized by clearly bounding them according to a modular logic that controls proxemic domestic relations. The relevance of all this for the films of Mizoguchi may be tenuous, but it is clear that Mizoguchi's efforts to personify and domesticate his images lends them a particularly Japanese flavor. They are particularly Japanese not in the tautological sense but in the specific work they perform, bridging distances between the Meiji era and the 1930s, between theatrical forms and film, especially in tiny details that lend a deceptively casual sense of intimacy.

The scene in which the geisha await Kiku's return from the theater is a model of seemingly chaotic movement, speech, and offscreen sound. The upper veranda of the inn is framed in long shot, showing the coming and going of geisha, the sound of their laughter, the swish of their garments. Offscreen it sounds like there is a rehearsal in progress. Somewhere, the plaintive cries of a *joruri* street singer rise from the darkness. Suddenly a geisha appears on the balcony, tosses a coin, and murmurs a word of appreciation. The singing stops, and from below comes a thank you. Apparently the *joruri* singer was not just in the neighborhood, but deliberately stationed himself below the geisha quarters whose clientele consists of actors and artistes. What seemed accidental turns out to be deliberate. In this way the distinction between dramatic action and mere atmosphere is undermined, because there is no way of knowing which "background" elements of set design or offscreen space may suddenly come forward into the limelight. This is especially pertinent in a film about the public and private lives of theater actors.

The attentive lingering on details of furniture, clothing, or light shows not just a concern with period detail but also an inscription of the Bazinian image of the usher's flashlight illuminating things that are but the barest fraction of a reality that lies beyond the pale. The synecdoche in Mizoguchi's technique evokes a whole world that lies just outside, or just yesterday, and suggests "a hierarchy of values almost the antithesis of that of the West, a world where the stillness of nature, the inanimate form, speaks strongest to the heart."[39]

If in 1939 the issue of loyalty in the arts was addressed in a Meiji-period setting, there is a certain logic to find in 1941–1942 a reexamination of loyalty, this time set in the Genroku period, with samurai protagonists rather than kabuki actors. It is telling that loyalty this time was framed in terms of warlike bushido rather than *geido*, the way of the artist. Mizoguchi's *Genroku Chushingura* was encouraged by the Education Ministry to continue the effort to stimulate a recognition of Japanese "spirit" through its most prestigious literary and artistic traditions. Though the film does not deal directly with the aesthetic life, it is suffused with aestheticism to a far greater extent than *Chrysanthemum*. Its aestheticism, moreover, is rigorous, uncompromising, and aims to redirect the perceptual faculties of the spectator in line with traditional Japanese art forms. Perhaps it is no accident that Arthur Koestler calls Chushingura "a tale of sheer dementedness."[40] Mizoguchi's *Genroku Chushingura* is nevertheless the avatar of the monumental style.

6

Genroku Chushingura
(1941–1942)

The excessive attention to historical detail which is sometimes obtrusive in *Genroku Chushingura* is certainly not true of the films on the subject, which follow oft-tried patterns of good and bad guys fighting and eliminate the shadings that Mayama was so careful to establish.

—Donald Keene, "Variations on a Theme: *Chushingura*"

Genroku Chushingura is the classic example of the monumental style. The film is not only exemplary, it is prototypical: any claims about monumental style should stand or fall by their plausibility with respect to this film. *Genroku Chushingura*, made in two parts on the eve of Pearl Harbor, is a model of technical virtuosity and restraint. The virtuosity of its cinematography, setting, and acting restrains the forward trajectory of its narrative and the stock character of its heroes. By the time Mizoguchi made his version of the legendary story of the forty-seven ronin (masterless samurai), there were already scores of filmed *Chushingura* renditions.[1] Before that, the story had been commemorated countless times in *rokyoku* and *naniwa-bushi* songs, in *kodan* ballads, and in the kabuki and bunraku puppet theater.[2] Because of this overwhelming intertextuality Mizoguchi could assume an enormous array of preconceptions and connotations about the myth of the loyal forty-seven, and so re-present the tale as an exercise in perceptual renewal.

Proposing to deliver all the connotations in *Genroku Chushingura* is presumptuous, similar to trying a definitive interpretation of the Easter passion or Passover. More than any other monumental film, *Genroku Chushingura* sacramentalizes Japanese tradition and Japanese perception. Since Mizoguchi takes for granted in his audience so many elements of plot, character, allusion and allegory, he is freed to concentrate his energies on the problem of defamiliarizing the *Chushingura* epic. This takes place in two registers or aspects, a thematic aspect related to the film's narrative structure and characterization, and a perceptual one that more directly inclines the spectator's attention to specifically Japanese forms of contemplation. Here Mizoguchi's style invokes the sacred by means of interlocking techniques like framing, camera movement, and long takes to encourage spatial and tactile explorations of the Genroku world. In abandoning oneself to these imaginary explorations, the spectator learns to perceive in a way consonant with traditional Japanese aesthetics and religion.

These "training exercises" in Genroku perception build an awareness of modular space as it is organized by Japanese interior design and an experience of how collective spectatorship can afford clues to deciphering a social situation. The perceptual provides a foundation for thematic lessons in discerning real from apparent motivations in specific situations. Style in *Genroku Chushingura* functions to plunge the viewer deep into a perceptual experience of the Genroku world in the hope that he or she may become conversant with its ways of seeing and perhaps take away the desire to practice them when the film is over. The intended effect, as a kokusaku project, is an inculcation of classical aesthetics for nationalist and militarist ends, and Mizoguchi was not alone in this effort. I have written elsewhere on monumental invocations of Japanese aesthetics for nationalist purposes, but what is revealing here is the function of style as training exercise in indigenous perception, a primer on seeing with Japanese eyes.[3]

Narrative Structure and Characterization

The idea that *Genroku Chushingura* is intent on sacramentalizing perception is related to its emphasis on the place of women in the tale. (Its full title is The loyal forty-seven ronin of the Genroku era, Genroku being a period of peace, dissolution, and artistic flowering between 1688 and 1704.) One commentator says that in *Genroku Chushingura* Mizoguchi is "a director at war with his own picture."[4] It could be argued that Mizoguchi's perennial preoccupation with women is the means by which he subtly sabotages the nationalism apparently promoted by the picture. Of all the ritual suicides that take place in the film, only a young woman's is honored by occurring onscreen. The implication is that the opportunity to witness a ritual suicide is an unparalleled privilege that legitimates the act and purifies the beholder.

However, a revisionist historical drama like *Genroku Chushingura* is not necessarily a subversive one. A samurai film that privileges perspectives of women, as this one does, is not necessarily a film that sabotages the traditionally martial themes of its genre. Far from implying some critical distance on the canons of bushido, *Genroku Chushingura* functions instead as an extension of the bushido ethos into home and family. Why should it be assumed that samurai home life represents some sort of haven from the bushido rigors that govern the professional relationships of samurai? There is no doubt that *Genroku Chushingura* questions the conventions of samurai jidai geki, particularly those of chambara and of prior Chushingura tales (pace Donald Keene, above). But it is an unwarranted leap to think that the film therefore questions bushido, nationalism, or militarism. Rather, *Genroku Chushingura*'s narrative structure, characterization, and stylistic strategies extend and refine the repertoire of jidai geki such that a broader range of connotations, such as the feminine, the religious, and the aesthetic, can be accommodated within it. A process of consolidation, not of criticism, is at work in *Genroku Chushingura* that tries to bring all of life, not just the martial and the masculine, under the bushido standard.

Bushido is the samurai "warrior way" that prizes loyalty to one's lord over all other virtues (see chapter 3). Bushido is especially evident in cases where loyalty calls for death, either in battle or by one's own hand, out of regard for one's lord or superior. One need think only of the massive self-immolation of kamikaze troops in World War II—singing lines from the eighth-century book of verse, the *Manyoshu*:

> If we go to the sea our corpses shall
> soak in the water.
> If we go to the hills our corpses shall
> rot in the grass.
> We will die by the side of our sovereign,
> We will never look back—

to remember the thanatotic foundations of bushido.[5] As for bushido's exhortations to women, consider Nitobe Inazo's classic statement of its feminine aspect:

> When a Japanese Virginia saw her chastity menaced, she did
> not wait for her father's dagger. Her own weapon lay always in
> her bosom. . . . She must know how to tie her lower limbs
> together with a belt so that, whatever the agonies of death
> might be, her corpse be found in utmost modesty with the limbs
> properly composed. Is not a caution like this worthy of the
> Christian Perpetua or the Vestal Cornelia?[6]

Onscreen, the figure of the self-immolating militarist woman dates back to
at least 1931, with a rash of *junshi* (loyalty suicide) films inspired by sacrificial patriotism in the Manchurian Incident. That year saw the release of *Shi
no sembutsu Inoue chui fujin* (*The Wife of Lt. Inoue Gives Her Life as a Parting Gift*,
Shinko Kinema, Kimura Kakichi), in which the heroine gives her husband
a farewell toast, then commits suicide to encourage him to die bravely at
the front.[7] Bushido therefore consisted of a warrior code that was extended
to nonwarriors (commoners, women, and children, even animals—see
chapter 7) and eventually appropriated as grounding for militarist jingoism
of the 1930s. Mass media policies saw to it that movies upheld the glories
of Japanese tradition, including samurai honor, loyalty, and bushido.

The motivation for this dissemination process was mainly political. *Genroku Chushingura* was one of the most prestigious in a series of government-
sponsored kokusaku (national policy) films that sought to edify the masses
and glorify non-Western Japanese heritage. If women at the homefront as
well as soldiers on the battlefield could be included in celebrated legends
that illustrate the principles of bushido, so much the better for the war
effort. But stylistic motivations also account for the catholicizing of
bushido in *Genroku Chushingura*: one is Mizoguchi's personal style—his concerns with women, with the artistic life, his penchant for the implacable
narrative culmination and the baroque opaqueness of his technique.
Closely related is another stylistic variable: the monumental style itself.

Since the Great Kanto Earthquake of 1923, jidai geki in the "American
style" had flourished.[8] Many of these films celebrated the criminal, the
ruthless, and the nihilistic, relying chiefly on dynamic techniques convey-
ing a dizzying sense of ferocity and violence (see chapter 4). The gentle
oyama (female impersonators) and performances of the *katsuben* (narrators)
were disappearing. By the early thirties authorities and press called for a
more positive role for the government in "stimulating, supporting, and
rewarding the industry's *autonomous* efforts to bring about a qualitative
improvement in our nation's cinema."[9] The "improvement" demanded here
required an amelioration of Japan's image abroad in addition to raising the
level of domestic entertainment. Wrote one film director in late 1932:

Here at home, our large film producers concern themselves solely with the domestic market. Is it not time for them to emerge from the protective cocoon of "entertainment value" and take up the task of making films which embody the National Mission (*kokka no shimei*)? We are now at the point in history when we must enhance the image of Japan and of the Japanese Spirit both at home and abroad. Film is the very best means for the promotion of that national image—I say this without hesitation. The industry needs guidance and leadership from the national authorities.[10]

The monumental style, one result of the kokusaku directive, was a propitious answer to the problem of resuscitating the flagging samurai film—giving it an important new political function to serve by means of a new stylistic mandate. The monumental style was more ascetic, more profound, more difficult than the erstwhile slapstick samurai films and thereby admirably served the purpose of rejuvenating a national identity, a market, an exhausted subject matter, and finally an interesting aesthetic challenge for period film directors. The elevation of jidai geki into a national policy charges the film industry with the responsibility to produce films that "1) exalt the spirit of the nation, 2) stimulate national industry and research, and 3) provide wholesome public entertainment," in the words of the 1934 mandate of the Greater Japan Film Association.[11]

The authoritarian tendencies implicit in the notion of "wholesome entertainment" were specifically directed at the riotous violence so typical of samurai films since the 1920s.[12] One place where wholesome exhortation might be found was in the adaptation of prestigious literary/theatrical properties. This was provided by Mayama Seika's monumental historical cycle, consisting of ten Chushingura plays written between 1934 and 1941 and performed by the Zenshinza kabuki troupe.[13] The flattening of dramatic effect (and affect) in Mayama's play cycle comes from his attempt to write a historically authoritative version of the story: "Mayama was eager to establish the authenticity of his treatment of the age, even at the risk of seeming dull."[14] Mayama's scholarly interest in producing an accurate rendition of the Chushingura tale is congruent with the nationalistic demand for cultural products that "embody the National Mission." In view of this requirement, the Mayama property was a presold product.[15] (*Zangiku Monogatari*, too, was a popular shimpa stage play when Mizoguchi and Shochiku bought the film rights. See chapter 5.)

The following discussion of the structure and textures of *Genroku Chushingura* tries to be alert to contemporary exigencies served by its austere tex-

tual design. The fact that women are privileged, or that suspense is suppressed, or that garden aesthetics are foregrounded, points toward an
imaginary Japaneseness, a role prepared for the patriotic Japanese spectator. The film is a form of Japanese fundamentalism, the paragon of a style
that seeks to express the essence of Japaneseness but still is no more nor less
Japanese than those that come from periods other than the late 1930s. The
norms that guide the narrative structure and characterization of *Genroku
Chushingura,* including its relative emphasis on women, find their most pertinent context in Mayama's concern with the historical actuality of the
Chushingura events. Mizoguchi's *Genroku Chushingura* is therefore a dual
rewriting of Chushingura. Through Mayama's play it works first as a corrective to the hackneyed formulae of Chushingura renditions and second
as part of a more general redirection of jidai geki film along historically
authentic lines. The search for authenticity in the face of deceiving appearances is a theme that organizes both the textual features and contextual
objectives of the film. Consider Oishi's exhortation to the Ako ronin who
are sceptical of giving up their master's castle: "Don't criticize the shogunate. Entrust your lives to me. It looks difficult but it's easy to hold the castle; all we have to do is fight against the shogun and die. But to give it up
and avenge our lord—it looks easy but is very difficult" (scene 18, segmentation).

Chushingura is a vendetta story whose culmination is complicated by the
legal repercussions of the ronin's act of vengeance. Because of his ceremonial inexperience, the lord of Ako loses his temper and wounds Kira, the
master of ceremonies, in the palace of the shogun. This is a capital offense,
and Ako is sentenced to commit ritual suicide. His estate is confiscated and
his now masterless samurai vow revenge against Kira. The samurai, now
ronin, are led by Ako's erstwhile treasurer, Oishi Kuranosuke, who must
deal with the dilemma of illegally taking the law into his own hands and
the obligation he is under as samurai to avenge his dead master. Where is
his primary loyalty? With the shogun or with his master? Is he bound by
the laws of the land or his personal relationship to his lord? Oishi's dilemma
is made more difficult by public speculation, even within the shogunate,
over whether and how the Ako vendetta will be carried out. The land has
been at peace for one hundred years, and there is an awareness that martial
discipline in the samurai classes is at low ebb. Oishi and his faithful ronin
must go underground for two years, pretending to lose themselves in drink
and dissolution, before they vindicate themselves and the bushido code
that binds them with a brilliant strike against Kira on the anniversary of
lord Ako's death. The story structure and characterization poses questions
about the codes that govern samurai ethics in a time when those ethics

seem most anachronistic. Chushingura, at bottom, asks the key question of what it means to be a true samurai when the very necessity of the samurai institution is in doubt.

Genroku Chushingura tries to tell the Chushingura story using a mass hero. Individualism was one of the cultural and political bugbears of the time and Mayama's play tries to avoid "heroizing" individual samurai at the expense of the forty-seven ronin who together perform their vendetta. It would be impossible to tell forty-seven individual stories of valor, so the film employs a serial structure with different protagonists dominating each part. Of course Oishi Kuranosuke has the lion's share of the responsibility for the honor and glory heaped upon the ronin; however, he does not dominate every part of the film. Other protagonists, such as Chamberlain Tamon (part 1), Sukeyemon, Lady Asano, and Omino (part 2), control the narrative with their respective acts of heroism. Each of these heroes and heroines take their turn in the spotlight, then move into the background. (This bears a structural similarity to the collective community artistry of the Zenshinza's own performance practice; see note 13).

The narrative is initiated by Asano's transgression, whose significance lies less in itself than in the chain of official and unofficial responses occasioned by his act. In fact, Asano's attack on Kira is not even included in Mayama Seika's original play.[16] In the film a motif of circularity governs the staging and shooting of the opening act of violence, ironically the only

Lord Asano's attack on Kira in Mizoguchi's *Genroku Chushingura* (1941–1942). Publicity still, Kawakita Memorial Film Archives.

physical conflict to appear in part 1 of the film. Asano's attack initiates the disruption of a harmonious state whose tremors shake the entire country and reverberate for centuries.

A prominent watcher in the opening attack is Lord Tsunatoyo, whose observance of the pandemonium is a preintroduction to the major role he will play in part 2. This illustrates a principle of linkage that governs the structure of the various sections: characters are often seen in the background, or with minor supporting roles, and only later figure prominently in the action. This linkage principle unifies the narrative and economizes on the need for exposition, while still contributing to the development of a collective hero. When Lord Tsunatoyo, for instance, plays the key role in the chastisement of Sukeyemon in part 2, our memory of his sympathy for the provisional hero of the opening section, Tamon, gives him added depth and complexity in his subsequent role. Similarly, Juroza, beloved of Omino at the end of the story, is introduced briefly toward the beginning of part 1 as one of the Edo belligerents whose loyalty Oishi is trying to command.

So before Oishi even appears, Chamberlain Tamon plays the hero's role in the events following Asano's attack on Kira. He helps in the interrogation of Asano (scene 3), who admits that his hotheaded attack was a personal grudge and expresses regret that he didn't kill Kira. By contrast, a cut to Kira reveals two things: that he is a coward, in the way he cringes at the sound of the shogun's arrival, and that he is a liar, when he says, "I did nothing to have Asano bear a grudge." Before returning to Tamon and Asano's imminent sentencing, we are shown Lady Asano's response to the news of her husband's transgression. Here again the plot introduces a character who will later perform the role of a provisional hero (part 2).

The sympathetic observances of Lord Tsunatoyo, the response of Lady Asano, and, especially, the entreaties of Chamberlain Tamon on behalf of Lord Asano depict the real heroes of the opening incident and investigation. Asano himself, apart from his rueful admissions (scene 3) and ritual suicide (scene 7), figures very little in the narrative. His primary function in the tale is to catalyze a series of events whose ultimate significance is a test of samurai loyalty in a time of peace and indolence. Chamberlain Tamon says as much in his impassioned defense of Asano, not only because the judgment on Asano was made by a distant relative of Kira, but also because Kira represents a selfish dissolution of samurai values: "We samurai do not consider him our equal; family and fief are first with him. Losing the samurai spirit, he thinks only of profits" (scene 3).

Tamon's sentiment is echoed by Councillor Tsunatoyo, who concedes that "these are peaceful times—samurai are becoming lax." But because of his bold intercession on behalf of Asano, Tsunatoyo compliments Tamon's

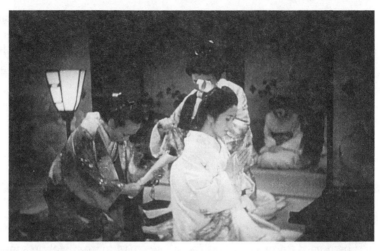

Lady Asano's response to her husband's sentencing. Frame enlargement, courtesy Shochiku Company, Ltd.

conduct as that of a true samurai. Tamon's dominance in this part of the film is confirmed by his bringing to the grief-stricken Lady Asano the news of Asano's death and the confiscation of his Edo mansion.

Two key aspects of the samurai character are introduced through the figure of Tamon: discipline and discernment. These aspects have a perceptual as well as a moral implication. From the first an emphasis is maintained on the vigilance that is necessary for samurai in times of peace and prosperity. An important aspect of samurai vigilance is to uphold the integrity of bushido by distinguishing those samurai who genuinely abide by it from those who merely pay it lip service. The shogun's prosecutors do not see the difference, and thus Tamon petitions for the opportunity to be heard by a higher authority. Later on Oishi hears that the emperor was apparently sorry that Asano failed to kill Kira; it turns out that there are those in the highest levels who realize the difference between spiritual commitment to bushido and mere due process. This distinction between spirit and law, between personal loyalty and invested authority, has disturbing implications for a society struggling to maintain a constitutional government in the 1930s. The logical conclusion of the distinction would seem to be situational, not constitutional, law.

Oishi Kuranosuke, whose decisions form the linchpin of the narrative structure, is not introduced until almost halfway through part 1. At first, his articulation of the Ako fief's priorities seems open to Tamon's ridicule of Kira's self-centered fixation on family and fief. The debate over Ako province's fortunes centers on whether rice quotas expected from tenant farmers and merchants should be maintained. Oishi takes a position of paternal egalitarianism, insisting that "the four Ako counties bolster us, not the other way around. The Ako farmers and shopkeepers must bear no losses" (scene 10). This, together with Oishi's reaction to the news of Asano's demise, serves to mark him as a man of "the people":

> Tokugawa scholars often voiced the Confucian principle that the common people, especially the farmers, should be treated with benevolence, but Kuranosuke's remarks at this point in the play seem an echo of the politics of the 1930s, when a love of the soil and sympathy for the farmers were an integral part of the philosophy of the young army officers who rose in rebellion.[17]

The regard for peasants initiates a pattern: a methodical presentation of Oishi, the ideal samurai, despite initial appearances. Events that have a direct consequence for the unfolding of the story, such as the fate of the Ako castle, the activities of dissenting Ako samurai, Oishi's petition to restore the Ako castle, and even the raid on Kira are systematically elided in the interest of concentrating on Oishi's character. An important exception to this occurs at the beginning of part 2, when Tsunatoyo chastises Sukeyemon for his hastiness in wanting to kill Kira independently of the

"The farmers and shopkeepers must bear no losses." Frame enlargement, courtesy Shochiku Company, Ltd.

other ronin. But the force of Tsunatoyo's argument lies in his appeal to Sukeyemon's loyalty to Ako, and therefore to Oishi, whose plan would be disgraced should Sukeyemon take precipitous action. So even this episode is about Oishi, even if he is not actually present.

Oishi's strategy is essentially reactive, even passive, involving a process of waiting (scenes 12–17), conscripting (scenes 18–20), dissembling (scenes 21–23), and finally reconciling (part 2, scenes 4–5). Overall, Oishi seems mainly to adjust his behavior to whatever vicissitudes come his way rather than actively campaigning to alter the outcome in his favor. Since Ako is by decree an outlaw clan, there is little that can be done in any direct way, save outright rebellion.

Rebellion is the course of action favored by the Edo members of the Ako clan. They are under the impression that if they peacefully turn over Ako castle to the shogunate, they are condoning its judgment and giving up the opportunity for vengeance. But Oishi knows something: the rumor that the emperor was sorry Lord Asano didn't kill Kira means the ronin have sympathy in high places. In the most histrionic of acting styles, Oishi and his messenger offer prayers of abject gratitude to the emperor: "You said you feel sorry for our lord. I'm saved" (scene 13).

Along with Oishi's sentiments about the peasantry's dependence on Ako benevolence, this apotheosis of the imperial figure also appears to be a theme peculiar to the 1930s. According to Donald Keene, no Tokugawa version of the Chushingura tale contains such abject emperor worship, and Mayama Seika, who usually documented his sources, supplied none for this particular scene.[18] The consequences are twofold: Mizoguchi's audience, in the post-Pearl Harbor period, were presented with a nostalgic representation of samurai loyalty, but one that transfers the object of that loyalty from provincial lord to emperor. Hence Oishi's expression of relief: his salvation, and that of the entire Ako clan, is secured by a rumor that the emperor has expressed sympathy. "Asano is dead, but he has been saved."[19]

But this information is not passed on to the rank-and-file ronin; nor is the fact that Oishi had asked his Kyoto messenger to apologize to Councillor Yanagiwara (Kira's distant cousin) and the other lords who prosecuted the Asano case. Already Oishi has suppressed information in order to lull the authorities into a false sense of security that what he appears to be doing—nothing—is what he is actually doing. But Oishi must also consider the danger that he appears to his own men, who are hungry for quick and bloody revenge, to be doing nothing. He must gain the trust and support of the Ako vassals while maintaining the secrecy of his real plans.

Oishi is portrayed as a master of *tatemae-honne* ("facade vs. true feeling") manipulation, in which one's outward behavior masks the inward intention. Oishi's intrigue is not played out for selfish reasons, but to protect the purity of his own motivations and that of his followers. He is shown as a broker of knowledge and ignorance in separate arenas of social inter- change. Despite showing a different face to his shogun, his followers, his family, and his community, he juggles each role according to how best it serves his ultimate master, the all-but-forgotten Lord Asano.

In the scenes depicting Oishi's attempt to conscript support for his plans, the narrative alternates between Oishi's professional solicitation of the ronin and the personal consequences of his choice. Oishi's deliberate vacillation, a disguised nimaime, is therefore reflected by the narrative structure. While rounding up the forty-six faithful Ako ronin, Oishi real- izes he faces the loss of his own family as well as his stake in the Ako fief. Oishi must count on the unconditional loyalty of the faithful ronin because the sacrifices are so high. But he refuses to tell the ronin what he has in mind: "There are many different opinions among retainers, so I cannot tell mine now. Promise me you'll follow my decision unconditionally" (scene 18). Oishi promises an opportunity for vengeance, but until he has the unconditional loyalty of the ronin (he asks them to sign in blood) he will not reveal his plan or how it will be accomplished. Absolute loyalty, after all, is the samurai's cardinal virtue; Oishi does not hesitate to call on it in his plan to respond to the crisis, knowing that a democratic compromise hardly suits the occasion.

A year goes by, during which Oishi dissembles, feigning dissipation and defeat. Several Ako ronin, including his son, believe that he has given up the cause and has no intention of avenging Lord Asano. Meanwhile Oishi has petitioned the shogunate for restoration of the Ako fief, thinking that his petition will be denied, giving just cause to his secret plan of vengeance. But he has miscalculated. His grief and dissipation persuade the shogunate, the community, and even the imperial adviser that perhaps his petition should be granted. This puts Oishi in a quandary. He and the other ronin have to "just sit and wait for the tide to change" (scene 21). Again, Oishi counsels more waiting, apparent passivity, reaction: the classic martial strategy of turning the enemy's weakness against himself rather than pre- vailing by direct superior force.

So far, Oishi's character problematizes the idealization of the dogged faithful retainer. The caution with which he proceeds shows that he is painfully aware, bordering on paranoia, of the consequences of his actions in the eyes of the community. Oishi's elaborate ploys and stratagems would have no meaning if the only issue were saving face for the Asano clan. Kira would have earned immediate retribution for his slight if the shogun and therefore the emperor were not involved. The Asano clan is hamstrung because Lord Asano's attack could only be construed as an outrage against the shogunate and possibly the emperor. As such, Asano's punishment was just and appropriate, but as many people knew, there was a private reality behind the public appearance of Asano's act. Accordingly, the dichotomy between the real and the apparent (as with the difference between the spiritual and legal aspects of bushido) finds its way into Oishi's behavior. To his chagrin Oishi discovers that public gossip has raised the status of the ronin of Ako to the *gishi* (righteous warriors) of Ako (part 2, scene 4). This is not only an embarrassment but a substantive blow to his plans, which are based on calculations of how they will appear prima facie. Oishi's strategy, then, is predicated on the presence of a community audience whose reaction to his pretenses are an integral part of his plans.

Oishi Kuranosuke is intent on using public opinion to his advantage, but Mayama Seika did not want to portray Oishi as a Machiavellian schemer:

> Kuranosuke was for Mayama the embodiment of samurai ideals which seemed of special importance in the late 1930s. He is determined to avenge his late master, but not if it involves stooping to base deceit. At one point he says, "It is desirable to search out weak spots in one's enemy's defenses and then attack, but I would not wish to satisfy our desire for vengeance if this involved luring our enemy into a trap."[20]

But it is a remarkably subtle distinction between "base deceit" and Oishi's willingness to allow people to believe that his intentions correspond to his behavior. Even the expository title that commences part 2 calls attention to Oishi's ploy: "He pretended he wanted to restore the House in order to shield his real intention. To his surprise, public opinion sided with him. If Asano House could be restored, his revenge couldn't be justified. It worried him."

The narrative structure and characterization of Mizoguchi's *Genroku Chushingura* plays up this issue of sincerity and deception, reality and appearance. Oishi's attempt to be reconciled with Asano's widow (part 2, scene 4) clinches this idea. Because of his dissolute lifestyle, Lady Asano's faithful servant does not want her to see him, especially on the anniversary of Lord Asano's death. The servant is overridden by Lady Asano, who agrees to speak to him. She and her companion, Lady Toda, pressure Oishi about Kira's imminent retirement and about his failure to avenge Lord Asano. She refuses to allow him to burn incense in Asano's memory, sighing, "No one wants to avenge him now." Ruefully, Oishi takes his leave, but, before he

goes, he delivers to Lady Toda a book of poems apparently written to commemorate the anniversary of Asano's death.

The next night the women open the book of poems to discover that it
is the account book of the Ako estate, whose fortunes Oishi used to over-
see. While puzzling over its significance, a message is tossed over the wall
that puts the women's perplexity to rest. It is a report written by an Ako
ronin detailing the raid on Kira's residence made by Oishi and the loyal
forty-seven the night before—just after Oishi left Lady Asano. An account
book masquerading as a book of poems; a loyal avenger masquerading as a
cowardly alcoholic—this is the moment at which Oishi's dissembling
finally ceases, but it is significant that this moment is not represented, but
only recounted by the two women. The key narrative moment in the film,
also the greatest opportunity for heroic spectacle, is given to the women.

Lady Asano's rebuke turns out to have been mistaken, but there is no
glorying in Oishi's successful subterfuge; instead they rejoice in his
accomplishment of that which Lady Asano had hoped for all along. Far
from being an unwitting dupe of Oishi's ploys, Lady Asano here plays a
heroic role. It is through her eyes that we learn of the decisive strike that
upholds the honor of the Asano house and the loyalty of the forty-seven
ronin. Not only have the Ako ronin settled their score with Kira and with
an unjust shogunate, but Oishi has settled accounts with those who
doubted his sincerity.

Oishi and Lady Asano on the anniversary of Asano's death.
Kawakita Memorial Film Archives.

Omino's Ruse

By the time Lady Asano reads Oishi's report on the strike against Kira, the vendetta is already over. Here Mizoguchi embellishes Mayama's play in an extended investigation of the role Genroku women play in the bushido scenario. Up to this point Lady Asano and Lady Oishi are casualties, even crucibles, of samurai loyalty to their various superiors. But once the vendetta is complete, there is an accounting due for these casualties. Because of their marginal status in the ethics of bushido, women are appraisers of samurai loyalty and make judgments on the cost of loyalty in real human feelings. Women make the final pronouncement on the excesses and manipulations in the name of loyalty, and function as a gauge that discriminates authentic from meretricious loyalty. Mizoguchi's contribution to the Chushingura myth is precisely this feminization of the warrior code, a recasting of the problem of authenticity in terms of human feelings (*ninjo*) not accountable to any official regime.

The denouement (scene 9–14) deals with Otomeda Omino, a young woman masquerading as a page in order to have access to one of the condemned Ako ronin, Isogai Juroza. Juroza was betrothed to Omino, but did so to gain information on Kira's whereabouts. On his wedding night he disappeared to join the raid on Kira. The heartbroken young woman comes to Oishi dressed as a page boy, asking permission to attend the ronin in their final hours before committing seppuku. Oishi is too good a deceiver himself to fall for this ploy and extracts the real reason for Omino's petition. She wants to find out if their relationship was strictly utilitarian, or if Juroza really loved her. We know already that Juroza is aware of the deception and hurt he has caused his beloved, because a brief transitional scene has his friend Sukeyemon (the rash attacker of Lord Tsunatoyo) counseling that he put away his regrets and soften his heart (scene 10). Ironically, Oishi tells the heartbroken Omino to harden hers, asking her to "please sacrifice yourself and despise him to the end."

But this is so much more pretense and deception. In an impassioned outburst Omino pits the protocols of samurai honor against the pain of her suffering, pointing out that it was the former that caused the latter. Rejecting Oishi's means-ends pragmatism, Omino identifies the cost in human feeling with which bushido is purchased—a bold statement in a film extolling "the National Mission." Oishi relents and allows her to see Juroza, who after an awkward hesitation admits that his devotion was not just a ploy (scene 11).

Is this subversive of bushido? It looks likely, in the Mizoguchian motif of exchange and redemption, maintaining the crosscutting between

Omino's ruse: cross-dressing to gain access to her lover, Juroza.
Kawakita Memorial Film Archives.

Omino and the formal sentencing of the loyal forty-seven (scene 13).
While they are about to die heroic deaths, Omino quietly kills herself
alone. As she lies dying, she is found by Oishi and Juroza, who assures her
that he did love her after all and considers himself part of her family. Her
death, she says, will make it the truth; the need for deceit is over. Further,
she asks that the Otomeda family be abolished, as if to dissolve it with
Juroza into a permanent unity in death. She dies, and it is time for Juroza
and Oishi to take their turns. A slightly black exchange has Juroza offering
to let Oishi go first so that he can pay his last respects to Omino. But Oishi
refuses, ever so gently, insisting that he must see through all forty-seven
seppuku to the last. A final dissolve to Omino lying dead is accompanied
by the droning announcement by the priest that Juroza has honorably
committed seppuku. This shot ranks with any of Mizoguchi's most melancholic evocations of the sacrificial power of a woman's love.

    Omino's suicide does not render the film subversive of its nationalistic
ideology. Rather, Omino is an absorption of official codes into personal
convictions, a conflation of bushido honor with a romantic myth of merging and apotheosis. But this presumes a distinction between official loyalties and personal yearnings (*giri* vs. *ninjo*) that the film maintains throughout. The wives and families of the loyal forty-seven ronin provide an ongoing account—in its fiscal as well as narrative sense—of the costs with

which samurai loyalties are purchased. This has a connection with the theme of deception that runs through the film because it is usually the women who are given key expository moments in the narrative. For instance, the recounting of the raid and Omino's exposé are the most memorable. Also, summaries of the situations early in the film are given by Oishi's wife's cousin (scene 15) and Oishi's wife—on the community's response to her husband's carousing (scene 23). If the women of *Genroku Chushingura* are the most reliable sources of information about the story, the film holds back from implying that it is precisely because they are partly outside the demands of official loyalties that they can assess the consequences of those loyalties more accurately.

More than this the women augment the code of bushido through their interventions. They purify, rather than subvert, samurai loyalty through their criticism of its distortions and abuses. They do this negatively, as when Sukeyemon's sister holds him back from an impulsive chambara attack on Kira early in part 2. More positively, women such as Oishi's wife, Lady Asano, and Omino put the principle back into bushido pragmatism. They authenticate it by exposing the deceit and disavowal with which bushido has become adulterated. They help samurai and spectators avoid hasty judgments and mires of deception that can confuse and distort. In sum, the women of *Genroku Chushingura* form the sinewy bonding of the delicate network of innuendo and obligation that constitutes the Japanese warrior code in a time of peace.

Style: The Primacy of Perception

Genroku Chushingura is a virtual catalog of monumental stylistic techniques. Other screen adaptations of Chushingura feel false because they lack the "theological" gravity of the Mizoguchi epic. In large part I have come to identify the Chushingura tale itself with the uncompromising, ascetic techniques of the monumental style. A contemporary audience, however, would have found *Genroku Chushingura* difficult and probably tedious because it lacks the bluster that typifies jidai geki generally and Chushingura vendettas in particular.

Since *Genroku Chushingura* shares with other jidai geki historically authentic sets, props, costumes, and other features of mise-en-scène, it is primarily technique that sets *Genroku Chushingura* apart. The film's use of shot scale, camera movement, and the long take gives the drama (such as it is) a whole new feel. Mizoguchi's insistence on the most expensively authentic period detail in materials, artifacts, and acting style is legendary. Part 1 cost

Mizoguchi's production company, Koa Uzumasa Studios, Y530,000, when the usual cost of a big production was around Y100,000, and caused it to fold.[21] Shochiku stepped in to underwrite the cost of part 2, Y520,000, and experienced "sticker shock" from a price tag ten times the going rate.[22] The government, however, was well pleased, and awarded the film a Special Education Minister's prize in 1942.

What sets this film apart in kind and not just degree is the camerawork and editing used by Mizoguchi to explore the space he so painstakingly constructs. It is a perceptual experience, not merely a recording of historical authenticity, that Mizoguchi seeks to convey. *Genroku Chushingura's* "stateliness was so majestic that Mizoguchi himself described it as transpersonal, derived from a historic and national aesthetic that ran counter to the usual personal and romantic spirit of the movies."[23] Its images are constructed in a way that prioritizes, and sometimes problematizes, the process of perceiving. Moreover, these images pass by in an almost seamless flow, arising "naturally" from the serenity of setting and design.

Genroku Chushingura is a masterpiece because it transcends drama, or rather brings drama into a perceptual realm that seems to have little to do with its overt subject matter. Although *Genroku Chushingura* is a deadly serious historical tract, Mizoguchi plays games with our perceptual apprehension of space and objects at a local level. He asks that we focus our attention on things that are not directly relevant to the story, which attenuates the narrative but concentrates the style. In so doing, we involuntarily come to regard the film as a whole, and the legend of Chushingura, with an intensive aestheticism that merges with the sacramental.

Why is this the case? Unlike a typical Hollywood film, *Genroku Chushingura* is a record of a spatial experience, not just a narrative unfolding within a fictional space. In painting or drawing three-dimensional space is an illusion; in sculpture, architecture, and film it is not.[24] But sculpture and architecture are site-specific and therefore articulate a spatial experience, whereas a film records a spatial experience. *Genroku Chushingura* is unusual in according the spatial experience a prominence as great or greater than that of the story. One can indeed think of this film as a story of perceptual discovery, because the issues with which the characters struggle are clearly exemplified in the style of the film, which in turn is determined by spatial articulations like architecture and landscape.

The opening sequence offers a good example of how spatial articulations can conceal or reveal social realities. The techniques that prize perceptual contemplation correspond with the issues raised by the foregoing analysis of narrative structure and characterization. This is not to contradict the point just made about style working against smooth narrative transmission, but rather to acknowledge the thematic implications of the monumental style.

Genroku Chushingura, in its style as in its narrative construction, encourages the contemplation and the practice of discernment, viz., the activity necessary to arrive at accurate, fair, and honorable judgments. We are called on to exercise judgments on actions and behavior, but also on motives, implications, and consequences. Thus we are presented with an ideal of practical judgment, Oishi, who deliberates and considers—dissembling if necessary—in order to carry out a sound plan based on noble intentions. The issue of appearance and deceit is also taken up by other characters, who either positively or negatively exemplify the standards borne by Oishi. Sukeyemon mistakenly attempts to co-opt Oishi's plan by trying to kill Kira at Tsunatoyo's noh performance; Lady Asano's mistaken assumptions about Oishi's intentions are transformed into gratitude and relief that her clan's honor has been restored; Omino's ruse is exposed, but she in turn exposes the suffering Oishi's pragmatic tactics have caused her. She is reunited with her lover, but only in death. Such episodes illustrate the process of sorting out valid inferences from prima facie appearances and choosing a fitting response.

The perceptual demands of *Genroku Chushingura*'s style do much the same thing. To illustrate, consider the opening sequence of the film, which concentrates on various points of observation on Asano's attack. Mizoguchi presents Asano's attack on Kira so as to favor Asano, but not so much as to allow the spectator to identify with Asano by sharing either his optical or emotional point of view. By using a combination of eccentric character blocking and misleading eyelines, Mizoguchi is able to firmly anchor our conviction that Kira provoked Asano but is also able to avoid a corresponding approval of Asano's outburst. Further, the circular motif that develops out of the subsequent pandemonium lends a sense of calculation and containment that is consistent with Oishi's deliberate style.

Garden of Stone

On the final day of ceremonies performed for an imperial envoy, Lord Kira questions the ceremonial competence of a provincial lord, Asano, who is entrusted with the task of communicating homages to the imperial messengers. Kira being a veteran master of ceremonies, his derision toward the more inexperienced courtier is merciless. In medium shot we see Kira bitterly denouncing the "ignorance and rudeness" of his colleague to another member of the court, Lord Kajikawa. Kira is talking about Lord Asano, and his agitation becomes more intense as he spits out the suspicion that Asano is a committee member "in name only, unable to carry out the various functions" according to the appropriate forms and rituals. In the absence of opportunities for valor on the battlefield, a high-ranking samurai could only show his cultivation through mastery of courtly niceties, and to be accused of barbarity in this was cruel gossip indeed.

The surprise is that this is not gossip at all, but open slander. As Kira's barrage of ridicule mounts, he looks to the left, away from the camera and Lord Kajikawa, as if his contempt for Asano knows no bounds. Then the two men move out of frame left to reveal a small figure crouching in the shadows less than twenty feet away. We suddenly realize that Asano has heard Kira's entire tirade against him, and moreover that Kira must have known of Asano's presence because of the direction of his glance.

Retroactively, it is revealed that Kira's invective to Lord Kajikawa was not aristocratic gossip about other courtiers, but a direct slap in the face, a deliberate insult to one whose stature and livelihood depend on his ceremonial relationships with shogun and emperor.

Mizoguchi initially prevents viewers from identifying the true significance of this action because he conceals it as a typical social interchange: "Two courtiers cast aspersions on the ceremonial competence of another." When these two move out of frame and the occlusion of the other is revealed, we can see that the interchange was anything but typical and that

Kira's insult: the slight that brought down a medieval fief.
Frame enlargements, courtesy Shochiku Company, Ltd.

Asano's sudden attack is fully motivated. Nevertheless, Mizoguchi maintains his camera distance on the outraged Asano, and even veils his face in shadow. We cannot identify or identify with Asano's emotional response due to the delay in the revelation of the deliberate, personal quality of Kira's remarks, the medium-long distance on Asano's figure, and the insufficient lighting of his face. The whole episode therefore takes on a more impersonal significance: an act whose importance lies less in its psychological causes than in its social consequences. The narrative problem of motivating Asano's assault and subsequent vendetta is established, but at the same time it is depersonalized, drained of psychological motivation, so as to encourage reflection not only on the commission of a personal injustice but also on the nature of injustice in a particular social formation.[25]

So much for the opening sequence shot. How does the rest of the introductory scene encourage perceptual concentration at the expense of narrative legibility? The style of the opening scene accentuates the explosive violation of the contemplative peace that ordinarily obtains in an imperial house. But working against this is a motif of circularity—in camera movements around the periphery of the courtyard and in editing patterns—that evokes a sense of quiescence and perhaps resignation. This sense of inevitability and stasis persists throughout the film, adding to the quiet calculation, claustrophobia, and even paranoia that stands in for overt onscreen action. Consider the way in which the camera moves around the palace (see diagram).

First, the camera is positioned obliquely to the corners of the structure so that two planes of action are simultaneously visible. With one exception (shot 4), action is staged in two places at once, a foreground and a background veranda. The action is intensified by the "empty" space of the garden between them. Next, the tracking and cutting of the first three shots are motivated by Kira's hasty retreat from Asano. Although the first tracking movement around corner no. 2 follows Asano in his headlong assault on Kira, Asano is actually following Kira, who motivates Asano's and the camera's movement. When Asano catches up, drawing his sword with a hair-raising yell, the shot breaks into a match-on-action to shot 2, elaborating the view of the attack from Kira's side. In this second shot, as in the first, the camera is placed obliquely to corner no. 2 in the same place as its initial position looking across corner no. 1.

Again, Kira quickly moves offscreen left, but this time a straight cut to shot 3 anticipates Kira's arrival into the space (rather than tracking with Kira's movement). The angle of shot 3 corresponds to corner no. 3 as shots 1 and 2 correspond to corners no. 1 and no. 2, i.e., showing two planes of action taking place at oblique angles to one another and separated by the

Asano's violent, unforgivable response.
Frame enlargements, courtesy Shochiku Company, Ltd.

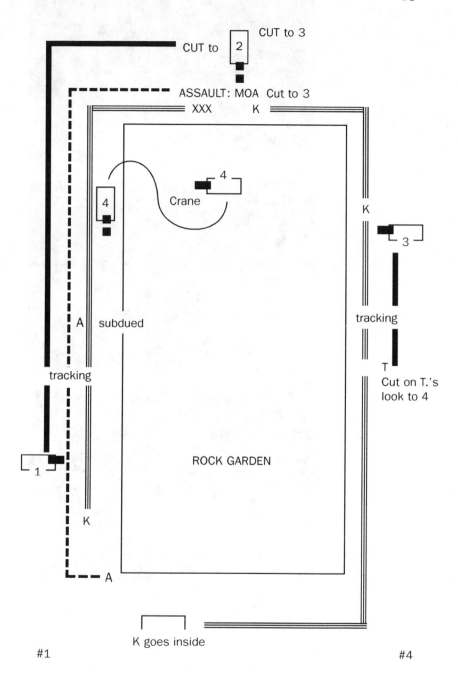

CUT to 3

CUT to | 2 |

ASSAULT: MOA Cut to 3

XXX K

CUT to

4

4

Crane

K

3

subdued

A

tracking

tracking

1

T
Cut on T.'s
look to 4

ROCK GARDEN

K

A

K goes inside

space of the rock garden. In shot 3 the camera briefly tracks along the corridor with Kira but is interrupted by the presence of a new character, Tsunatoyo, who steps into the frame and momentarily controls the angle of view. Rather than following Kira, a cut to shot 4 puts us inside the garden looking in at Asano's hysterical struggle. This is in clear violation of the circular tracking and cutting pattern initiated by Kira's flight around the courtyard. With a complicated crane movement, the camera follows Asano as he moves, kicking and screaming, around corner no. 2 in a counterclockwise direction, opposite that of Kira. The struggling Asano moves left, while the camera swivels around with him until it is positioned looking straight down the corridor toward corner no. 1, where the entire incident began. Since in almost every shot Kira is shown scurrying out of frame left, and since he has already gone around three corners, it is no surprise to see him in shot 4 hurried into the background and out of sight through fusuma sliding doors. Meanwhile, the sputtering Asano lies on his face in the foreground while an official reprimands him and asks for his ceremonial robe.

The pattern of circular camera movements and shot changes established from the outset is therefore fulfilled, in a way. What was apparently a violation of the circular pattern in the cut on Tsunatoyo's look is really a shortcut to the original place where everything began. Kira's insult takes place in corner no. 1, where he eventually disappears after running around the entire periphery of the courtyard. This gives the episode spatial as well as narrative closure—but with some differences. First, there is no oblique angle that segregates two planes of action by means of the empty garden space. Asano's arrest and Kira's disappearance are separate planes of action, but they are spatially continuous. Second, the frantic movement of characters and camera have subsided by the end of shot 4, as if the initial camera position inside the garden has a "cauterizing" effect on the rapid lateral tracking movements of earlier setups. The circularity and closure of this sequence is hardly reassuring, however; the style evokes finality, but also futility. One gets the sense that this was a disaster waiting to happen, an inevitable paroxysm borne of long, steady, implacable repression. If one has to specify the precise moment of explosion, one would have to choose the match-on-action device that heightens the intensity of the assault. This is significant with respect to Noel Burch's contention that Mizoguchi's tendency to use "centripetal" camera movements is a sustained challenge to the prosceniumlike frontality of Western codes of camera/figure placement.[26] The match-on-action is a privileged *departure* from the norms of Mizoguchi's style, which accounts for its accentuating function here. In Western editing codes the match-on-action is a nearly infallible way of smoothing over a potential disruption in the spatial flow; in *Genroku Chushingura* it intensifies the disruption initiated by Asano's attack. While the viewer assimilates the revelation of Asano's presence and infers the deliberateness of Kira's insult, she or he is confronted by a sudden shattering of the stately serenity of the opening moments. The assault itself, the match-on-action, the sudden flooding of multiple planes with shouting, milling samurai: this adds up to a perceptual barrage whose motivation is not psychological but social. What kind of society is it where a breach of etiquette causes mayhem and unraveling of the social fabric? Because the perceptual plenitude of the opening moments is so fragile, we expect further violent disruptions. But they are not forthcoming in the rest of the film, and this conveys an edginess, a heightened perceptual vigilance in the expectation of more paroxysms of repressed passion.

A change of location completes the sequence in a sort of coda to the actual attack and shows the respective places where Kira and Asano are taken. A characteristic tracking shot of Kira being hurried through the back rooms of the palace is a good example of what Burch calls a "scroll shot," a successive interpenetration of spatial modules intermittently blocked by grills, shoji screens, and pillars. The shot recalls the credit sequence, a traveling series of landscape images, and the delicate rightward tracking movement in the first shot inside the palace. Finally, there is a high-angle shot in the Palm Room, the place of Asano's interrogation. Structurally, the shot brackets the very first shot of the film, a static oblique

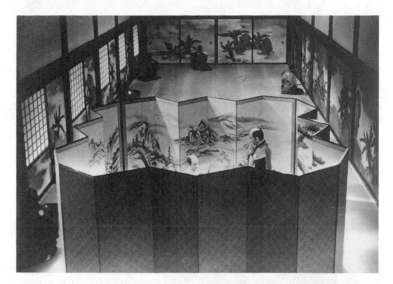

"Scroll shots," bird's-eye views, and vanishing points: circling in and around the palace. Frame enlargements, courtesy Shochiku Company, Ltd.

angle on some imperial ceremonies. Visually, the high angle shot in the Palm Room is composed using parallel perspective, i.e., two vanishing points define the perspective of the large room in the style of medieval Japanese paintings of the *Tale of Genji* and other classical works. The opening sequence forms a relatively self-contained cell, a structure of circularity in time and space:

(Credits)
1. Stasis: oblique shot of ceremonies (figure 6.15)
2. Long take: shattering of perceptual plenitude
    a. rock garden: tracking right
    b. Kira insult
    c. revelation and attack of Asano: tracking left
3. Match-on-action: Kira circles left
4. Straight cut: Kira's flight, circles left (cut on Tsunatoyo's glance)
5. Long take, crane in: Asano's struggle in foreground; Kira goes out in background
6. "Scroll shot": tracking left (figure 6.13)
7. Stasis: high angle shot of Palm Room (figure 6.14)

The structural and spatial symmetricality of the sequence gives it a closed, hieratic quality consistent with its dual function of initiating the narrative trajectory and providing the rationale for a demonstration of bushido vitality.[27]

In compressed form this dual function is contained in the opening shot of the rock garden (2a), framed by two posts of the palace veranda. With painstaking slowness the camera tracks rightward past two or three of the posts before swiveling right to show the Kira-Asano interchange. This is the canonical way of experiencing a *kare-sansui* garden, like the famous Ryoanji rock garden in Kyoto, which synthesizes the contemplative practice of Zen Buddhism with the design principles of *shoin* architecture.[28] The garden itself consists simply of pure white pebbles raked into straight rows, a textured plenum punctuated only by the black posts that slowly traverse its surface. This setup clearly shows a concern to reproduce the *kansho*, or *zakan*, a central compositional view of the garden "suggestive of a picture and suitable for long and studied viewing."[29] The *kansho* evokes Zen practice of prolonged, intensified perception as a way to heightened consciousness, and the posts that intermittently frame our view call attention to the intervals/relationships between objects, or *ma*, which in turn form the central principle of traditional domestic architecture in the Muromachi period. Specifically, the intervals between the posts are called *ken* (written with the same character as *ma*), whose distance of around six feet eventually was standardized at 1.8 meters, the standard length of tatami mats and of all other measurements (columns, beams, shoji screens, etc.) necessary for building a Japanese house.[30] The majority of shots taken around the palace use oblique angles that separate the action planes with the garden between them. This shows a foregrounding of intervals, of relationships *between* things as well as things in themselves. The moving camera also emphasizes the proprioceptive, or bodily aspect of perception. A static "view" is established and held, then everything moves in a vertiginous flux, only to resolve itself again into a new tableau open for perceptual scrutiny. It demands perceptual participation to become involved in *Genroku Chushingura's* intrigues and second-guessing. When we accept this we find our perceptual arsenal and our endurance strengthened. This is consistent with the film's ideological project: the training of a certain perceptual facility with traditional Japanese forms and designs.

To sum up: the opening sequence of *Genroku Chushingura* is anomalous in its spectacular burst of murderous violence, but its circular structure telegraphs the subsequent containment of chaos through perceptual concentration. Hollywood films domesticate the irrational through the proposal and eventual solution of a narrative enigma. *Genroku Chushingura* does it through displacement of narrative by perceptual, aesthetic, and religious contemplation. Style serves narrative in Hollywood, but in *Genroku Chushingura* style renders narrative peripheral. The primacy of Genroku perception is fully established in the opening sequence. By exploring spatial arrangements more than character psychology, our perception is both constrained and opened up, and we begin to realize that in the realm of Genroku ethics, as in aesthetics, less is more.

The Poverty of Drama

What kind of perceptual experience, then, does the monumental style invite us to have in Mizoguchi's Genroku world? More than anything else, our perceptions are solicited by the slowness and gravity of monumental evocations. Because of the story's conventionality, there is little puzzling over the overall narrative chain. We are left with a critical appreciation of ritual exchanges, objets d'art, interior design, architecture, and the very space of the Genroku era. David Bordwell says of the narrational strategies of revolutionary Soviet cinema that "the conventionality of the large-scale narrative articulations promotes a moment-by-moment 'microattention' to the unfolding syuzhet [or plot]. . . . The task is to make these givens vivid, or as the Soviet directors were fond of saying, *perceptible*."[31]

A similar process obtains in *Genroku Chushingura*. The default back to per-ceptual style from narrative comprehension might even be more pro-nounced for Japanese spectators who know the details of the Chushingura story by heart. He or she would be less "distracted" by the narrative atten-uation of Mizoguchi's version, though I suspect the slowness of it would surprise anyone.

At the highest level, the macrostructure of the narrative, cause and effect are stretched apart, if not exactly displaced, because of the story's tendency to serialize the heroism of the vendetta. The plot is goal driven, but Oishi shares heroic status, and therefore narrative development, with several other characters. Because of this, spectators will find it harder and less pro-ductive to try to fit a given segment into a neatly intertwined structure of motivation and suspense. A classical Hollywood film will seem to move quickly, because the spectator is constantly comparing the information in a segment with what has gone before and revising expectations about the resolution. This is not a norm to which *Genroku Chushingura* cleaves, but it helps explain why it seems so slow.

The drama of Chushingura takes place at the level of the scene—for two reasons: the narrative attenuation that comes from the serial hero, and the legendary status of the Chushingura tale, which takes for granted a knowledge of the story and the consequent *"confirmation* of the permanence of certain values, certain symbols, certain structures."[32] In the locality of its

The space of the Genroku era. Frame enlargement,
courtesy Shochiku Company, Ltd.

A Daughter of the Gods (1918).
Private collection.

Graphic "rhyme" in *I Was Born But . . .*   Courtesy David Bordwell.

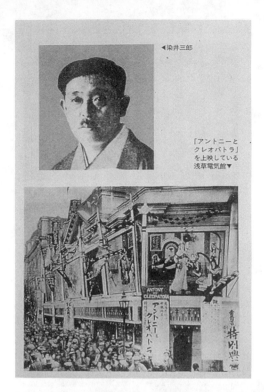

◀染井三郎

「アントニーと
クレオパトラ」
を上映している
浅草電気館▼

Antony and Cleopatra at
the Asakusa Denkikan
(March 1914).
Private collection.

Ero-guro-nansensu: Ozu's *Days of Youth* (1929). Kawakita Memorial Film
Archives.

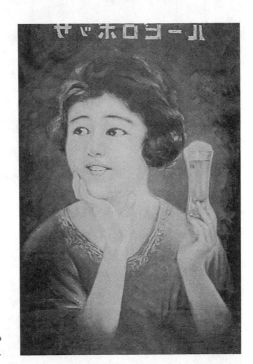

Ad for Sapporo
beer, 1905.

Five Scouts (*Gonin no Sekkohei*, Tasaka Tomotaka, 1939) Kawakita Memorial
Film Archives.

Tasaka's *Mud and Soldiers* (*Tsuchi to Heitai*, 1939)
Kawakita Memorial Film Archives.

Okochi Denjiro as
Tange Sazen in
Yamanaka Sadao's
*Pot Worth a Million
Ryo* (*Hyakuman Ryo
no Tsubo*, 1935)
Kawakita Memorial
Film Archives.

A simple thief outwits a samurai in *Hitohada Kannon* (*The
Mercy Goddess of Hitohada Shrine*, Kinugasa Teinosuke, 1937)
Kawakita Memorial Film Archives.

Enomoto Ken'ichi (Enoken) burlesquing Kondo Isamu
(*Enoken no Kondo Isamu*, 1935) Kawakita Memorial
Film Archives.

A highly sublimated
Miyamoto Musashi
(Inagaki Hiroshi,
1940). Kawakita
Memorial Film
Archives.

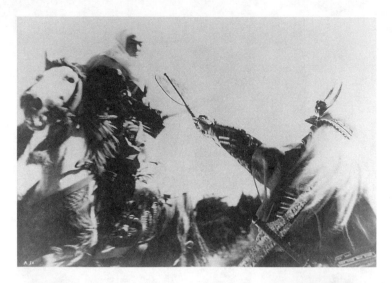

Kawanakajima Kassen. Kawakita Memorial Film Archives.

Mother's encouragement of suicide:
The Abe Clan (*Abe Ichizoku*, 1938). Frame enlargement, courtesy Toho Company.

Mud and Soldiers (*Tsuchi to Heitai*, Tasaka, 1939). Kawakita
Memorial Film Archives.

Omino's ruse: cross-dressing to gain access to her
lover, Juroza. Kawakita
Memorial Film Archives.

Kira's insult: the slight that brought down a medieval fief. Frame enlargements, courtesy Shochiku Company, Ltd.

The palace erupts into pandemonium. Frame enlargements, courtesy
Shochiku Company, Ltd.

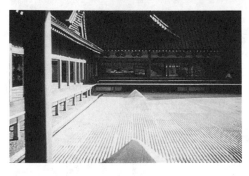

Kare sansui: dry
sand-rock garden as
perceptual plenitude.
Frame enlargements,
courtesy Shochiku
Company, Ltd.

Asano en route to his ritual suicide. Frame enlargements,
courtesy Shochiku Company, Ltd.

Rack focus in Kumagai's *The Abe Clan*. Frame enlargements, courtesy Toho Company.

The Abe Clan: the home of a retainer favored with ritual suicide. Frame enlargement, courtesy of Toho Company.

Offscreen battlefield performance, *Kagemusha*. Museum of Modern Art Film Stills Archive.

Outdoor ritual in *Ran*. Museum of Modern Art Film Stills Archive.

dramatic focus, *Genroku Chushingura* is in step with its kabuki and puppet theater lineage. After centuries of variations and refinements, audiences are less interested in the narrative resolution of the stories than in the renditions of key scenes requiring extra virtuosity (e.g., Benkei masquerading as Yoshitsune's master in the famous checkpoint scene of the kabuki play *Kanjincho*). But while early Chushingura renditions sought virtuosity, *Genroku Chushingura* is marked by (dramaturgical) austerity. In virtually every scene of the film, *nothing happens*. With the exception of Asano's assault on Kira and Sukeyemon's abortive attack on Tsunatoyo, the only action in every scene is talk. News is received by various characters, discussions ensue about responses to the shogun, the politics of the situation are debated, strategies are formed, condolences expressed, rituals observed . . . . . The action in the Chushingura story takes place offscreen, leaving Mizoguchi to concentrate on character reactions as if the events that constitute the vendetta were in some way a fait accompli—which in many ways they are.

The drama consists in the conversations and declamations of the film, if we attend to them as conventional gestures of a bygone era, as expressions of "grace under pressure" that are governed by codes no longer in existence. Ultimately, however, the perceptual invitation offered by *Genroku Chushingura* calls the pertinence of *drama* into question. The demands and pleasures of this film are mostly extradramatic, in the way that dance or religious rites are extradramatic forms. There are stories in such forms, but usually they are pretexts for other kinds of artistic or spiritual activity (e.g., ritual as community consolidation). The forms and designs of traditional Japaneseness beckon like forgotten ancestors, and the gate through which one enters is perceptual.

Perceptual Address

By what techniques and to what ends does Mizoguchi open up our perception? As I have argued, there is a negative side to this in the "poverty" of narrative, action, and drama. More positively, Mizoguchi uses interlocking techniques of framing, camera movement, and the long take to encourage spatial and tactile exploration of the Genroku world. In abandoning oneself to these explorations, the spectator learns a mode of perception that is consonant with traditional Japanese aesthetics an religion.

Mizoguchi's "flying" crane shots, for instance, propel us straight up into the air as much as twenty feet, affording a bird's-eye view on the action below. Given the preponderance of interior setups and modular spaces, these crane shots have quite a liberating quality. There is still another reason for this quality, and that is the way in which these shots transcend the boundaries—fences, curtains, wall, etc.—that modularize the space below. Finally, these shots are reminiscent of the high parallel perspective found in classical screen paintings.

According to Margaret Hagen, a perceptual psychologist, the perspective system used by *Yamato-e* classical painting is marked by aerial views that combine a station point distance of infinity (there is no vanishing point in these pictures) with perspective lines that are parallel.[33] This contrasts with European "natural" perspective which uses a middle distance station point with converging lines of perspective. The very great height of the station point lends a "God's-eye" view that is impartial and detached. It also necessitates the depiction of roofless and wall-less buildings in order to show any human activity, as in the anonymous Kyoto genre paintings of *rakuchu-rakugai*. Unlike the scientific reproduction of optical perspective in the Renaissance,

the Japanese artist is not placed by perspective in the composition of the picture, nor is the observer. The work of art created

Rakuchu, rakugai: or, scenes in
and around Kyoto.
Private collection.

is a separate entity unto itself, an object of contemplation, not
an extension of the self. A Japanese composition does not
depict a personal, momentary view through a window, subject
to change from the slightest of observer movements.[34]

It is reasonable to assume that Mizoguchi wished to pay homage to the
technical hallmarks of classical Japanese painting because of his training as
a painter and because his crane shots simply resemble these paintings. But
these shots have a more important role to play than mere citation. If Hagen
is correct in assigning to this perspective system an evacuation of both
painter and observer from the depicted scene, these shots may function as
perceptual anomalies with respect to Mizoguchi's other techniques that so
strenuously guide the observer's activity. If these shots express or embody
a "theological" self-sufficiency, they are consistent with the overall ideological project of the film but inconsistent with the ongoing solicitation of
spectators' perceptual faculties. The shots are a kind of release from the
relentless cultivation of perception through glance, blocking, and interior
design.

As with other kinds of camera movement, the flying crane shot always moves with deliberate slowness, directing attention to the unfolding transformation of vision rather than to the sensation of movement as such. One of the best examples is a shot of a grief-stricken vassal, Gengoyemon, who meets Lord Asano at his place of suicide (scene 7). A high-angle crane shot along a wall shows Asano approaching, then descends and stops as Asano greets his loyal vassal. He gets ready to step through a gate in the wall, leaving his vassal behind. As he goes through, the camera moves straight up, allowing a view of two actions separated by a barrier: Asano walking bravely across the courtyard to the curtained area where he will disembowl himself, and his retainer kneeling at the gate, stunned with grief and shock.

This sequence and that of Asano's interrogation in the Palm Room function as norm-establishing shots, because they underscore the boundaries that divide space. In the Palm Room (scene 3) an outer boundary is constituted by elaborately painted shoji and fusuma, and is accentuated by the bodies of outward-facing guards stationed at intervals along the periphery. Within this space an inner boundary is fashioned by high paper screens set up to form a makeshift interrogation space for Asano. The smallness of this bounded space is belied by the opulence of Sesshu-inspired splashed ink paintings on its inside walls. After the interrogation, the makeshift modularity of Genroku interiors is signaled by the same high angle on Asano's departure into custody with the accompanying disassembly and removal of the Sesshu screens (scene 6).

Oishi is introduced by way of a spectacular crane shot that starts high over the Ako castle walls and gradually descends to follow him as he moves inside among the stewards taking inventory (scene 10). The offscreen sounds of the counting and sorting is associated with Oishi before we even see the source of the noise. Oishi appears as a tiny lone figure standing contemplatively outside the castle walls. This invests him with an authority

Sesshu splashed ink painting. Private collection.

Oishi contemplating the Ako estate. Frame enlargement,
courtesy Shochiku Company, Ltd.

carried along as the shot follows him through the more mundane surroundings of the castle inventory. Oishi's stature is magnified by the perceptual concentration lavished upon him as a lone figure in such a large
visual field.

A virtuosic swooping crane movement down onto the noh performance
opens part 2. According to Andrew and Andrew, the noh's "stately tempo
and ritualized violence key the tone of the entire movie."[35] But it is not so
much the play itself as Mizoguchi's handling of it that gives it such an otherworldly aura. A typically oblique aerial shot of the roofs and buildings
opens the sequence; a gliding motion downward briefly shows the performance onstage, the camera then pans to reveal the gallery audience along
the periphery of the courtyard. Finally it reaches the place of honor, then
cranes in before coming to rest and cutting to a medium shot of Tsunatoyo.
What is striking about this shot is the concentration on the audience more
than the performance itself. One might imagine that Mizoguchi would
linger on the play a little longer, since the sequence is the first in part 2 and
would present few motivational problems for the narrative. But performance is forthcoming in Tsunatoyo's spear dance; for now, it is the layout
and scale of the audience's gallery that takes center stage. It is not the performance itself but the whole spectacle—performance, audience, physical
arrangement, atmosphere—that alerts us to a characteristically Genroku
scene.

Having introduced the perceptual address of one of the film's more com-

Ako vassal Sukeyemon apprehended at a noh performance (part 2).
Kawakita Memorial Film Archives.

plicated techniques, it is time to fill in the functions of *Genroku Chushingura's*
more basic means of perceptual work. In terms of shot scale and framing,
there are two principal kinds of setups in *Genroku Chushingura*. One is a
medium shot capable of accommodating two to three seated figures, and,
like these figures, the shot is placed about three or four feet above the floor.
After the French term for American medium shots, I call these plan japonais, which also happen to be an ideal position for viewing Japanese objets
d'art. The other main setup is an extreme long shot, with or without camera movement, that usually emphasizes a configuration of congregated figures, as in shots of the assembled ronin. In each kind of shot the spatial disposition of objects and people contribute as much to the scene's significance as does dialogue or action. It is fair to conclude that the camera's
organization of the spatial field is not hierarchical, that is, it does not subordinate background to object, negative to positive space. The most interesting elements in the shot will be configurations, not just figures, i.e.,
combinatory *patterns* of space, people, and objects rather than clearly delin-
eated things sitting or moving in neutral surroundings. There is an egalitarianism in the shot composition of *Genroku Chushingura* that is at odds with
the hierarchical compositional legibility of Western shot scale and framing.
As with *Chrysanthemum*, again we see the meticulous indiscriminateness of
Mizoguchi's cinematography.

Consider Noel Burch's description of the articulation of space in Japanese film images:

> In the projected image . . . depth cues, such as axial character movement and receding, converging lines are, in the most common instances, *overridden* by the effect of surface, due primarily to the predominance of the quadrilateral. Thus, the film image becomes, *predominantly*, the planar projection of the three-dimensional cells, static in each of their succcessive arrangements, which constitute the pro-filmic dwelling-space.[36]

Burch's italics reveal his preference for attributing flatness and surface orientation to Japanese cinema's articulation of space. This is simply substituting one hegemony for another: Japanese cinema allegedly promotes a two-dimensional field, in opposition to Western cinema, whose codes encourage a three-dimensional diegesis. In *Genroku Chushingura* both the plan japonais and the collective compositions in the long shots do not suppress three-dimensionality but play with it as one element among others.[37]

For example, two instances in which long shots articulate collective compositions of assembled ronin have thematic as well as graphic significance. A meeting between Onodera Chuzaemon, Oishi's trusted aide, and

Mizoguchi's spatial indiscriminateness: patterns of space, people, objects. Frame enlargement, courtesy Shochiku Company, Ltd.

some agitated Edo vassals is not going well (scene 14). They insist on immediately striking at Kira, or failing that at least staying in Ako castle and defending it against the advances of the shogun's army. An impasse is imminent, and Onodera counsels unity under Oishi's guidance. The Edo vassals find this intolerable and show their disdain for Onodera's counsel by petulantly turning away from him in sullen, speechless rage. They had earlier eagerly encircled Onodera; then they turn away, fuming, all facing different directions in a graphic display of frustration and disunity. It is a rather unnatural, artificial configuration, but it is an appealing one because the visual discord caused by their pouting is so mutually interdependent. The Edo ronins' arrangement of their bodies seems dependent on the shared coincidence of their frustration with their lot—something of an irony in light of Onodera's advice.

The other example depicts the unity of the ronin following the successful completion of their vendetta (part 2, scene 12). The ronin have gathered to hear the formal pronouncement of their sentence by a representative of the shogun. Legally they are criminals, but they face their judgment together with composure and serenity, secure in the knowledge that they have honorably discharged their duty to bushido. On this formal occasion they sit in neat rows, waiting to hear the verdict. When the judgment of punishment by seppuku is pronounced, they perform a deep bow in perfect unison, collectively expressing their heartfelt gratitude and relief. Since the time of Asano's death, a new shogun has been installed who obviously sympathizes with the ronins' course of action, illegal though it is. This is confirmed beyond all doubt when the messenger conveys an informal message, that Kira's son has been deprived of his fief and his house abolished. As the camera inches forward congruent with this added intimacy, the Ako ronin bow again, weeping in their shared joy. They turn and together bow twice more in two other directions, first to the right in farewell to the shogun's messenger then away from the camera in gratitude to their custodian, Lord Hosokawa.

These collective compositions are conveyed through carefully selected shot scale, framing, and the long take. There are even more striking instances of collective configurations in the use of moving long shots that appear to be motivated according to perceptual lines generated by a group of spectators. I call these images objectified spectatorship because it is the collective perception of characters engaged in ritual contemplation (e.g., mourning, praying, performing, or even admiring some art object) that determines, first, the arrangement of the group and, second, the distance and movement of the camera. Objectified spectatorship is not different in kind from the collective compositions just described, only more elaborate.

It is as if onscreen perceptual contemplation, collectively undertaken, spills over its designated narrative and thematic functions to control the disposition of the camera itself, and our perceptions with it. Just as one is powerless to resist the impulse to look in the same direction as a surrounding crowd, so Mizoguchi's camera in *Genroku Chushingura* appears seduced by, or exists for the sake of, configurations of objectified spectatorship.

A good example is the scene in which shocked Ako vassals are officially informed of Lord Asano's sentence and demise (scene 11). An extreme long shot from the back of the hall shows some score of samurai kneeling and waiting for the news from Edo. When the messenger is formally introduced to Oishi at the front, the samurai all inch forward on their knees to hear and see better. The overall appearance of the scene is one of unsettled organic movement, as first one part of the group shifts and fidgets, then another. Since the samurai are all dressed and coiffed alike, their fragmentary movement resembles a swarm of tiny creatures whose repose has been disturbed.

A sequence of medium shots follow, which lend more intimacy to Oishi's bewilderment at the sudden death of his lord. Then a 180-degree reverse angle shows a deep focus view of Oishi grieving in the foreground, with the mass of samurai huddled behind, mirroring Oishi with his dark costume, bald pate and *chonmage* topknot. As he reads Lord Asano's farewell poem ("More frail than petals scattered by the wind / I bid a last farewell and leave spring behind") the mass of shiny heads and topknots drop out of sight as the samurai begin to weep and lower their heads to the floor. Oishi then does the same.

It is a very odd scene for its graphic qualities, and might even be comic were the grief not so intense. Perhaps we find such collective orchestration of gesture and feeling improbable. In *Genroku Chushingura*, however, it is the most emotionally wrenching scenes that employ configurations of objectified spectatorship. Perhaps we are approaching something culturally specific in such representations, in that expressions of great feeling are magnified by objective echoes of its impact on other people. However, both *Shogun and Mentor* (chapter 4) and *The Abe Clan* (chapter 7) show an awareness of the comic, or at least satirical possibilities of objectified spectatorship.

A tour de force of objectified spectatorship occurs in the entertainment scene performed by the ronin while waiting for their judgment from the shogun (part 2, scene 8). They are in custody at Lord Hosokawa's mansion, and flowers arrive from Lady Asano. Oishi correctly perceives that they signify imminent judgment, and so expresses his gratitude that the waiting period is over. The scene crosscuts between Oishi's solemnly bowing group and a second, younger group who merrily mount an impromptu entertainment. Since the two rooms are spatially contiguous, a rather incongruous effect is achieved with an image of the stolid older ronin giving ritual thanks, accompanied by the offscreen singing and dancing of the younger ronin. The crosscutting continues, alternating between Hara's *rambo* (rough stuff) kabuki dance and Oishi's group listening in the next room. A 180-degree reverse angle shows Hara's dance from the front of the room, with the ronin audience in the background. The shot is held as Isogai Juroza gets up to play his bamboo flute. As Hara moves off left, we are left with a view of the audience in which Horiuchi, the ronins' custodian, is noticeably melancholic. Dressed in mournful black, he sits in the center with a tired slump, surrounded by young white-clad smiling samurai anxious to continue their entertainment for him. When the young Juroza sits to play, his back is to the camera and his body precisely blocks Horiuchi's entire body, except for his face, which looks like it is perched on Juroza's shoulder. The remaining ronin flank Horiuchi and attend to the mournful, rustic sound of the flute. In the background two white fusuma sliding doors are open exactly equidistant from the sides of the frame and lend a remarkable compositional symmetry to the setup.

The shot continues by axially moving around Juroza's left shoulder to linger on his classically Japanese features. In this veritable icon of traditional Japaneseness, a panel from the *Tale of Genji* paintings depicting Genji's exile is all that is visible in the background. Occupying the foreground is a medium shot of Juroza's serene face as he plays his flute. A panning movement back to Horiuchi reveals his deepening melancholia and sorrow for the plight of the ronin. As the sad notes rise and fall, Horiuchi slowly gets up and leaves the room to weep. The long shot of the hunched old man weeping hotly in the cold hallway is among the most moving in this film of formal ceremony and restraint. The visual and aural raptness of the ronin indicate the triumph of form over feeling, a triumph Horiuchi cannot share. The scene abundantly illustrates the contrasting styles of spectatorship between the beatific ronin and that of the sad old man. In the next scene, moreover, we discover Horiuchi's ploy to smuggle Omino into the company of Juroza, and this adds a layer of dramatic significance to Horiuchi's breakdown.

The collective compositions of objectified spectatorship serve as markers of distinct nonverbal expressions. Behavioral cues for expressing ineffable feelings are visually articulated and magnified by technique. In similar fashion the flying crane shot and active role of space magnify indigenous design and decorum. In *Genroku Chushingura* space enjoys a more active role in the composition than merely a neutral background. In the long take and

Detail from Tale of Genji handscroll. Courtesy Goto Art Museum.

in Mizoguchi's camera movement, duration similarly comes forward as a dimension that is radically slowed down, if not quite arrested. The moving camera and the long take "stretch" time similarly to the way the framing of the mise-en-scène magnifies space.

A dual intensification takes place with the static long take. A long take encourages something like a mental close-up in that we begin to see that a denotative function is being overtaken by some other purpose. We start to look for connotative meaning in the shot, especially as an indication of expressive intensification. When Chamberlain Tamon bravely appeals the hasty judgment on Lord Asano in part 1 (scene 5) and Lady Asano reads about the attack on Kira in part 2 (scene 5), the emotional pitch of the dra-

maturgy rises as the shot is held. These extremely long takes (five and two
and a half minutes, respectively) show a correlation between dramatic
intensity and duration.

In addition to dramatic intensification encouraged by the static long
take, a perceptual intensification takes place as well. The long still shot is
not without movement of the spectator's focus of attention. The longer a
shot is held, the more time there is to "decompose" the composition. There
is plenty of time for this, as *Genroku Chushingura* has an average shot length
(ASL) of about one and a half minutes (compare this with ASL in 1939's
Chrysanthemum, about one minute, in 1936's *Sisters of Gion*, thirty-three seconds, and in *Naniwa Elegy*, twenty-two seconds).[38] One begins to analyze
facial expressions, background objects, spatial relationships, shadings of
light and dark, shapes, lines, and textures. In *Genroku Chushingura* the sustained perceptual concentration encouraged by the long take always pays
off, and does so in a way consistent with stylistic and ideological goals of
the film. A particular shot early in part 2 can illustrate.

The sequence (scene 2) has Lord Tsunatoyo interrogating Sukeyemon
about his real intentions concerning the vendetta. The long take of the
interview lasts over three minutes, though it breaks down into three static
shots linked by crane movements. The final setup is a deep focus composition, dominated by the back of Tsunatoyo's courtesan, in which Sukeyemon, on the extreme right, appears to be three times smaller than Tsunatoyo and his courtesan because he is so far away. In the background over
the shoulders of Tsunatoyo and his courtesan is a line of more attendants,
including Suke's sister, looking across at Sukeyemon.

The perceptual force of this composition clearly favors Tsunatoyo; the
effect of the eyelines and perspectives is to practically push the hapless
Suke right off the screen. Compositionally, the body of the courtesan
forms a massive barrier between Tsunatoyo and the remote Suke, lending a
sense of disproportion and futility to the exchange. The shot is composed
using an angular-isomorphic perspective, typical of Edo-period courtesan
woodcuts, in which an angular corner illusion organizes the space while
maintaining a picture plane isomorphic with the plane of the screen.[39] In
Edo woodcuts (e.g., Torii school, Harunobu) the lines stretching deep into
the picture do not converge, but remain parallel.

More than this, there is a concealed geometry to the shot whose central
axis is covered by the body of the courtesan. The shot actually shows the
inside corner of a rectangular room, flanked on one side by a line of courtesans and on the other by Sukeyemon. But because the huge figure of the
courtesan blocks the view, this is hard to see. Perhaps this is the way
Mizoguchi tries to approximate the isomorphic perspective used by wood-

Parallel perspective in Edo
woodcuts. Courtesy Honolulu
Academy of Arts.

cut artists. He compels us to *infer* the geometry of the room for it to make
visual sense. But, at the same time the perspective, composition, and speaking role lend perceptual priority to Tsunatoyo's side of the frame. The only
thing to catch our interest over on Sukeyemon's side is a small puff of
smoke from his pipe. This very unbalanced composition eventually cranes
over to a smaller scale plan japonais again, this time with Tsunatoyo and
Sukeyemon in medium shot.

Such an elaborately composed serial shot underscores the organiza-
tional work of perception. Burch says that such visual fields, whose design
may be indebted to the *e-makimono*, the *kare-sansui*, or the kabuki stage,
demand a "reading."[40] But this does not involve a Brecht-like distanciation
effect; on the contrary, the spectator's attention is *solicited*, not alienated, in
order to work out the spatial configuration of the scene. In these compositions a constant that encourages perceptual involvement is the presence of
perceptual forces inside the picture—e.g., eyelines and body positions—
that visually complement, or confound, the empirical spectator's activity.
The cues with which spectators work invite them to put themselves into
the scene, assuming, of course, a suspension of their awareness of the pla-
nar properties of the images (pace Burch). Often there are spectator-surro-
gates in the image whose sole purpose is to contribute their bodies and
attention to the overall perceptual design, and to extend an implicit invitation to spectators to do likewise. Robert Cohen and Dudley Andrew,

among others, have noticed the "inscribed observer" convention in Mizoguchi's work and have speculated about its status as spectator and authorial surrogate.[41] The latter emphasizes the duality inherent in many Japanese arts that represent an observer reacting along with the scene or spectacle calling forth the reaction. In Japanese landscape art, bunraku puppetry, kabuki, haiku poetry, and in cinema (through the benshi), the sympathetic observer is integral to their form and meaning. Thus there is a "necessary interplay between distance and identification at the heart of Mizoguchi's method and world view."[42]

Camera movement that links various views are also used in a way that approximates shot-reverse-shot constructions. Rather than alternately cutting between appropriately positioned talking heads, the camera will reframe in a leisurely way to include an offscreen interlocutor. When the camera moves from a plan japonais of Tsunatoyo around the courtesan, the result is a strangely composed deep focus shot of Tsunatoyo and Sukeyemon facing each other from opposite sides of the frame. When Tsunatoyo gets up to join Suke, the camera reframes to follow him before settling into another plan japonais that shows the two men earnestly matching wits.

Cutting patterns in this segment clearly play an accentuating, rather than a structural, role. Normally, there is a series of medium shots linked by camera movements, with cuts reserved for moments of surprise. Oishi's confrontation with Omino shows an arresting use of camera movement because it violates axes of action established by cutting. It is also a good example of the "mood and rhythm" of noh theater that Burch finds reflected in the film.[43] It is an extremely long scene (over nine minutes) punctuated by only two cuts, both motivated by heightened dramatic moments. The creeping, drifting crane movements so typical of the film begin the sequence as the camera slowly reframes from three-shots to two-shots of Horiuchi, Omino, and Oishi. As Horiuchi fills in background details of Omino's engagement to Juroza (after Oishi has seen through her ruse), Omino breaks down in tears, which is cut with a match-on-action to a camera position almost directly behind Oishi. Recall the use of match-on-action in the opening attack on Kira: a device that intensifies, rather than smoothing over the action and the change in angle. As Omino continues the story, the camera drifts back out past Oishi, whose broad back momentarily blocks the frame. The shot is held, slowly reframing between distant and close views of the scene, as Omino becomes more passionate in her demand to see Juroza. On a tight medium shot of Omino's entreating look offscreen right, there is a sudden cut to Oishi over her right shoulder as he tries to persuade her to give Juroza up. This cut, along with the match-on-action, establishes the nohlike rhythm of the scene, whose slowly rising passion is punctuated by flashes of action through cutting and dramaturgy. This cut also introduces a "false" axis direction that is inconsistent with the axis established by the match-on-action over Oishi's right shoulder.

For the second cut to match the first, i.e., to maintain a consistent axis of action, the camera should have been placed in position 3." Instead, the cut crosses the axis on the reverse shot, then glides behind Horiuchi just as it glided by Oishi before. The shot is held more or less in area 1 as the scene plays out. Here Omino tells her lie and exchanges Juroza's lie for the truth, and Oishi eventually grants her request.

The eccentric cutting of this scene is not at all disorienting, which reveals the essentially expressive function of Mizoguchi's editing. Far more important for the revelation of space and face are the creeping camera movements around the periphery. These movements simultaneously pivot the camera's angle even as it is moving back and around the space. The result is rather protean in that the perceptual forces that organize the space—body positions, direction of looks—can be instantly transformed by a simple reframing, a lateral movement, or both. This is important because it emphasizes the "embodiedness" of perception. The camera's activity is never allowed to become invisible, neither as an overarching code of conventions nor as a stand-in for a character's point of view. Craning movements behind a character are especially useful for situating certain perspectives within the scene and playing off others, including that of the empirical spectator through the camera. But what is the broader significance of such techniques?

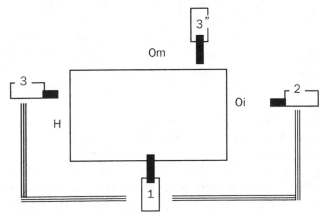

"Omino's Ruse," scene 9, part 2

One way of accounting for them might be to see them, with Noel Burch, as "an absolutely unique *ceremonial commentary* on the representational system of the Western film . . . a specific transformation of a set of Western codes, comparable, at the level of the individual artist, with those cultural modes of transformation observed earlier."[44] Burch sees these techniques as essentially experiments with style performed by an outstanding auteur. This is a mistake, I think, because the historical moment in which Mizoguchi found himself provides the occasion and the means with which to integrate Japanese aesthetic form so thoroughly into film style. It is precisely because the film is so fixated on Japanese forms and traditions, not because it offers a commentary on Western conventions, that it is sublimely indifferent to Western modes. Mizoguchi is interested in forging a uniquely Japanese film style that operates on its own terms, inherited from the indigenous heritage. Everything about *Genroku Chushingura* is hypertrophied Japaneseness. Its cinematography indefatigably emphasizes the artistry in Japanese architecture and design, costume and manners, paintings and gardens. More than this, the systematic patterns of decoupage invite a mode of perception that reflects the serenity, decorum, and tenacity of the depicted historical world. I say "tenacity" to indicate that *Genroku Chushingura* is not a mere indulgence in nostalgia, but a serious ethical and political exhortation. Its aesthetic devices, especially its framing, camera movement, and the long take, are "training exercises" in Genroku perception: encouraging an awareness of the modularity of space, especially as organized by Japanese interior design, the experience of collective spectatorship and how it offers clues to deciphering a situation, the austere pleasure of duration and its concomitant virtues of patience and discernment. This is not a claim that these are ploys to induce our identification with Oishi and other heroes of the tale. There may be instances of this, but, mostly, style operates independent of character. Style instead functions to plunge us deep into a perceptual experience of the Genroku world—one that most emphatically refuses the pyrotechnic excesses of chambara. The ideological project of the film is the chance that spectators may absorb the unusual style of *Genroku Chushingura* and take with them into everyday life an "eye" for its daily manifestations.

Generally, Mizoguchi's use of the long take and moving camera has a perceptual rather than a directly dramatic or expressive function. Through placement of expectations in the spectator's mind, these techniques saturate the diegesis with a sacred, deliberative aura whose outcome is never in doubt. The perceptual "address" of the monumental style ultimately works on spectators more than story or characters because *Genroku Chushingura* can assume so much knowledge from its audience. Sometimes eccentric techniques of this kind have allusive connection with the content of the drama, but most often they will not—except insofar as spectators are encouraged by technique to see the drama with new eyes. In this sense the film offers a mode of perceiving along with its represented world that affords those who wish a new way of seeing and the opportunity to indulge in a Genroku feast for the senses.

If *Genroku Chushingura* is a feast, it is one that requires some fasting from the satiation of narrative appetite. The structure of the film discourages an approach that seeks a tight-knit causal chain, because, first, it can assume a fairly complete knowledge of the story and, second, *Genroku Chushingura* is based on a literary property distinguished by historical accuracy, not high drama. This, together with the highly conventional nature of the story and its genre, privileges the drama of individual episodes over that of the whole film. The film does not work up to a grand summation that synthetically unifies all its motifs, issues, and heroes. Instead, it works on the spectator incrementally, encouraging small-scale intensive scrutiny of things that do not necessarily further the plot. *Genroku Chushingura* promotes the primacy of perception over narrative trajectory due to the poverty of drama and to the solicitation of close perceptual scrutiny. *Genroku Chushingura* solicits perceptual attention that is consistent with the sacramental impulses of traditional Japanese artistic forms. Decoupage and cinematography replicate the perceptual modes most fitting to the indigenous art forms so prominent in the mise-en-scène. Shot scale and framing exhibit characteristic setups that express a sense of restraint and decorum toward its subjects. The long take helps arrest the forward motion of action and reaction and preserves the continuity of space, inviting perceptual contemplation that is embodied, proprioceptive, and exploratory. The moving camera coaxes the viewer into this unaccustomed perceptual experience and reveals the play of forces that come about through objectified spectatorship and collective compositions. These techniques both express and compel a mode of perception that is overwhelmingly classical. The gravity, restraint, and uncompromising rigor of *Genroku Chushingura*'s style points to a way of seeing and absorbing that is ineffably Japanese. Its subject matter, narrative attenuation, and historical detail go a long way toward this destination, but it is technique—especially the bond forged between individual and collective, spectator and performance—that really provides the sine qua non of cinematic Japaneseness. Walter Benjamin, speaking in a different context, said, "The collective perception of the audience can make the individual modes of perception of the psychotic and the dreamer its own."[45] *Genroku Chushingura* is the fullest elaboration imaginable of the dream of pure Japaneseness.

Genroku Chushingura *Segmentation*

PART 1

1. Credits
2. *Edo*: Asano attacks Kira in the Pine Corridor for his insulting remarks on Asano's ignorance of court etiquette.
3. In the Palm Room Chamberlain Tamon interrogates Asano, then the cowardly Kira.
4. Lady Asano is told of the attack.
5. Tamon pleads for leniency, but the shogun's counselors have con demned Asano to commit suicide.
6. Asano is held in Tamura's castle, while the dissenting counselor, Kofu, praises Tamon for his courage and support.
7. Asano's vassal Gengoyemon gets permission to see his master for the last time. Gengo and Asano exchange farewells outside the place of ritual suicide.
8. Lady Asano's maids cut her hair.
9. Asano's men receive word that his Edo castle is to be confiscated.
10. *Ako*: At the Asano castle Oishi Kuranosuke, Asano's chamberlain, is criticized for calculating the fief's assets, but he explains that he must think of the people in Asano's domain.
11. Messengers arrive with word of the shogun's verdict. Oishi reads Asano's last words and a poem to the bereaved samurai.
12. Oishi broods and keeps his wife and family ignorant of his intentions.
13. Onodera arrives from Kyoto to tell Oishi that other lords, and possibly the emperor, support him. Oishi is overcome with relief.
14. Edo retainers complain that Oishi is delaying the revenge out of cowardice.
15. Oishi's wife, Riku, and children are apprehensive. Riku's cousin summarizes the situation. An old friend, Tokubei, and his son arrive and ask to help with any plans, but Oishi refuses.
16. Edo retainers demand to know Oishi's plans and refuse their support in blood.
17. Tokubei and his son wait outside the castle, chagrined at their exclusion.
18. Meeting of loyal retainers. Oishi's proposal: surrender the castle and disband, but bide their time to kill Kira and avenge Asano.
19. Tokubei has killed his son and stabbed himself outside the castle. On finding them, Oishi confides his plan to the dying man.
20. At Oishi's home retainers Yasubei and Kazuemon are angry that he is

not there. Oishi's son Matsunojo leads them to Kyoto while Riku declares her intention to stand by her man.

21. *Kyoto*: Yasubei and Kazuemon find Oishi drunk in a geisha teahouse. They witness his offensive behavior to a highly placed lord who wishes to retain him. They leave in disgust. Oishi throws off his feigned drunkenness and recalls his son, telling him that they must patiently wait.

22. At Oishi's home loyal retainers arrive to tell Oishi that since the Asano house has no hope of being restored, they must proceed with vengeance. He agrees.

23. Riku asks Oishi for a divorce on account of the community's disapproval and he consents. She and the younger children leave Oishi.

PART 2

1. Credits
2. *Edo*: During a noh performance, Lord Tsunatoyo wonders whether to ask the shogun to restore the Asano house. Sukeyemon, an Asano retainer, sneaks into the performance because he knows Kira will be there. He is recognized and brought before Tsunatoyo, who questions him about the vendetta. Suke only criticizes him for allowing the shogun to pass such harsh judgment on Asano. Kira arrives and Suke rushes impetuously to kill him. His sister restrains him and promises to help him kill Kira at that night's noh performance.
3. That night Suke attacks a noh actor he believes to be Kira, but after a scuffle discovers it is Lord Tsunatoyo himself. He upbraids Sukeyemon for his impetuosity and the young man accepts the criticism. Tsunatoyo then goes to perform before an audience that includes Kira.
4. At Lady Asano's home Oishi arrives to pay his respects to the memory of Asano on the anniversary of his death. Oishi meets with some resistance from the old servant Godayu, but he is admitted by Lady Toda. Lady Asano sees Oishi, but she criticizes him for not avenging her husband and refuses to let him burn incense to his memory. Before he leaves Oishi gives a packet of poems to Lady Toda for Lady Asano.
5. That night Lady Asano talks with Lady Toda. They discover Oishi has left not poems but an account book. A message is thrown over the wall: the forty-seven ronin have attacked Kira's mansion and killed him.
6. Lord Asano's grave: the ronin arrive and offer thanks for their victory, placing Kira's head on the grave. Oishi declares they must surrender instead of committing suicide on the spot.
7. *Kumamoto*: At Lord Hosokawa's mansion flowers arrive from Lady

Asano. They are taken to the imprisoned ronin. The elder group of ronin express their gratitude and the younger group offer to entertain the messenger, Horiuchi. After the flowers have been arranged on the altar, all bow in thanks to Lady Asano.

8. Crosscutting: Laughing, the younger group asks Hara to dance. Oishi and his group sit gravely. Hara finishes his dance, and Juroza plays the flute. This sends old Horiuchi out weeping.

9. Omino's ruse: Horiuchi tries to pass off Omino as a page boy, but Oishi is not taken in. She says she must see Juroza.

10. Juroza and Sukeyemon discuss Omino, who was used to spy on Kira. Suke tells him to soften his heart.

11. Horiuchi and Omino explain to Oishi that she has been disowned by her family because Juroza failed to marry her. Oishi finally agrees to let her see Juroza. He arrives and pretends not to know her. Then he calls himself her father's son-in-law.

12. The sentence arrives from the shogun: the ronin must commit suicide. Hosokawa provides a farewell meal, for which they express their thanks.

13. The execution procession is interrupted by Oishi's discovery that Omino has killed herself.

14. Horiuchi prays over Omino's body as the ronin commit suicide one by one. Juroza offers to let Oishi go first, but Oishi must go last, smiling as he meets his fate.

7

Historical Uses and Misuses:
The Janus Face(s) of
The Abe Clan

There is a scene in the 1938 film *The Abe Clan* (*Abe Ichizoku*) that is splendid for its poignancy or its absurdity—it's hard to know which. It is 1641 and the Hosokawa daimyo has just expired. To show their loyalty a large number of his prominent retainers perform junshi. More than an extreme form of mourning, these suicides starkly showed the lengths to which samurai would go to demonstrate the depth of their gratitude for their lord's favor. It is said that even the daimyo's favorite falcons plummeted to their deaths to show their devotion to their erstwhile keeper.

The daimyo's dog handler, Gosuke, is also about to commit junshi. Sitting quietly under a tree, he spends his last moments talking to one of his dogs:

> Since you're a dog you may not understand, but our lord, who
> used to pat you on the head, has now passed away. That's why

the high retainers who have enjoyed his favors will all commit seppuku today. My own status is lowly, but I am no different from them in owing my life's sustenance to his favor. I too have been honored by his personal affection. So I am going to commit seppuku today. After I am gone you will be free to roam. I feel sorry for you. Our lord's falcons have plunged into the well at the Shuunin and killed themselves. How about you? Maybe you prefer to go with me. If you prefer to live as a stray, then eat these rice balls. If you prefer to die, don't eat them.[1]

The dog is not hungry, and pays for it dearly. Happy that the dog prefers to accompany him into the netherworld, Gosuke promptly eviscerates himself. A friendly woodcutter assists Gosuke by beheading him.

Gosuke's last words ring portentously down through the years into the late 1930s. His death represents a profound and fanatical devotion to his daimyo. By virtue of his lowly status, Gosuke's death also extends this thanatotic devotion (the supreme token of bushido) to a nonwarrior, and in turn extends it further still into the animal kingdom, like a Greater East Asian Chain of Being.[2] In 1938, Japanese war propaganda exhorted audiences to sacrifice themselves for the greater glory of the emperor and the fatherland. In cinema the Home Ministry encouraged historical epics like *The Abe Clan* that glorified the self-sacrificial, authoritarian values of feudal Japan. It is likely that Gosuke's celluloid death illustrated a blind alle-

Gosuke the dog-handler. Frame enlargement, courtesy Toho Company.

giance to authority that would make the Home Ministry censor weep for joy.

But Gosuke's suicide could also be seen as a black joke, an ironic subversion of junshi that shows the ridiculous excesses of the warrior code of loyalty; at least this is how it might appear to someone who does not accept the warrior code. It is testament to the evenhanded subtlety of Mori Ogai, who wrote the original novella, that the excesses of junshi are so apparent, yet so matter of fact. Yet in the film the problem of junshi fanaticism is represented with far more bile. Surprisingly, though, the object of its biliousness is obscure. It is only through a careful consideration of the film's style that its ideological sympathies are revealed—and only sometimes.

For the most part *The Abe Clan* cleaves to the reverential gravity of the monumental style. The film valorizes feudal Japanese history by lingering on traditional Japanese art, architecture, dance, and the virtues of the hierarchical family system. Using characteristic techniques like the long take, graceful, fluid camera movements, and opulent historical settings, *The Abe Clan* sets out to canonize Japan's pre-Western past. This was meant to help the war effort by representing the strength, dignity, and spirit of Japaneseness that the monumental style extols. *The Abe Clan* is a good example of the monumental style, except for curious disturbances like the death of Gosuke the dog handler and other anomalies that I will presently describe.

Because canonization of the past is central to the monumental style, it is not surprising that Mori Ogai's historical novella of 1912 would appear on the screen in 1938. The seventeenth-century Abe family incident, a true story, had different meanings in 1938 from the ones it had in 1912. Thus the film is a dual historical appropriation of a feudal incident and a Meiji literary meditation on that incident. The narration and technique of the film further replicate and complicate this historical dialectic. The film is two generations removed, in time and in medium, from the historical Abe clan.

In the quest for the mass mobilization of war resources, *The Abe Clan* looks to the traditional Japanese cultural heritage for inspiration. By 1938 the country was on full military footing and was operating under the National Mobilization Law, which mandated a military priority for industry and business. The National Mobilization Law gave the government control over labor, resources, production, prices, and wages on the assumption that a major consolidation was required, both material and spiritual, in order to speed the war effort to a victorious conclusion.[3] In 1939 large private industries were practically nationalized under the Major Industries Association Ordinance, which formed a government cartel of big industrial companies. An analogous consolidation of the independent political parties, formed by the Imperial Rule Assistance Association, occurred in 1940.[4]

This process, which consolidated, centralized, and nationalized in the name of war unification, was well underway in Japanese foreign policy. The first articulation of the "New Order in East Asia" was seen in 1938: the prospective formation of a unified Asian bloc that opposed Western imperialism.[5] Each country within the New Order, including China, Korea, Taiwan, Indonesia, the Philippines, and even Australia and India, was to have its "proper place" under the benevolent headship of Japan. This idea soon became an explicit government policy, culminating in the 1942 formation of the Greater East Asia Ministry, which initiated what was to be called the Greater East Asia Co-Prosperity Sphere.

In the thick of these muscular exercises, *The Abe Clan* gives pause. The film is a chilling depiction of Tokugawa ethical conundrums centering on the appropriate uses of junshi. The film asks, Who is entitled to commit junshi? What is the proper motivation for taking such a drastic step? What are the consequences of junshi for a society that elevates it to the level of a high honor, a privilege, and an art? Most disturbing, the film raises the issue of distinguishing between authentic and meretricious expressions of junshi. In the framing of these questions with such dramatic force, *The Abe Clan* is an exercise in Japanese casuistry (i.e., the branch of legal philosophy that deals with the application of ethical doctrines in specific cases).

As an exemplary film in the monumental style, *The Abe Clan* invests Japan's feudal history with a spiritual aura and so upholds hierarchies of mutual obligation between inferior and superior. But *The Abe Clan* holds out for an idea of "proper place" that does not quash the dignity of subordinates. It does this by interrogating bushido codes whose application is capricious and unnecessarily inhumane. Both film and novella represent the side of bushido that wears a death mask and exposes it as a potentially vain and dangerous orientation. The samurai in the Abe clan show their protest in increasingly extreme ways. In the end rebellion takes the form of self-immolation, as a way to question the application of ethical codes. But neither bushido nor junshi is condemned outright; rather, *The Abe Clan* draws a distinction between a sincere and an abusive application of these codes, and so reminds its audience to stay true to its spiritual heritage as *Nihonjin* (people of Japan). The monumentalism of *The Abe Clan* is both an affirmation of and challenge to Tokugawa norms of proper place because they are represented as authoritative norms that can sometimes, through misappropriation and misapplication, go awry.

Historical Appropriations

As a screen adaptation of Mori Ogai's 1912 historical novella of the same name, *The Abe Clan* (Toho) is about a disastrous political transition in a seventeenth-century fief. The Abe family is arbitrarily disavowed and eventually annihilated because of an unjust transfer of power from a feudal lord's administration to that of his inexperienced heir. The film seizes on the ethical problem of junshi and its appropriateness as an indication of a samurai's depth of regard for his lord.

The plot of the film runs as follows: Abe Yaichiemon, the daimyo's poison-taster, is in a quandary because although he also wishes to join his late lord in death, the daimyo expressly forbade him to do so. Now Abe is shamed before his samurai peers, who ridicule him for lacking the proper loyalty to the late daimyo. They feel that Abe's hesitation betrays an unwillingness to make the ultimate expression of samurai loyalty: to die for one's lord. This interpretation of Abe's position seems to be echoed by the new Hosokawa daimyo, who redistributes the Abe stipend to each of its separate family members, thereby fragmenting the clan's fortunes and vitiating its administrative integrity.

Abe has had enough and decides to commit junshi anyway, to salvage the damaged reputation of his family. Abe's last words before he kills himself are an exhortation to his sons to "stick together." Junshi is represented here as a gesture of exasperation, if not quite defiance. The rest of the film shifts over to the surviving sons' increasingly tense relations with the new daimyo. The eldest son Gombe scandalizes the community when he publically cuts off his topknot in protest of his clan's mistreatment. When he is imprisoned his four brothers must decide on a plan to appeal for his release. They ask a visiting priest to intercede on Gombe's behalf, but Gombe is nevertheless soon executed as if he were a common thief. The remaining Abe clan cannot abide this, and since they openly defy the daimyo's judgment, a punitive force is sent to massacre the entire clan. Some of the Abe clan's closest friends and neighbors are forced to lead the massacre and to act, against their better judgment, as the daimyo's scourge. The end result of what was originally a ceremonial technicality is the extermination of an entire samurai household.

Before jumping to the conclusion that this film is an object lesson in the excesses of bushido militarism, we must recognize the importance of the film's sources. Due to the topicality of Ogai's original story, the film depicts seventeenth-century historical events and indirectly refers to the historical conditions surrounding the composition of Ogai's 1912 story.

Ogai wrote the story on the occasion of the junshi suicides of General Nogi Maresuke and his wife, who killed themselves on September 13, 1912, the day of the Meiji emperor's funeral ceremonies.[6] "Abe Ichizoku" is actually one in a cycle of historical works beginning with "The Last Testament of Okitsu Yagoemon," representing Ogai's first reaction to Nogi's suicide, and ending with "Kuriyama Daizen" and "Sansho Dayu," a title familiar to Mizoguchi devotees.[7] Many of the stories in this cycle deal with three generations of the Hosokawa family, an influential *han*, or fief, based in Kyushu. There can be no doubt that Ogai was personally moved by General Nogi's suicide, for both Nogi and Ogai had participated in the imperial funeral ceremonies and had fought in the same campaign during the Russo-Japanese war, of which Nogi was the undisputed hero.[8] While the two versions of "Okitsu Yagoemon" are fairly straightforward celebrations of junshi and feudal loyalty, "Abe Ichizoku," written about six months later, is a more ambivalent work. In this story Ogai is sympathetic toward the impulse to take one's life out of gratitude to one's late lord; however, he also "sustains his mordant and penetrating irony through his delineation of the psychology of those who die for reputation in this world rather than in devotion to their former master."[9]

Ogai's ambivalence toward junshi seems to have both an ethical and historical aspect. Ethically, Ogai draws a distinction in the story between an authentic and a hypocritical attitude toward junshi, because he describes in detail all of the prestige and perquisites a samurai can expect if he is favored with officially sanctioned junshi. Junshi is one of the highest manifestations of the samurai spirit, and a clan whose patriarch commits junshi could expect to be revered by the daimyo and community alike. This was reflected in the custom of daimyo providing for the families of junshi samurai with extra care:

> The heirs of the households of the eighteen men who committed junshi were allowed to succeed their fathers without complication. No heir, however young, was bypassed. The widows and elderly parents of the eighteen were granted stipends. Residences were conferred upon them, even when in some cases this meant building new quarters. These were households whose deceased heads had been particularly favored by Tadatoshi, and who had even gone to attend their lord on his journey to the next life; therefore even if these families were envied by the other retainers, it was not malicious envy.[10]

Ironically, there were very real material and social benefits to be gotten through junshi, and through this emphasis Ogai subtly suggests the accompanying potential for dissembling, obsequiousness, and envy. Ogai's story captures the venality of the junshi code by emphasizing its prestige and its rewards.

A related ambivalence in the story concerns the tide of history. If Ogai's stories about the Hosokawa daimyo largely uphold samurai traditions and values, it is also true that they were written in response to a profoundly anachronistic event. Writes David Dilworth, "At the time of his suicide, some interpreted Nogi's action as appropriate to a warrior, while others felt considerable apprehension at this manifestation of the vitality of feudalistic morality in the twentieth century."[11]

Ogai's story ingeniously incorporates both interpretations of the significance of junshi, lending an equivocal flavor without literally reproducing the anachronism of Nogi's suicide. The emphasis on Gosuke's suicide is a structural parallel, a social anomaly rather than an historical anachronism that marks an ethical irregularity. Significantly, Ogai's junshi cycle was written at the turn of the Taisho period, marking the country's irrevocable accession to a modern, international phase. Therefore Ogai's subtle homage to junshi is best seen as an elegy for a departed age rather than a reactionary endorsement of feudal solutions to modern problems. The historical ambivalence of "Abe Ichizoku" involves a simultaneous recognition of the transcendence attainable through junshi and the meaninglessness of junshi to an uncomprehending generation. The uneasy coexistence and overlapping of ethics deriving from succeeding historical eras finds an inscription in the Abe's predicament, caught as they are between succeeding, conflicting regimes. Ogai's own position also exemplifies the dialectic between universal and contingent so admirably expressed by the historical relativity of General Nogi's suicide. Ogai's story suggests that its significance is entirely governed by which side of the Meiji restoration one chooses to look at it. In this elegy for a departed age, the story is a meditation on the evanescence of things, and despite its vacillation between feudal and modern, the story's elegiac understatement gives it a traditional Japanese feel.

If Ogai's novella is an elegy to Tokugawa ethics, Kumagai Hisatora's 1938 film is revolutionary. It resumes the historical dialectic of the 1912 novella and adds yet another layer. A film that dwells on the intricacies of junshi was congruent with the reactionary Showa restoration movement of the 1930s, even if its representation of the practice was not completely enthusiastic. Contemporary critics of the film thought Ogai's cool treatment of junshi was lost within a celebration of right-wing, pseudofeudal, militarist sentiments: "Where is the original Ogai in this piece?" writes one exasperated critic. "We can only find here the sinister side of director

Kumagai himself."[12] The "sinister" side of Kumagai was his radical conversion from muckraking liberalism in the early thirties to fanatical nationalism as the war intensified.[13] Another critic praises Kumagai for his "high-pressure realism," remarking on his use of the romance between two servants to criticize samurai ethics. But that critic also thinks the director "suffers from a tendency toward the ideological."[14] Kumagai's film repudiates the balanced perspective of Mori Ogai in favor of the "noble failure" of the Abe family's apotheosis: "The cry of frustrated indignation sent up by the film's bushido purists clearly echoes the similar cry of the young militarist fanatics of the thirties."[15] Or so many critics thought at the time.

Though the contemporary critical consensus was that the film glorified junshi and, by implication, military sacrifice, ultranationalist critic Sawamura Tsutomu stubbornly demurred:

> What breadth! What density this work has! If I may be allowed the expression, what violence of vision! Kumagai has thrown a bomb into the sluggish Japanese film world, blowing open a hole for fresh breezes to enter. He dazzles us with the fury of his iron determination to cut through the Gordian Knot which has strangled our nation's cinema. This work tosses and turns with the tempestuousness of Kumagai's passionate convictions about life. Writhings of this sort are of course far from the coolness of the Mori Ogai original. Yet it is clear that the present era demands from us just this sort of tumult. That this is so lacking from our presentday cinema is one of its chief flaws.[16]

It is easy to see why Sawamura is a champion of cinematic "spiritism" (seishinshugi), an idealist ignition of the Japanese Spirit that insists on the victory of spirit over physical force.[17] Thousands of Japanese soldiers and civilians died in the Sino-Japanese and Pacific wars as a result of seishinshugi ideology. Such rhapsodies of praise from Sawamura, who later began to write scripts for Kumagai, justifies treating *The Abe Clan* in light of the Showa restoration movement.

The ideological processes surrounding the Meiji restoration (1868) are marked by strategic historical appropriations made by the restoration architects, the samurai bureaucrats. Conceits like the sanctity of the imperial institution and pseudoarchaic touchstones like kokutai (the mythicized national body politic) were mobilized for the encouragement of spiritual and racial solidarity among Japanese subjects.[18] The Meiji restoration was a benchmark of Japanese nationalism in its idea of a divinely sanctioned authority sweeping away an outmoded, exhausted regime, the shogunate (*bakufu*). The idea of imperial restoration could be harnessed to many different calls for reform and was later repeatedly invoked in various social and political causes. Movements in late Meiji dealt with the problems of individualism and communism by establishing a nationwide shrine merger movement (1906), publishing ethics textbooks that glorify the kokutai and traditional family structures (1910), and celebrating military loyalty by forming an imperial veterans' association (1910).[19] These were all reforms justified by appeal to imperial fiat. Through the years themes of historical continuity, divine right, and racial solidarity recur, recirculate, and recycle into a dense condensation of imperial ideologies used to advance causes in the name of Japan.

By the 1930s the ruling consensus had settled on a course of steady military escalation, and this was the cause to which the Showa restoration was devoted. The Showa restoration was invoked, among others, by the young army officers who tried to overthrow the government on February 26, 1936.[20] They were unsuccessful, although they assassinated one senior minister and wounded several others. Their story is immortalized by Yukio Mishima in his novel *Runaway Horses* (Homba, 1969), which emphasizes the young men's fanatical devotion to emperor and to traditional values. In the novel, and in the story "Patriotism" (*Yukoku*, 1961), Mishima also brings out the chilling fascination with self-immolation as a badge of loyalty to the cause. A devotion that welcomes death as a vindication of one's sincerity is a mark of the religious purity of the young men's cause. In the 1930s, as in late Tokugawa, "it seemed to some people that they were in the midst of a general breakdown of traditional morals and denigration of the spirit of self-sacrifice."[21] Mishima's story of the young officers' death cult is disturbing not only in its linkage of youthful vigor with sacrificial loyalty but in its acknowledgment that there was considerable public sympathy for the young officers' efforts. Mishima's central character is an ordinarily dispassionate judge who becomes fascinated, then implicated, in the youthful passion of the army officers. The judge eventually resigns his post to defend the officers and their ideals.

Not accidentally, Mishima centered his novel on the "conversion" of a distinguished judge to the fanaticism of the young officers, for it was the powerful justice minister Hiranuma Kiichiro (1867–1941) who publically called for a "Showa restoration." Significantly, Hiranuma diagnosed the roots of Japan's condition in the Taisho era. In response to widespread political corruption, Hiranuma called for renewed efforts to expel corrupting foreign ideas and return to the purity of traditional Japan.[22] Through the Taisho and early Showa years the Justice Ministry prided itself on its moderate conservatism and successful prosecution of political corruption.

Given its reputation, the fact that the Justice Ministry was caught up in the tide of ultranationalism sweeping Japan is testament to its irresistible surging power. The Showa restoration movement was both reactionary and revolutionary in its call for national self-purification as well as its extreme sacrificial manifestations.

The Abe Clan deals with immolation, too, but it also investigates the boundary between willing self-sacrifice and sacrifice of a minority element in order to safeguard the hegemony of the majority. As a lightning rod for ultranationalism all over Japan, the young officers of 1936 conflated their desire for purity with their righteous anger toward those who spoil the purity of "their" kokutai. The young officers justified their assasinations by distributing a manifesto written by the ultranationalist Kita Ikki:

> There have appeared many persons whose chief aim and purpose have been to amass personal material wealth, disregarding the general welfare and prosperity of the Japanese population, with the result that the sovereignty of the Emperor has been greatly diminished. The *Genro*, senior statesmen, military cliques, plutocrats, bureaucrats and political parties are all traitors who are destroying the *Kokutai*. . . . The Imperial work will fail unless we take proper steps to safeguard the Fatherland by killing all those responsible for impeding the Showa Restoration and slurring Imperial prestige.
>
> May the gods bless and help us in our endeavor to save the Fatherland from the worst that confronts it.[23]

The crucial assumption in such sentiments is that the kokutai is a preexistent collective body whose continuing purity is threatened by corrupting "outside" influences. That is, the weight of history is attributed to "the Fatherland" by associating its purity with the imperial lineage and its unbroken continuation over two millennia. It is the monumental weight of history, exemplified by the imperial lineage, that sanctifies the kokutai. Just as the young officers confused personal purity with collective salvation, they also confused their historical moment with a teleological culmination of history.

Much of this comes down to the not very enlightening proposal that the young officers of 1936 were subject to delusions of grandeur. Maruyama Masao has a more pointed observation concerning the essential innocence, naïveté, and "mythological optimism" of the young officers' credo:

The content of their ideology was extremely vague and abstract, being the principle of accepting the absolute authority of the Emperor and submitting humbly to his wishes. One of the reasons that the participants' plans covered only the violent stage of the operation and were not concerned with the aftermath is that their thoughts were based on the principle of the absolute authority of the Emperor. In other words, any attempt at formulating plans of reconstruction would be tantamount to surmising the will of the Emperor and thus an invasion of the Imperial prerogative. This leads to the mythological sort of optimism according to which, if only evil men could be removed from the Court, if only the dark clouds shrouding the Emperor could be swept away, the Imperial sun would naturally shine forth.[24]

The kokutai concept is essentially mythological in the way its force overrides its sense.[25] For the meaning of the kokutai idea—its sense—is subordinate to its force: the kokutai idea as a gesture of national solidarity, an ideograph or shorthand for cultural identity that was disseminated at the time of the Meiji restoration. Since kokutai was one of a number of notions proffered to the Japanese to consolidate support for the new Meiji regime, its importance lies in its conjunction of archaic conceits with contemporary exigencies.[26] Therefore the meaning of kokutai is less important than the recognition that, as a Japanese, one "belongs" to it. Such concepts were spoon-fed to youngsters from their earliest schooldays.[27] As a form of national interpellation, kokutai ideology served to raise or, better, to impose a recollection of national consciousness, always in service to some pressing contemporary cause. The fact that imperialists in the 1930s could sincerely champion a Showa restoration indicates the flexibility of concepts like kokutai and *tenno heika* (the emperor); they could be used to justify disparate programs within different historical contexts. It also takes nothing away from the sincerity of those who proposed a Showa restoration, for the fact that the same strategies were used in the Meiji, Taisho, and Showa eras only shows how deeply ingrained the Meiji indoctrination process had become. The Showa restoration, then, was an appropriation of not only the ideas but also the strategy of the Meiji restoration, which in turn was a selective appropriation of Tokugawa ideals.

The Abe Clan exemplifies this process of historical appropriation not only because it harnesses Tokugawa ethics to calls for a Showa restoration but also because its Taisho-era source by Mori Ogai is aware of the uses and misuses of history. *The Abe Clan* is an instance of a Showa reconstitution of the Meiji appropriation of Tokugawa history. Essentially this comes down to a rhetoric of analogy: as in the Meiji period, "our" kokutai is in danger of foreign contamination that can only be withstood by restoring the divine prerogatives of the emperor. The presence of the same terms—e.g., *kokutai, tenno heika, bushido, junshi*—serve to legitimate disparate policies in the Meiji, Taisho, and Showa periods. Whatever the specific objectives of those who were attempting to mobilize a national consciousness, whether the objective was to modernize or educate, mandate or militarize, it seems that a self-consciously unified national consciousness was a means to those ends.

The Showa restoration movement saw a languishing people whose farmers bowed under the weight of tenant servitude and falling prices brought on by the policies of Tokyo capitalists; it visualized the emasculation of traditional Japanese ideals in the cities, where dissolute young mobos and mogas sported Harold Lloyd glasses and frequented jazz parlors, in which taxi dancers worked until dawn, perhaps sending a part of their wages to beleaguered family back in the provinces (see chapter 3). In Tokyo such visions were hardly paranoid fantasies; they signified to many people a divided, debased kokutai. It was time to reunify Japan in the name of the emperor, the unassailable bastion of the national tradition.

To sum up, it is essential to attend to the historical dialectic embedded in a text like *The Abe Clan*. We are used to thinking of period drama as a dodge away from topical claims of the present, but the ethical imperatives of the historical imagination, as opposed to the religious or scientific, have a strong claim on Japanese thinking. As anyone knows who has ever witnessed the Japanese festival of the dead, *O-bon*, in some sense history *is* religion, insofar as the past is personalized and venerated as a spiritual act. The appeal to history, moreover, does not necessarily lodge neatly into a reactionary political slot. The bewildering political dualism of the Showa restoration is commented on by Ben-Ami Shillony: "On the face of it, [the Showa restoration] was a rejection of the present and the recent past, in favor of a remote and supposedly ideal one. But within these traditional terms of reference there was a revolutionary content, the intention to destroy the existing regime and build a new society, based on a greater degree of social equality."[28] *The Abe Clan* takes up these contradictions. Its adaptation of Ogai's novella was denounced at the time as reactionary, but now it looks pacifist, or at least humanist.[29] Its narration simplifies the temporal convolutions of its literary source, but complicates the ideology of the story. And its style cleaves mostly to the monumental pace and gravity of other nativist historical films, but sometimes veers off into unexpected and idiosyncratic directions.

Narration and Technique

Just as Mori Ogai appropriates the historical record in the composition of his novella, so Kumagai's film appropriates Ogai's novella. Ogai's story begins with the Hosokawa daimyo's death, giving plenty of background detail on the Hosokawa fief, its ancestors, and funeral arrangements, including the junshi code: "The code governing *junshi* had arisen naturally, rather than having been established by someone for a specific reason at some point in time. No matter how much a retainer may esteem his lord, he could not commit *junshi* at will."[30]

By immediately introducing the issue of junshi, the novella takes the tone of a tendentious historical chronicle—even a moral tale—that aims to illustrate a lesson through the benefit of hindsight. In doing so, Ogai weaves a tapestry of contradictions occasioned by the code of junshi. In his mordant, understated style Ogai exposes an instance whereby a code meant to regulate a private interpersonal relationship between samurai and lord becomes a crucible by which the stature of samurai is publically judged. As the previous section suggests, the distinction between private and public junshi reveals the narrator's ambivalence toward junshi relative to its historical situation. But the contemporary reception of the film suggests that the narration minimizes this ambivalence in favor of traditional bushido loyalty.

Far from minimizing the novella's ambivalence toward junshi, the film substitutes an ambivalence of a different sort. Kumagai clearly delineates the distinction between junshi as private devotion and as public spectacle. Like Ogai, the film favors the former. However, the narrative structure of the film privatizes junshi as a familial gesture rather than an expression of loyalty to the daimyo. That is, Abe's suicide is clearly performed to save face to the surviving family. Thus the film privileges representations of the immediate Abe family and its neighbors over Abe's status as a Hosokawa vassal and perhaps even as samurai. Junshi becomes a prerogative taken by the Abe family in *opposition* to its official significance as the ultimate act of samurai fealty. The destruction of the Abe clan bears fiery testimony to the sacrificial power of junshi to chasten and redeem a wayward, capricious authority. Still, *The Abe Clan* is exemplary of the monumental style because it reaffirms the sacramental function of junshi and bushido.

The film's linear structure contrasts markedly with the interwoven temporal structures in the novella. This structural difference determines the respective ambivalences maintained by each version of the story. Both stories concern the steady decline in the Abe clan's reputation, fortunes, and key members. In the novella the decline is explained through digressions that recount (R) historical background information and authorial speculation that comments (C) on the motives and goals of characters. In the film the Abe clan's decline is more precipitous and arbitrary than in the novella. This lends a capriciousness and even absurdity to the clan's tragic fall. A comparative narrative structural breakdown looks something like this:

film	novella
1. Hosokawa's death (title)	1. Hosokawa's death
2. Chojuro, Gosuke, Ihara	2. Chojuro, et al.
3. Stipends (spear boasting)	3. R: Hosokawa's animus
4. Abe's suicide	4. Abe's suicide
5. Tasuke the servant ("Shut up, kids!")	5. C: Stipends
6. Memorial services	6. C: Memorial services
7. Decisions, supplications	7. Decisions, supplications
8. Gombe's execution (offscreen)	8. Gombe's execution
9. hunting party	9. family's response
10. spy and formation of punitive force (Kazuma's assignment)	10. formation of punitive force and spy
11. neighbors' warning	11. neighbors' warning
12. Yagobei's commemoration (cf. 4.)	12. preparing for death
13. preparing for death (crosscutting: Tasuke and Matashichiro's decisions)	13. C: death ritual
14. death ritual	14. R: Matashichiro's decision
	15. R: Kazuma's assignment
	16. R: Takami's assignment
15. Massacre	17. Massacre
	C = commentary by narrator
	R = recounting the past

The narration in the film departs from the novella in three important ways: the film minimizes the temporal suspensions in the novella by eliminating the recounting (R) of strategic background information; the film manipulates the order of events and even adds events to straighten the narrative trajectory; the film dispenses with Ogai's copious commentary (C) on the action in favor of commentary of a more organic, less intrusive kind. What follows is, I hope, less novel-into-film description than an analysis of the ways in which Ogai's story is both simplified and problematized (more than it already is) by the film's structural manipulations of its narrative material.

The most striking omission of background information in the film is the Hosokawa daimyo's animus against Abe. In the novella the daimyo refuses Abe's request for junshi because he intensely dislikes Abe. The reason for this irrational antipathy is only speculated on by the novella's narrator:

> Every man has natural likes and dislikes. If he tries to understand them, he often cannot tell exactly why he feels as he does. This was the case in Tadatoshi's aversion to [Abe] Yaichiemon. Somewhere in Yaichiemon, however, there must have been something which made it difficult for him to relate to others, as evidenced by the fact that he had few close friends.[31]

The passage goes on to describe how Abe's elders had always thought that "somehow—Abe is completely locked inside himself,"[32] despite his reputation for being a most worthy and punctilious samurai.

I shall argue that the film compensates for the absence of this crucial stipulation—Hosokawa's dislike of Abe—by emphasizing the quality of Abe's home life and thereby motivating the community's antagonism. This is reinforced by another constitutive absence in the narrative of the film, the recounting of background information on Matashichiro (Abe's neighbor, played by Kawarasaki Chojuro, of Zenshinza, cf. *Genroku Chushingura*) and Kazuma (Abe's fellow samurai for the late Hosokawa daimyo). In the novella these two are not even introduced until after the Abe clan's death ritual (13) when there is a description of the leaders of the punitive force that wipes out the Abe clan. The narrative retardation in this structure—the story working up to a bloody climax (13) only to be interrupted by a long digression on the genealogies and motivations of the punitive force (14–16)—is typical of the novella. This is similar to Mizoguchi's suppression of key moments in the plot of *Genroku Chushingura*, especially those with physical action. But where Mizoguchi suppresses, Ogai merely delays, and Kumagai displays all in chronological order. In Ogai's digressive sequences the narrative takes a temporal detour into the past perfect that in the film is presented directly, without suspending the story's temporal progression:

> Matashichiro had been on familiar terms with the Abe family, and not only the masters of each house, but their wives as well,

had frequent contact with one another. This was also true of Yaichiemon's second son, Yagobe, and Matashichiro. Yagobe took special pride in his skill with the spear, and after Matashichiro also took up the same art, they would trade boasts with one another among friends. They would say, "You may be quick, but you're no match for me," or "Never! How could I lose to you!"[33]

In the film the subjunctive detour is unnecessary because this particular scene is enacted at the very beginning of the film, before Abe Yaichiemon's suicide (4). This has two consequences. First, the narrative is linearized, eliminating the distinction between main story (past) and background recountings (past perfect). Second, Matashichiro's character is introduced as part of the Abe clan in the spear-boasting scene (film, 3) rather than as a participant in the punitive force (novella, 14). In other words, the film's narrative manipulation of story order promotes Matashichiro's status as neighbor over his status as henchman. It is precisely because he is neighbor and family friend that his decision to disobey the daimyo's warning (11) and engage his old friends in battle is so bewildering. One might expect Matashichiro, as close family friend, to fight with the Abe clan against the daimyo; but since the daimyo tells him to stay out of the fray, his entrance into the battle—even to fight

Abe Yagobe and his neighbor Matashichiro as sparring partners . . .

and as enemies. Kawakita Memorial Film Archives.

against his friends—defies the daimyo and upholds his friendship with the Abe clan.

The film similarly manipulates Ogai's introduction of Kazuma, who is assigned to lead the punitive force against the Abe clan (15). Again, in the novella this is revealed through narrative recounting that situates Kazuma's assignment in the nefarious political intrigues hatched by Geki, the new daimyo's prosecutor. There follows Kazuma's agonizing rationalizations and self-incriminations, made worse by a message from the daimyo that Kazuma take care not to injure himself in the assault. Kazuma becomes hysterical wondering whether Geki's order that he lead the assault and the daimyo's solicitation of his safety are barbs aimed at one who may have been expected to commit junshi but didn't. As the dubious hypotheticals proliferate, the narration shifts into first person: "[Lord Mitsuhisa] was telling him, in effect, to take care of his cowardly life. His solicitude was too ambiguous. It was like flailing an old wound with a whip. I want to die now, right now. My disgrace cannot be washed away by dying, but I want to die—die even like a dog."[34]

In the end Kazuma gets his wish and dies, but out of frustration rather than loyalty—the furthest thing from the sacrificial decorum required of a proper *bushi*:

> Kazuma was now completely beside himself. He informed his
> wife and children that he had been ordered to direct the attack

on the Abe, and then feverishly hurried with his preparation by
himself. Whereas those who had committed junshi had done so
with serenity, Kazuma was pursuing death to escape the
anguish in his heart.[35]

A more pathetic picture of junshi can hardly be imagined.

In the film Kazuma's primary significance is his role as a fellow sufferer
in the community for not having committed junshi. He is introduced as a
close friend of Abe's just before the scene where stipends are reapportioned
(3). Since there is no indication in the novella that Kazuma knew the Abe
clan, it is important that the film fabricates an ally for Abe within his circle
of colleagues at the castle (Matashichiro is never seen in his professional
capacity).

Although Matashichiro figures more prominently in the story overall,
Abe's alliance with Kazuma, a fellow poison-taster, shows (pace Ogai) that
Abe is not alone in his disfavor with the administration. This means that in
addition to smoothing out the temporal digressions in the story order, the
film introduces Abe's predicament *along with* his personal and professional
sympathizers in the community, rather than presenting his sympathizers at
the end of the story in asides. The result is a greater poignancy in watching the Abe clan massacred by its closest friends and associates; but the relative salience of the Abes' friends and family also presents an aspect of loyalty that is personal, not political, and thereby an implied threat to the
absolute fealty demanded by daimyo, shogun, and emperor. It is precisely
the closeness of the Abe clan that motivates the daimyo's paranoia and
desire to wipe out even the illusion of a concerted resistance to absolute
authority. As in *Story of the Last Chrysanthemum*, the hierarchal family system
cannot tolerate a nuclear family within its ranks because it introduces a
potential rival for loyalty. Surrogate family gestures in *Kawanakajima Kassen*
and in contemporary war films can also be attributed to the absence of the
nuclear family.

On the one hand, the film omits important background information that
helps to explain the Abe clan's predicament; on the other, the film adds
characters and events that reinforce the communal aspect of Abe's persecution. First, children figure prominently in the Abe household. There is a
characteristic informality associated with the Abe backyard, where children play, the wives gossip, and neighbors indulge in good-natured sparring with their lances. Yagobe in particular is fond of cavorting wildly with
the children of the neighborhood. We see him charging across the yard in
an elaborate horse costume with delighted, squealing children clambering
on his neck. It is an indication of his mental state when, shaken by the

death of his father, he rudely tells the children to shut up (4–5). The children's prominence toward the beginning of the film is gruesomely reiterated at the end in a sequence crosscutting shots of the servant digging a mass grave for the soon-to-be executed children with a scene in which Matashichiro's wife arrives to the delight of the children, bearing presents and kind words (13).

Even the Abe clan itself, the father and his five sons, have a childlike, playful aspect, since they engage in such unpredictable behavior, unbecoming to typical samurai. The youngest son is himself a child, no more than twelve or thirteen. Ichidayu, the darling of the new daimyo, is soft, effeminate, and a little cowardly. Godayu is slovenly, constantly picking at himself and seemingly indifferent, but is actually a stalwart warrior. Yagobe, as we have seen, is often associated with the children, and Gombe, the gruff samurai heir, nonetheless shows himself subject to fits of filial caprice when he breaks down at his father's memoral service and cuts off his topknot (6). Despite the Abe clan's supplications, Gombe's breakdown leads to his public execution, which in turn is the insult that brings on the massacre.

The film also introduces a completely new character, Tasuke (Kato Daisuke), the Abe servant who wishes to do well by his clan in committing junshi after his dismissal from the elder brother's service. Tasuke wants to be a samurai in the worst way. He deports himself with gruff disregard for the entreaties of the maid Osaki who wants to run off with him and start a

The Abe Clan. Publicity still, Kawakita Memorial Film Archives.

Tasuke the manservant,
played by Kato Daisuke.
Publicity still, Kawakita
Memorial Film Archives.

new life (5). One of the strangest shots in the film is an extremely long take
of Tasuke scrambling under the cow that the maid has led onto the road to
block his path, then running away down the road for the better part of a
minute—running away from the offer of love and domesticity in search of
bushido. Tasuke later proves himself when he kills a Hosokawa spy sent to
infiltrate the Abe household (10).

Tasuke's importance to the film's interrogation of bushido lies in the
class origin of the warrior codes. Just as the innocent women and children
of the Abe clan are unhesitatingly sacrificed for the honor of the family, so
the family servant professes his terminal loyalty to a code governing a
group to which he does not belong. Recall for a moment the class issues
around which the Showa restoration was elaborated: the plight of the rural
constituency from which most of the young army officers hailed, the disgust with the abuses of capitalist speculators, the apparent loss of traditional Japanese ideals from institutions of both conservative and left-wing
quarters. It is significant that the film adds a servant character, Tasuke, to
expose the venality of the samurai commitment to the warrior code. Like
Gosuke the dog handler, Tasuke takes bushido more seriously than his
superiors.

Tasuke resisting the appeals of Osaki, the maid. (Tsutsumi Masako). Kawakita Memorial Film Archives.

Some provocative parallels are made in the scene crosscutting Tasuke, who digs a mass grave for the children, with Matashichiro's wife offering presents and comfort (13). As Tasuke digs with alacrity, the maid Osaki comes to him and again tries to persuade him to quit the suicidal obsessions of the Abe clan. She says, "Friendship is friendship, loyalty is loyalty." Cut to the neighbor Matashichiro's house, where he sits brooding on the Abe clan's fate. Suddenly he jumps up, having come to a decision, and tells his wife to go pay her respects to the Abe clan. Then he goes to prepare his lance for his unauthorized dawn battle with his neighbors, saying to himself what the maid said to Tasuke: "Friendship is friendship, loyalty, loyalty."[36] Cut back to Tasuke still determinedly digging, who replies, "I must show people how to die as samurai." Tasuke honors his word the next morning, and the film ends with a series of bleak views of the Abe clan's charred remains, mourned by a melancholic Osaki.

In a way, this film is told from the servants' perspective, because the first glimpse we get of the Abe clan is Abe reproaching Tasuke for being overly impressed with the performance of junshi by his fellow retainers. Both Tasuke and the even more peripheral Osaki are given some of the key moral pronouncements in the course of the film, and Osaki alone survives the sacrificial carnage of the Abe çlan. The presence of this "outsider" perspective is very difficult to judge, because it is hard to know

Destruction of the Abe household. Frame enlargement,
courtesy Toho Company.

whether Tasuke, for instance, is genuinely heroic in his steadfast loyalty
or symptomatic of the misappropriation of samurai ideals. And if he is
symptom rather than exemplar, does the misappropriation of samurai
ideals signify a debasement of those codes that is to be rectified or an indication that samurai codes are harmful (to whom?) and should be eliminated? The incorporation of marginal characters, together with a manipulation of the story's temporal structure and devices for drawing parallels
such as crosscutting, are the means by which the film substitutes its own

form of judgment for the overt continuing commentary provided by the narrator in the novella.

The film makes a final addition to the novella's plot in the commemoration of Abe Yaichiemon's death by his second son Yagobe (12). Besides being an addition to the original story, this sequence exactly replicates the black comedy of Abe Yaichiemon's suicide (4). In this remarkably sacramental scene, the Abe patriarch meets with his sons to discuss *bushi no hon*, the essence of the warrior. "Since the rumor is everywhere in our lord's house," he tells them, "you yourselves have undoubtedly heard it. That my belly is so soft it can be opened with an oiled gourd. I have resolved to kill myself in exactly that manner. I want you all to witness it to the end."[37] In farewell Abe exchanges a solemn cup of sake with his sons, yet another, and still another. Then Abe performs an impromptu noh dance, lugubriously intoning a pitiful ballad about his tribulations. The style of the scene underscores the depth of his humiliation by moving to a high-angle long shot of Abe performing, oblivious to the rain driving down around him and the bewilderment of his sons. As Abe praises the name of Buddha for his imminent release, the mixture of ceremony, grief, and black comedy add up to a very strange farewell indeed. The poignancy of Abe's departure comes from his embrace of the community's ridicule rather than his rejection of it: Abe does not literally disembowel himself with an oiled gourd, but he nevertheless accepts the inevitability of disgrace, even in death:

> Now, when I have died, contrary to expectations, others will probably ridicule you as the sons of one whose suicide was unsanctioned. It is your fate to be my children. Nothing can be done about it. When disgrace comes, face it together. Do not fight among yourselves. Now mark well how one cuts himself open with a gourd.[38]

No sense of righteous indignation, no outrage over a breach of justice informs these parting words.

The manner of Abe's action betrays no hope of future glory; the only consolation to be taken is in prospects of facing disgrace together. Thus Yagobe's commemoration of his father's death (12) reiterates the solidarity of the Abe clan because he mourns not only the passing of his father but also the imminent massacre of the entire clan. Yagobe also adds a macabre element of burlesque to his father's original turn, because the identical sequence of sake drinking, noh dance, and farewell song is employed by Yagobe with an exchange of knowing looks with his brothers. With the same shot sequence as in Yaichiemon's performance, it is almost as if

Abe Yaichiemon . . .

about to disembowl himself
with a gourd. Publicity still,
Kawakita Memorial
Film Archives.

Yagobe's black comedy mocks his father the way Yaichiemon mocked his antagonists. This gives the film an implied cyclicality that the novella lacks, although the burlesque of junshi ceremony in both cases is consistent with the novella's mordant understatement:

> The four Abe brothers ordered their retainers to assemble in the main hall from which shoji and fusuma had been cleared away, where they chanted the name of Amida Buddha to the accompaniment of gong and drum until dawn. The Abe clan said this action was taken to mourn the elders and the women and children, but it was actually a precaution against their lower retainers losing heart.[39] (13)

The heavy irony conveyed in the last sentence of this passage is left out of the film's depiction of the death rituals (14). Instead, the scene is played with maximum gravity, using an extended tracking shot combined with panning movements across the melancholic faces of the Abe clan. The lighting is dark and eerie while the Buddhist priest beats out a steady, ominous cadence that could only herald one thing. When the scene ends and is replaced by a title giving the date of the massacre, October 21, 1642, the drum continues its implacable beat.

A scene like this is typical of the monumental style, which uses long takes, long shots, slow, fluid camera movements, and plenty of pageantry and ritualized action. But the asceticism of the film's technique is offset by playful variations on the somber gravity of monumental norms. This gives the style of the film flashes of irreverence and levity, as if a repression of stylistic idiosyncracy were taking place. "Monumentalism with a human face" might be one way to describe the style of *The Abe Clan*; another might be to call it "schizophrenic monumentalism," because the stylistic variations on the usual figures of monumental style are sufficient to form a kind of counterweight. The ethical conundrum of junshi, then, waffling between apotheosis and apostasy, appears in the film style of *The Abe Clan*. For the most part technique conforms to canonical features of the monumental style, but the presence of anomalies and variations gives the style a knowing, deliberate, and self-conscious aspect. *Shogun and Mentor* contains similar breaches of monumental protocol, but they consist mostly in behavioral breakdowns that serve to humanize the shogun. In *The Abe Clan* the anomalies usually consist in a monumental stylization of nonmonumental subject matter, or technical anomalies in a sequence that is "properly" monumental in both style and subject.

For instance, the opening scene of the film depicts Chojuro's suicide. He is one of the favored retainers. Details of the suicide ritual are presented in a series of static close-ups: a mother's proud face, a grief-stricken young wife, a farewell sake cup. Long takes punctuated by 180-degree cuts between mother and son sitting in different wings set a somber tone for what is to come and prominently showcase the opulence of house and garden. Everything is hushed, save for the occasional chirping of a bird. A slow pan through the room reveals a sleeping Chojuro and a retroactive ellipsis as his wife comes into the shot to wake him in time for his seppuku appointment. Chojuro makes an extremely formal little speech of farewell directed primarily at his mother and the scene concludes with an Ozu-like series of "pillow shots" (spatially indeterminate transitional objects) based on the following passage from Ogai's novella:

> His mother, bride, and younger brother, in their separate rooms, were sunk in thought. The head of the house snored away in the sitting room. At the open window of the sitting room was suspended a hanging fern to which a wind chime had been attached. The wind chime tinkled from time to time, as if remembering what was going to happen. Beneath it, there was a hand basin hollowed out of the crown of a tall rock. A dragonfly had alighted on the wooden ladle resting on the basin, its motionless wings forming the shape of a mountain.[40]

A high angle extreme long shot of Chojuro and his retainer moving off toward the place of immolation is accompanied by the mournful tolling of the temple bell. The melancholy formality of these junshi preliminaries is maintained in the following scene depicting the death rites of Gosuke the dog handler. This scene is paradigmatic of the film in that the gravity of its style is sometimes out of step with its subject matter. Gosuke's ritual with his dog is shot with all of the dignity and grace afforded to Chojuro's canonical act of junshi. The temple bell peals out its mournful toll, the shots of Gosuke's beatific face are held, then the camera slowly moves away from the scene of grisly sacrifice. Whether the parallels drawn between these two are ironic is hard to judge, and the novella is too understated to offer much help: "Though Gosuke's status was low, his widow later received an allowance comparable to that received by the high-ranking families of those who committed *junshi*. . . . A nephew took the name Gosuke and thereafter his house served in the capacity of surrogate for various *han* offices for many generations."[41]

Gosuke's case is also paradigmatic of the film in its foreshadowing of the class issue taken up by the servant Tasuke in the very next scene. Although the character of Tasuke does not appear in Ogai's novella, the issue of junshi and social class is specifically addressed in Gosuke's case by describing his resistance to the elder statesmen's advice to spare himself, even though he had obtained Lord Tadatoshi's permission. Ogai here raises the issue of junshi as ruling class canard by describing the elders' condescending advice, and Gosuke even mentions it in his farewell poem![42] Ogai's story also makes a point of reporting Gosuke's wife's final words: "Gosuke, you too are a man. Show that you are not inferior to those who are prominent retainers."[43]

Another monumental sequence is the scene in which stipends of the surviving Hosokawa retainers are reapportioned (3). This is a classic instance of objectified spectatorship, a figure of style that makes a spectacle of a ritual collective configuration. The scene begins with an extreme long shot of the hall in which the audience with the new Hosokawa administration takes place. The shot is held as samurai enter from the wings, and held further as the new daimyo and his retinue take their places at the front. When the space is fully occupied, the unity of the congregation is graphically emphasized by orchestrating a deep formal bow to the new daimyo in perfect unison, like some graceful collective organism or samurai "wave." The action is striking in the grace with which it is orchestrated and executed as well as its scale, including at least 150 samurai congregated in the space.

The orderliness, opulence, and formality of the occasion is quintessentially monumental because the samurai are not presenting themselves to the camera, as is the case in a Western-style collective spectacle (e.g., Busby Berkeley). Rather, this particular configuration is justified by the presence of the daimyo seated in the far background. Yet the camera's position at the back of the hall offers a unique perspective on the action in the way that each row of samurai bows just after the rows immediately ahead, resulting in that striking, dominolike illusion of collective, concerted motion. The wave also moves its way back up to the front in reverse, i.e., the samurai rows in the rear raise their heads first, then the succeeding rows in the middle, with the front rows finally uplifting their faces at the very end to complete the collective gesture. This reversal of the motion makes its orchestration all the more remarkable because in raising their heads from rear to front the samurai are not just timing their action according to movements of those sitting before them, but behind them where they can't see—a sense of perfect correspondence is maintained between decorum and deference, between the time that it is appropriate to remain bowed and the distance between samurai and lord.

A samurai "wave" as objectified spectatorship. Frame enlargement, courtesy of Toho Company.

Such pro forma collective configurations are belied, however, when the stipends are announced, indicating which families are favored with raises. Such configurations apparently have deliberate thematic meanings in addition to a decorative function. The Abe clan is shocked by the new administration's decision: its allowance is to be broken up between Abe and his several sons, thereby fragmenting the fortunes of the family and hence its status as a unified clan. By this time the shots originate from the front of the space where the announcements are made and are fragmented between shots of the daimyo and the startled faces of his retainers.

Significantly, the order of the stipend scene is changed in the film to make it come before Abe's suicide, whereas in the novella it comes after Abe kills himself. The order of story events in the film implies, therefore, that Abe commits junshi because and in protest of the breaking up of the clan fortunes. In the novella the redistribution of the stipends is a confirmation of the futility of Abe's suicide. Ogai, however, faults the narrow-minded inconsistency of the new administration in its handling of the affair. "Although the younger brothers gained individually in stipend, they now felt a difference, for while they formerly stood under the protection of a more than one-thousand-*koku* main-branch house as under some large, sheltering tree, they now stood equally in stipend but the sheltering tree was gone."[44]

Through the fragmentation of the household's fortunes, the household itself is broken up. This implies a veiled rebuke by the new daimyo to

Gombe, who otherwise would have succeeded as heir to the Abe clan. The rebuke therefore sanctions the daimyo's contempt toward Abe for not committing junshi, then committing unauthorized junshi. Ogai, then, is very specific in his condemnation of the daimyo's inconsistency as the occasion and perhaps a cause of the Abe clan's humiliation in the eyes of the community. Perhaps this is why Kumagai chose to have Abe commit junshi after the redistribution of stipends, as a way of identifying the policy decision that publically slaps the face of the Abe clan.

In the film Abe's response is suicide. His suicide is occasioned not by misery, as in the case of Kazuma, nor by bushido glory, as in the case of the eighteen who committed authorized junshi. His suicide is a carefully considered response to the community that saddled him with such an unreasonable Catch-22. It is a defiant gesture, but also one of self-abnegation. It is a sacramental ceremony, a covenant Abe makes with his sons, reminiscent of the religious significance of the Last Supper.

Yet it lacks the piety of the junshi sequences that open the film, because Abe's self-mockery lends a levity to the episode that humanizes the monumental tendencies of the scene. Full of high angle shots through the rain and misty lights of lanterns, the technique conveys a sense of reverence and repose, a fitting farewell to a venerable samurai about to join his master. But Abe prances around the space drunk, cracking jokes and singing silly songs in a most unsacramental fashion. Abe is a scapegoat, taking on himself the absurdities of a world where one must have permission to die as much as to live. In the black comedy of Abe's suicide there is an undercurrent of bitterness, but there is also a sincere hope that his exhortation to his sons to stick together will yield a more just outcome. This does not happen. Instead, a new generation of scapegoats arises, the sons cavorting in absurd farewell ceremonies and dying like "a swarm of bugs in a dish devouring one another"[45] (12).

The ambivalence toward junshi at work in the narrative finds its way into the most monumental sequences of the film. Conversely, there are numerous variations on the monumental style that playfully call attention to themselves as departures from the usual figures of monumentalism. These are mostly experiments in framing and shot scale that are at odds with the highly composed iconography of the monumental style.

Following the prologue, which introduces the theme of junshi, Abe and his retinue are introduced when they meet yet another junshi prospect. As Ihara, the samurai in question, ascends the temple steps, a reaction shot from his spatial point of view reveals Tasuke the servant and his master Abe gazing up after him. The perspective of this two-shot is peculiar and striking, with Tasuke standing in center foreground smiling up at the camera and Abe in the right background looking up in apparent suspicion. Since Tasuke is standing on the lower steps and Abe is standing on the ground behind him, Abe appears much smaller than Tasuke and actually looks like he is perched on Tasuke's shoulder. The background accentuates this illusion by flattening the perspective, since the ground appears as if it is rising up behind Abe like some angular expressionistic theater set. With the combination of high-angle shooting and low-angle lighting, the shadows are very prominent, dwarfing the impotent figure of Abe in the background.

Thematically it is a strange and emblematic shot because what looks like Abe's suspicion toward Ihara actually turns out to be envy, couched in disapproval of Tasuke's open admiration. More than this, the scale and perspective of this shot privileges it as a marker of meaning that is central to the film: if junshi is a performance, who is it done for? Does it solidify the relationship between samurai and lord? Is there greater regard between members of the surviving community? Is it essentially an exclusive gesture of kinship between members of a privileged class? How is one to approach the spectacle of junshi? With admiration? Scepticism? Envy? Nostalgia? The optical distortion of perspective in this shot cues the viewer to attend to such questions and to take care that one's judgment rests on reliable perceptions.

If this is stretching the significance of a single reaction shot to the break-

"A swarm of bugs in a dish devouring one another":
Mori Ogai's *Abe Ichizoku*.

A new generation in the Abe clan takes up the gourd.
Kawakita Memorial Film Archives.

ing point, we can leave it at this: thematically and perceptually, the shot
calls our attention to the conflicting meanings that can be attached to the
practice of junshi. The fact that the conflict here is one of class, that a servant takes one point of view and his master the opposite, points toward a
fundamental disturbance occasioned by junshi's function as an ideology of
the ruling class, as a fiction foisted upon the mass of people who are not
samurai. In a review essay on the origins of democracy, the historian Keith
Thomas writes,

> To subdue a people and keep them subdued, a ruler needed his
> subjects' acquiescence; and that acquiescence was usually
> secured not by a show of force but by propagating a theory, or
> fiction, that gave the ruler legitimacy. Most of these fictions por-
> trayed rule by the few as natural and normal. The authority of
> royal dynasties and governing elites was sanctioned by religion
> and justified by tradition. The rulers were portrayed as inher-
> ently superior persons, whether by virtue of their descent, their
> innate ability, their special training, or their semidivinity.[46]

In the case of samurai about to commit junshi, all four of these tests of superiority apply. Samurai perpetuated their prerogatives not just by virtue of
their divine right, or their socialization, or aptitude, or their pedigree—but

The servant Tasuke admiring the serenity of a retainer favored with suicide. Frame enlargement, courtesy of Toho Company.

Tasuke and Yaichiemon at the same location. Publicity still, Kawakita Memorial Film Archives.

Tasuke pays his respects to the favored retainer.
Kawakita Memorial Film Archives.

by all means. Thus for a commoner to be granted permission to commit junshi was a rare privilege indeed. But one must ask, who benefits from the "privilege" of such fanatical loyalty?

I hasten to add that the disturbance to which I refer—junshi as ruling class canard—is a symptomatic meaning, not an implicit one.[47] That is, in no way can *The Abe Clan* be considered a deliberately subversive film; it is rather an ambivalent film, a film whose style and narrative structure carve out an ideological position whose implications are not consistent with its apparent sympathies. Another way of saying this might be to consider *The Abe Clan* an overdetermined film in that its promotion of bushido and junshi protests too much: the lengths gone to show samurai valor permeating every social relationship—those with family, friends, potential lovers, domestic help, even pets—betrays problematic areas the film might be trying to hide.

There are a few other departures from monumental techniques. Several "intrusive" cuts in the course of the film, like mismatched concertina, 180-degree cheat cuts, and matches-on-action whose shot scales do not at all match. This last instance involves Tasuke again (5). As a result of the stipend redistribution, the eldest son Gombe has informed Tasuke that his services are no longer required. Devastated, Tasuke is about to kill himself before the grave of his erstwhile master, Abe Yaichiemon. In close-up, he prepares the dagger, and is about to thrust it home when he is interrupted by Yagobe, the second son. As he jumps up in surprise, there is a cut to an extreme long shot of Tasuke and Yagobe across the empty courtyard. The cut is noticeably flashy and disjunctive, motivated perhaps by Tasuke's surprise and delight at being told he can work for Yagobe. A more "canonically" monumental way of handling the transition would be a painstakingly slow dolly, or better, crane movement backward until the opulence of the castle courtyard dwarfs the two figures. This would monumentalize the episode by granting it a scale larger than life. But Kumagai prefers a slightly less oblique technique.

He also employs rack focus, a technique beloved by chambara potboilers. Rack focus is generally used in dramatic scenes of tension or argument, and especially in the final scene of combat. When Yagobe and his neighbor Matashichiro square off on either side of a hanging brazier, the camera repeatedly refocuses on the fraying rope between them. It snaps, and Matashichiro lunges into the plane of focus to deliver the mortal thrust. Meanwhile the rest the of Abe clan is being massacred by the sharpshooters brought in by the daimyo. A point of view shot shows Abe soldiers falling and dying, cut down by bullets spewed out of the rifle barrels at the bottom of the frame. A reverse angle reveals the tense faces of the riflemen concentrating on their targets, then a rack focus brings the lethal ends of the rifle muzzle to the very center of attention.

These techniques certainly dynamize the action, but they are more typical of Sam Peckinpah than of the monumental style. The fact that *The Abe Clan* has action sequences at all is a concession, if we take the ascetic, spirit-centered monumental style as our standard. Still they are anomalies in what is mostly an austere, reserved samurai film with a serious purpose rather than a chambara escape vehicle.

The Abe Clan is nevertheless an entertaining film. Its hieratic aspects are bent to the purpose of telling a powerful, sometimes bitter story. It contrasts markedly with its impassive literary source. This is surprising for a film in the monumental style, whose sacramental gravity often tends toward the rarefied and the pious. The monumental style is typically concerned more with exhortation than with entertainment, but *The Abe Clan* is entertaining because its departures from the monumental style give it a verve and restlessness just short of the perverse. Still, it serves up in the end its ideology in a style that makes a sacrament of sacrifice, and in this way upholds "traditional" values. The childlike character of the Abe family is very appealing. It gives the family an idiosyncracy and intimacy that earns it the ire of the daimyo and eventually leads to its destruction. By the end, we sympathize with the "noble failure" and hate the daimyo, whose concern with official samurai protocol translates into a cruel massacre of all the children, women, and men of the Abe clan. As a result we are left with the impression that the true keepers of bushido are not the daimyo or samurai but the children and the childlike, the servants, maids, and dog handlers.

8

Other Manifestations of the Monumental Style

Monumentalism, Orientalism, and Gate of Hell

In the introduction I suggested that an important aspect of the monumental style is its legacy in subsequent jidai geki. Monumental style, in its exemplary works from the late 1930s, consists of fewer than a dozen strong examples. But this does not compromise the integrity of monumentalism as a stylistic category. Rather, like other extreme stylistic movements in the history of art (Futurism, Fauvism) or film (Soviet montage, German expressionism), monumentalism entered mainstream film practice in relatively diluted form. Although the monumental style screens a vivid picture of an official Japanese national identity between 1936 and 1941, the films were not popular enough to spawn great numbers of imitations, the sincerest form of compliment in any film industry. Nonetheless, the films were highly regarded by critics and had an influence on subsequent films out of proportion to their lack of popularity. The fact that there are relatively few "pure" monumental films means only that the style was diffused through films that balance monumental elements with more conventional elements like linear narrative, dramaturgical spectacle, and cathartic melodrama.

But there is still a paradox in the postwar development and degeneration of monumental style. In 1940 pictures like Kinugasa's *Kawanakajima Kassen* portrayed the feudal battlefield as a place of awesome beauty and its warriors as members of a family caught up in something like an act of God. Kinugasa's contribution to monumental style consists in the deification of battle by humanizing its participants and naturalizing its spectacle as something sublime and implacable (chapter 4). Considerations of motive and culpability are evacuated by the aestheticizing of war, to borrow Walter Benjamin's conceit. Starting in 1945, Occupation censors banned the production and distribution of jidai geki on the grounds that they harbored vestiges of feudalism. Films in the monumental style are indeed "feudal," but the SCAP authorities could not conceive of jidai geki that might be critical of feudalism, as in Kurosawa's 1945 *Tora no o o fumu otokotachi* (*Men Who Tread on the Tiger's Tail*), which was not released until 1953. All jidai geki, therefore, were ipso facto suppressed in the name of democracy and free speech until the early 1950s.[1] With *Rashomon* (1950), Kurosawa showed that jidai geki could be self-critical and appeal to a broad art house audience around the world. But *Rashomon* is too existential in its themes and modernist in its technique to be much in debt to the monumental style. Mizoguchi's *Saikaku ichidai onna* (*The Life of Oharu*, 1952) and *Sansho Dayu* (*Sansho the Bailiff*, 1954) and Kobayashi's *Kwaidan* (1964) and *Seppuku* (1963), similarly feted on European festival circuits, also take a critical stance toward feudalism while maximizing the pictorial appeal of exotic settings.

Kinugasa's *Jigoku Mon* (*Gate of Hell*, 1953), touted as the first period film in color, "cashed in on an international hunger for delicious illusions"[2] and garnered a Best Foreign Film Academy award and the Grand Prize at Cannes. Its success is attributable largely to the use of techniques pioneered in the prewar period film, especially in films of the monumental style. The irony of Kinugasa's success lies in the postwar recuperation of a style forged to express an indigenous national identity free from foreign adulteration. Kinugasa himself had a major part in creating the "Japanist" associations of the monumental style. He had also been among the most experimental of directors in the 1920s with his surrealist classic *Kurutta ippeiji* (*Page of Madness*, 1926).[3] What began as a stylistic movement to purge jidai geki of alien influences evolved into a shorthand stylization of things Japanese for Western consumption.

Like SLR cameras, videodecks, automobiles, and silicon chips, *Gate of Hell* flows with that ever widening river of postwar goods Japanese-designed for Western consumers. A high-profile production of Daiei, the studio that released both *Rashomon* and Mizoguchi's *Ugetsu*, the film is a repackaging of jidai geki to suit art house tastes for exotica. From the start it is easy to identify what made the film a festival favorite. Based on a story by an author with an international reputation (Kikuchi Kan), the film uses big stars with worldwide popularity (Kyo Machiko had appeared in *Rashomon* and *Ugetsu* and Hasegawa Kazuo was on his way to becoming the "grand old man" of the Japanese cinema).[4] Akutagawa Ryunosuke, the author of the story on which *Rashomon* was based, had also written a version of the Kesa and Moritoh story. The newly introduced Eastmancolor process is prominently featured; its speed and economy made it an attractive alternative to Technicolor and also produced more muted, "natural"-looking colors. *Variety* could not resist pointing out the superiority of the Eastman process over locally developed color systems by Toho and Shochiku.[5] Finally, the opening musical theme sounds like a Japanization of a score for a John Ford Western, complete with harps and strings in a minor key, following the somber cadences of a deep drum. Like *Rashomon*, the richly orchestrated score conforms more to someone's idea of the "mysterious Orient" than to any authentic reproduction of Japanese music. The *New York Times*'s Bosley Crowther and the *Variety* reviewer were full of breathy words like "weird and exquisite," to describe in particular the formality of movement and music, which possessed a "weird eloquence and grace that are profound."[6]

Gate of Hell tells the story of a valiant samurai, Moritoh, who distinguishes himself in the rebellion of the Genji clan in the twelfth century, commemorated in the famous epic *Heike Monogatari*. His is an exemplary sense of royalist loyalty since he helps crush the rebel faction in which his own brother is fighting. But his military valor does not serve him well in peacetime. He falls in love with the woman who acted as decoy for the empress during the fray, and is not dissuaded when finding out she is married to a prominent retainer at court. The majority of the film details his attempts to forcibly win her over, and when he threatens to kill her husband she outwits him and saves her virtue by sacrificing herself in her husband's stead.

While prewar monumental films try to integrate their traditionalism within the diegesis, *Gate of Hell* explicitly anchors it within a discrete graphic and aural exposition. A scroll depicting the 1160 Heiji revolt is rolled out by a disembodied hand while a voiceover tells of the perennial struggles between the Taira and Genji clans. In the twelfth century the lat-

Lady Kesa gripped by obsessive desire in *Gate of Hell*. Museum of Modern Art Film Stills Archive.

ter tried to overthrow the former by staging a rebellion and abducting the imperial family. The first thirty minutes of the film dramatizes this background material, but except for the fact that the protagonist Moritoh meets his obsession, Lady Kesa, in the course of the rebellion, this background remains just that: gratuitous spectacle with little plot justification.

Compared to the battles in Kinugasa's earlier *Kawanakajima Kassen* (see chapter 4), the revolt is rather cosmetic, a short history lesson and mood piece illustrating the colorful ferocity of Japanese costumed swordplay. Though not unified within the main plot, the revolt does establish key aspects of the protagonist's character. Moritoh (Hasegawa Kazuo) distinguishes himself as a loyalist in the suppression of the revolt, even against his own brother. Moritoh's heroism, however, is framed by the bookend depiction of the Heiji handscrolls themselves at both beginning and end of this background episode.

Moritoh's valor is therefore consigned to the picturesque antiquity of a twelfth-century handscroll, and his subsequent behavior in the "real" (i.e., nonhistorical, diegetic) story of his infatuation with Kesa becomes a cartoonish throwback to bushido theatrics. The "backcountry samurai," as he is derisively called by Kesa's attendants, is a dangerous figure in a peaceful court society when he brings his obsessions into the domestic sphere. While his bullish perseverance can initially be tolerated, perhaps even admired, his peers and superiors gradually withdraw in irritation, then alarm, when Moritoh's desire seeks satisfaction in bloodshed. On the one hand, the historical material on the Heiji conflict is a segment that establishes a discrete time and ethos; on the other, its uncompromising ferocity is carried into the main story of the ménage à trois by the figure of Moritoh. In this way it is similar to the ambivalent historical dialectic of *The Abe Clan*, with its meditations on transitional ethics, or indeed the transitional postwar situation of *Gate of Hell* itself.

The narrative gratuitousness of the historical prologue, then, does have an important place in the overall structure of the film. In the peaceful aftermath of the revolt's suppression, the martial fanaticism shown by Moritoh is an anachronism, a passionate, anarchic aberration. This is how Moritoh looks to modern spectators, partly because the Heiji revolt is so clearly marked off as an event, and an artifact, of remote antiquity.

But this is also how Moritoh looks to Lady Kesa and her husband, Wataru, and increasingly to Moritoh's fellow samurai. The historical and ethical fixation of Moritoh is abandoned by the same characters who shared with him the conflict dramatized in the Heike scroll. In the first section of the film Kesa, Wataru, Lord Kiyomori, and others are part of that ancient diorama dominated by Moritoh's heroics, but, subsequently, they

Moritoh, the shell-shocked veteran of *Gate of Hell*. Museum of Modern Art
Film Stills Archive.

share the modern perspective on Moritoh as a shell-shocked veteran fixated on his wartime exploits. The historical irony is that Moritoh's code of
bushido is the one that eventually wins out. *Gate of Hell* could profitably be
seen, then, as a cautionary film about the historical origins of bushido in
the twelfth century. Metaphorically, the film also offers a veiled suggestion
on the psychic aftermath of the war: we ignore the aftershocks at our
peril—not only those of the war itself but also of the abrupt transition from
a desperate war to a desperate economic catch-up. The film appears to
denounce bushido heroics as inappropriate in peacetime, but the denunci-
ation itself depends upon a monumental militarism beaten into Orientalist
ploughshares.

   If *Gate of Hell* appears to be a broken-backed concatenation of historical
spectacle with obsessive love story, a closer analysis of the "hinge" between
these parts reveals a more intricate structure. Shortly after the revolt breaks
out, we first see the eponymous gate from a low angle. The camera slowly
tilts and pans down to reveal a group of peasants gossiping about the rebellion's outcome. In this plain homage to *Rashomon*, they explain how the gate
got its name—from the hundreds of beheadings necessary to ensure the
security of the existing regime. To the eerie strains of a samisen played by
a blind priest, there is a slow pan past the wall painting of a hideous vision

of hell, rather like a Japanese version of Bosch's inferno. The painting serves as a touchstone image of chaos and degeneration, because it serves no apparent purpose in the plot or in the development of character. It sets a mood that is designed to permeate the rest of the film; as Anderson and Richie note,

> The influence of the graphic arts, always strong in Mizoguchi's work, was readily apparent but was quite different from that seen in, say, *Gate of Hell*. In the Kinugasa film, the influence consists of literal copying of the attitudes and tableaux seen in Japanese paintings; in the Mizoguchi film, the graphic arts have been fully "cinematized."[7]

The imposition rather than integration of traditional graphics is easily seen in the transition cut from a tilt up to the clouds within the wall painting to real clouds in the sky. The transition is smoothed over by a sound bridge provided by the samisen music; the inference to be made is that the world inhabited by Moritoh is in some sense the same as the hell screen depicted on the wall of the Gate of Hell. This interlude, begun by tilting down from the sky, depicts Moritoh riding down the couriers sent to Lord Kiyomori to report on the rebellion. The segue from the hell screen is

Itsukushima noh performance. Museum of Modern Art Film Stills Archive.

bracketed by another quick cut to the famous torii of Itsukushima (whose cultural associations remain implicit),[8] then a close-up on a wildly gesturing performer in a demon mask from the noh.

For a moment there lingers a long view of the performance space on the famous open-air platform. But unlike the noh performance in *Genroku Chushingura*, the noh representation lends only the cachet of Japanese theatrical practice. Instead of emphasizing the whole congregation in long shot, the audience ranged around the stage is immediately fragmented into one-shots of individuals. Rather than concentrating on the perceptual force of collective, objectified spectatorship in long shot, the figures of individual characters such as Lord Kiyomori and a Minamoto spy-priest, are isolated, and thus introduced, by the framing. The composition and blocking of the shots are designed for maximal clarity of exposition rather than the maximization of a traditional theatrical aura.

The same effect occurs in the scene at Rokuhara where the loyal samurai are being rewarded by Lord Kiyomori. A high angle prevails on the congregated samurai, which clearly lays out the orderly rows in which they sit and wait for the bounty from their lord. But the shots of Moritoh pick him out from the end of a row of samurai to show his face in exact profile. Each samurai is asked to name his reward. At first, Moritoh asks for a married woman, Kesa, and the assembled samurai in the background chuckle. But Moritoh only glowers. He insists that Lord Kiyomori honor his word and refuses to back down. This time, Moritoh's rigid profile is flanked by outrage and disbelief from the samurai who kneel in the background. In both cases the congregation is used as a device to highlight the behavior of Moritoh. Objectified spectatorship is used here, but its function is not a collective representation of group feeling but rather a configuration that spotlights the main character.

Gate of Hell is full of such classical Hollywood-style appropriations of Japanese manners and design for the purpose of character exposition. The film is primarily a character-centered romantic conflict against a historical backdrop. The antiquity of its setting is a device to secure the appeal of the remote and the exotic; even the symbolic functions of its graphics and architecture (the Heiji handscroll, the hell painting, Itsukushima Shrine) are merely expressive, rather than referential. Kinugasa makes little effort to bend the conventions of classical cinema to those of classical Japanese design, as is done in films of the monumental style. In *Gate of Hell*, he does just the opposite.

Since proving himself so adept at making films in the monumental style, what better figure than Kinugasa to purvey monumental techniques to a post-*Rashomon* international public? The irony is exquisite when we recall that the monumental style, as the most prestigious offering in the kokusaku campaign, was designed to be a corrective to the excesses of chambara and other decadent (American-style) influences. In *Gate of Hell*, as in other post-war jidai geki, militarism is neatly dropped and pictorialism is intensified. The monumental style thus became exoticized, strategically, for export in postwar jidai geki.

This is not simply my interpretation of the film, but a point made by the Japanese consul general, Tsuchiya Jun, at the opening of the film in New York:

> The successful entree of Japanese films in the world market may well have not only cultural, but also, I venture to suggest, economic consequences for both our countries. . . . [the] export of superior films will greatly help my country in its present unremitting struggle to become self-sufficient, to rely on trade, not aid. We will continue to strive side-by-side with the United States for human betterment and freedom in Asia.[9]

Kinugasa's earlier film, *Kawanakajima Kassen*, contains premonitions of an internationalized monumentalism that is taken up explicitly in Kurosawa's *Kagemusha* (1980). We now turn to Kurosawa's role in attenuating the monumental style.

Theatrical Appropriations: Kagemusha *(1980)* *and* Ran *(1985)*

In technique and theme *Kagemusha* conforms closely to the monumental prototype. It is a samurai film emphasizing the lavish design, costume, and decorum of feudal Japan, using an austere cinematography and editing to bring out the majesty of the historical period. It is unusual for Kurosawa, but standard procedure for the monumental style, to take a story directly from the established historical record. Though the conceit of a "shadow warrior," or double, for the famous warlord Takeda Shingen is no more than a historical footnote, Kurosawa nevertheless incorporates into the film well-known persons, events, and details from the late Sengoku (Warring States) period, from 1467–1568.[10] Ingeniously, Kurosawa also integrates into his technique key issues from the reconstructed historical record. As in *Kawanakajima*, the monumental style in *Kagemusha* takes shape partly as a function of the technological dynamics of war. Kurosawa goes further than Kinugasa, however, in identifying the specifically European provenance of killing technologies. At the same time, the film modernizes the touchstone issue of the monumental style, the problem of historical authenticity, by transforming it into a more existential problem of personal identity. *Kagemusha* is a modern updating of the monumental style by appropriating classic tropes of the historical record for the purpose of questioning their status as authorized classical icons.

Tanizaki's elegy for a doomed age of traditional Japanese decorum and indirection, *In Praise of Shadows*, questions the headlong mechanization of urban life (see the quotation in the introduction). But Kurosawa goes further by questioning the adequacy of the tradition itself, asking how the signs and signals of tradition became so privileged in the first place. The film centers on a thief who happens to possess identical features to that of the famous warlord Takeda Shingen. Shingen is wounded and dies early in the film, and the thief is forced to play his double in order to maintain the stability of the realm. The shadow warrior is presented to his men, then to his clan and attendants, and finally to his women, grandchild, and favorite horse. His performance is so spectacular that he begins to earn the envy of other warlords who know his true identity. The film concludes with a trivial incident that exposes the ruse, destroys faith in the Shingen clan, and leads to a pitched battle in which the clan is destroyed. David Desser has written that *Kagemusha* is an an elegiac allegory of the samurai genre itself: "To Kurosawa, the Samurai film, perhaps even his own, is a mere sham . . . in showing so clearly that film, history, and myth may be reduced to mere signification, Kurosawa is denying us a sense that these are also more than signification."[11]

The American version of *Kagemusha* runs about 160 minutes (the Japanese version about twenty minutes longer), and its pace makes it seem longer still. A shot sequence of perhaps five minutes opens the film prior to any credits or other expository information. In long shot we are introduced to the warlord Takeda Shingen, his brother Nobukado, and a common thief, whose face is virtually indistinguishable from that of Shingen (in fact they are played by the same actor, Nakadai Tatsuya). As Shingen and Nobukado calmly discuss the potential usefulness of the thief as a double, he sits on the floor, bound and brooding. Due to the scale of the shot and the costumes of the players, the three men appear as mirror images of one another: a weird visual contrast to the absolute power wielded over the thief by the two lords. The thief is reminded of his fate, death by crucifixion, for the crime of malingering and looting. He laughs bitterly as he spits out the irony of his crucifixion for petty theft while his captors enjoy honor and glory for mass murder and the pillage of entire provinces.

The long immobile take, the "triplication" of the characters, and the arbitrariness of the divisions between them set the stage for the rest of the film. The leisurely deliberation of the sequence, along with its visual and dramatic austerity, plainly marks it in the tradition of the monumental style.

But things here also initiate motifs that work against classical, monumental evocations of feudal history. The Takeda family crest carved in a heavy, dark wood dominates the wall space behind Shingen, overwhelmingly resembling the imperial chrysanthemum crest. The totem looms over the three figures and links them in a common symbol that overrides the individual differences between them. The metonymic and metaphoric power of totems and talismans, especially as it obtains in the figure of the *kagemusha* (shadow warrior), is the central theme of the film. It is also important to note the absence of the most crucial totem in the samurai arsenal: the sword. Despite the film's delirious battle footage, the use of the traditional longsword (*katana*) is conspicuously missing. This is a constitutive absence with respect to *Kagemusha*'s emphasis on history, technology, and signification.

Finally, the three men are linked by their costumes, which all have a bit of red-orange sash tucked away in their folds. This color is almost fluorescent in its insistence, dragging the eye away from the total configuration to these seemingly irrelevant red flashes. Both these motifs, the Shingen totem and the red flashes, introduce elements that open a wedge for the entry of nonclassical, perhaps antimonumental themes into the film. As the sequence ends, however, the power of ceremony again asserts itself. Shingen gets up to leave, having enjoined Nobukado to begin training the thief for his duties, and as he walks off, Nobukado and the thief both bow deeply in the direction of his departure. The monumental pace and deportment of the scene is maintained as it cuts to the title credit.

A perennial figure in monumental style, objectified spectatorship, also enjoys a prominent place in *Kagemusha*. The wounded Shingen addresses his retainers in a formal audience at which he insists that his death must be kept secret for three years. The long shot/long take is shot from the back of the hall facing Shingen, and when his will has been formally pronounced, the assembled warlords characteristically bow their heads low to the floor in unison. Here, as in the opening shot sequence, the orange-red hues of the retainers' costumes take on an exaggerated prominence. By this time the color has taken on a specific connotation: that of the spilled blood spattered over the lower levels of Tokugawa's Noda castle. The castle had been under siege by the Takeda army until Shingen was shot by a nighttime sniper. The hot reds of the samurai undergarments evoke an unmistakeable visual rhyme with the blood-red carnage spilled along the steps and passageways of Noda castle.

Kagemusha: the thief and "his" grandson. Museum of Modern Art
Film Stills Archive.

In other places objectified spectatorship takes on a more important role
in the plot. Scene 16 has two parts: first, the thief must fool Shingen's
grandson into thinking that he really is the boy's grandfather; second, the
thief is introduced to the guards and attendants in his private chambers.
These five know who the thief is, so there is no need for deceit. Yet the
framing of this sequence in private chambers is more formal than that of
the sequence with the grandson in the main hall, which is rife with tension
and suspense. In chambers the thief takes the elevated place of honor at
extreme right, while guards, attendants, and Nobukado arrange themselves
before him in the central part of the frame. It is here, in private where there
is no need to pretend that the thief is a lord, that Nobukado exhorts them
all to maintain the illusion of the shadow warrior. Here it is revealed that
Nobukado himself once performed the *kagemusha* role for his brother Shingen. He stresses the difficulty of maintaining someone else's identity in
one's own body (comparing it to crucifixion) and demands complete dedi-
cation: "The shadow of a man cannot desert that man."

Nobukado leaves on a lighter note, by warning the thief not to get lost
in his own house, and all present bow deeply as he departs. The guards and
attendants introduce themselves to the thief, and as they do so relax their
posture and sit crosslegged instead of in the more formal position on their
knees. They laugh at the thief's buffoonery for a minute, but then he strikes
a certain reflective pose, hand on chin, and suddenly they change their

behavior markedly. Rising again to their knees, they stare in disbelief, then break into tears, as the thief's demeanor transforms his gestures from mere mannerism of the late lord into genuine presence. The thief has found a congruence between his ability to impersonate Shingen and the typical Shingen behavior called for in this particular situation. The witnesses are aghast and react with their body language in unison to this uncanny reproduction of their late lord's personality. They are transformed instantly from suspicious, churlish pages to genuinely devoted retainers—even though they still know the identity of the thief. Their collective spectatorial activity is what confers a kind of authenticity on the illusion of Shingen's presence. For them Shingen's personality is called forth by a collective invocation of Shingen that flies in the face of intellectual knowledge of the thief's real identity. Presence here becomes a contractual relation between personalities, observers, and a specific situation, rather than a simple matter of individual personal identity.

Later there is a still more harrowing episode involving objectified spectatorship. A formal council is called concerning the Takeda clan's response to Tokugawa's attacks on outlying strongholds. All the Takeda warlords, and their retainers, are present, and only six of them know Shingen's true identity. The camera cranes rightward over the heads of the assembled retainers, then cuts in to a long shot over Shingen's head at the line of warlords arguing what to do. Suddenly Shingen's son Katsuyori asks his "father's" opinion, knowing full well who he really is. Up to this point all we have seen of Shingen is the back of his broad figure presiding over the discussion. Now the discussion ceases and all faces look earnestly at the place where Shingen sits (out at us). But the thief again rises to the occasion. Drawing on a lesson learned from one of his pages, he draws himself up, takes a deep breath and says, "Do not move. The mountain stays put." And, with a flourish, the thief concludes the meeting and departs, having dispensed sound advice to the clan not to be drawn into a protracted conflict with Tokugawa. The camera cranes back along the congregation of retainers as they bow in deep gratitude, secure in the shadow of their imperturbable lord. But Shingen's son Katsuyori has been humiliated, and this eventually leads to the fall of the Takeda clan.

The sequence is perhaps the most monumental of any in the film, but it is built on a lie. The long takes, graceful camera movements, and formal arrangements and declamations are all indications of the film's complicity with the central deceit. Rather than chop the sequence into suspense-stretching close-ups of the central antagonists, Katsuyori and his "father," the sequence is filmed de rigueur, with appropriately dignified monumental devices (i.e., long takes, long shots, emphasizing the congregation and suppressing facial expression). The spectator is blessed with superior knowledge that allows him or her to appreciate the significance of Katsuyori's challenge. But most of the congregation present, the gathering of samurai whose ceremonial presence calls forth the monumental treatment of the episode, remain oblivious. Because they do not know Shingen's real identity, the *in*appropriateness of the monumental style here makes no difference. In this case the monumental style cannot derive from an authentic outpouring of leadership and loyalty, as is the case in prewar exemplars. The monumental style here is a form of "stylistic self-interrogation" used as an invidious exposure of the conventionality of bushido decorum.[12] The use of stylistic markers of sincere samurai dignity is undercut by its coupling with a phony surrogate. Kurosawa here drives a wedge between a typical stylistic device and the thing it conventionally represents.

Evocations of history and personality become a form of shorthand wherein certain techniques, like objectified spectatorship or displacement of action through cutaways, stand in for the substance they supposedly represent. Like *Kawanakajima*, the film is full of spectacle, but the action is often displaced. At the final battle at Nagashino three battalions of the Takeda clan are mowed down by Oda Nobunaga's matchlockmen. Each battalion charges to the left and is intercut with shots of the riflemen firing

Graphic displacement of violence in *Kagemusha*. Museum of Modern Art Film Stills Archive.

right from behind their long barricade. Instead of showing the impact, the conflict is displaced onto the ashen-faced thief, now forced to bear witness to the slaughter of his surrogate clan. After the massacre there is a leisurely pan along the wide expanse of the plain where thousands of bloody bodies lie dead and dying. The carnage is magnified with close-ups of horses and men struggling in very slow motion, writhing in pain, stumbling through the blood and mud of the battlefield. The horror of battle is suggested precisely through the refusal to dwell upon the moment of killing; we linger in grotesque close-up and slow motion on the aftermath, like the maid in *The Abe Clan* and Neya in *Kawanakajima*.

But there is something excessive, even spurious about these shots, as if they came from an Arthur Penn, a Sam Peckinpah, or a John Woo battle climax. This is a deliberate nod at the "catholicizing" of monumental style by the optical manipulation of the image necessary in a slow motion shot or even in the exaggerated red color of the costumes and gore. In a 1980 film super slow motion footage of battle carnage has little specific national or ideological connotation. (Aside from this, there is the further irony of Penn, Peckinpah, Leone, Woo, Lucas, and many other directors' debt to Kurosawa's technique, particularly his use of horses and slow motion in *Seven Samurai*.) The spuriousness or meretriciousness of the coda is in keeping with monumental rendering as a way of propping up an outmoded regime with a patriarch long dead. In the three years since Shingen's death, what is it that allows the clan to survive and even prosper?

The displacement of physical action onto an observer is matched by its displacement by technique. Like the climax of *Miyamoto Musashi*, Kurosawa stretches the anticipation of battle to the breaking point. Once it is clear that the Takeda clan is going to war, an entire scene is composed of preliminaries. We see a clash of spears as a gesture of solidarity and farewell between the Wind, Fire, and Forest battalions. Then the waiting begins. Like the waiting line of knights in Eisenstein's *Alexander Nevsky*, the film fixates on shots of windswept cavalry, fluttering banners, and anxious lancers squinting in the swirling dust. These shots have a precipitous tension about them because they are at the very cusp of the Takeda immolation to the tide of history and technology. We wait, holding our breath, for the inevitable confrontation of bullets and flesh. This stillness in the moments before death is a classic monumental device, one that Kurosawa exploits to the hilt. The surprise, or black joke, is that he fails to deliver the moment of impact, and instead signifies it metonymically through the eyes of the thief and the deadly crackling volleys of musket fire. The impact is displaced onto a stray soldier manqué, a shadow warrior who only belatedly runs onto the battlefield and falls, mercifully, to a stray musket ball.

The battle of Kawanakajima, fought only a few years earlier than Nagashino, was also decided by the deployment of muskets and cannons. Kinugasa's film is parallel to Kurosawa's in that the army with the guns prevails, while the apotheosis belongs to the army that loses. In *Kawanakajima*, the crafty, technologically superior Takeda clan overwhelms Uesugi Kenshin (recall the almost sacreligious eavesdropping of Uesugi's "moonlight serenade" by a Takeda spy), while *Kagemusha* has Takeda succumbing to the technological craft of Oda Nobunaga. Nobunaga is consistently associated with Western, specifically Jesuit, customs throughout the film. Not only does he build his military strategy on gunpowder, he drinks red wine (and laughs at Tokugawa's sour face when he tastes it), uses a cardinal's scarlet hat for a herald, and keeps Portuguese Jesuits on the payroll to ensure a providential outcome in times of war. In his embrace of foreign technology, customs, and religion, Nobunaga is obviously the advance guard. But within a few years it is the more circumspect, thoughtful Tokugawa who ushers in almost three hundred years of stifling unification. Under the Tokugawa shogunate firearms were banned, Christianity stamped out, and foreign barbarians either expelled or killed.

It is too easy to conclude, therefore, that Nobunaga's embrace of Portuguese gunpowder and Jesuit priestcraft is only a veneer of Westernization over an implacable Japanese heritage.[13] When Nobunaga hears of Shingen's death three years after the fact, he slowly rises and performs an impromptu noh turn, singing in classical verse, "Man's fifty years / Are but a phantom dream / In his journey through / The eternal transmigrations."[14] While some might see this as proof of Nobunaga's Christian hypocrisy, it is less ethnocentric to take it literally, a lament for the passing of a great warlord and for the credulousness of those who overlooked it. Furthermore, Nobunaga's song, especially its implied self-recrimination, has an appropriate ring in view of his violent suicide in Kyoto at age forty-eight (1582). Nobunaga is a virile, eccentric foe fully worthy of his role as antagonist of Shingen, but then he is apprised of the fact that he has been fighting a dummy daimyo all these years, and in fact was defeated at Takatenjin—by a shadow warrior. It is clear that Katsuyori's victory at Takatenjin is made possible by the enemy's belief that Shingen, the mountain, was there to reinforce Katsuyori's advances. Though Nobunaga is intriguing and full of panache, it is left to the more retiring, plump Tokugawa to prevail over his perennial rivals and unify the country.

The monumental style in *Kagemusha* functions as a swindle or red herring. While the monumental films of the late 1930s use style as an expression of bushido loyalty and historical authenticity, *Kagemusha* uses style to expose these ideological props as a sham. In a bizarre twist on the Christian doctrines that Oda Nobunaga professes, the thief is told to attend to the pile of dead bodyguards that surround him after the battle of Takatenjin: "Look. They died for you." The Japanese word used for "you" is *kisama*, or bastard. The speaker practically accuses the thief of responsibility for their deaths, but it is precisely these deaths that persuade the enemy that the impassive figure sitting beneath the Takeda banner is indeed Shingen. Whether or not the person occupying Shingen's spot is really Shingen simply does not matter. Daimyo will scheme, generals will plot their strategies, samurai will profess their undying loyalty, families will be proudly fatherless, and the whole spectacle will still be presented in the epic proportion, scale, and gravity of the monumental style. The reason it does not matter is that the significance of these things is a matter of spirit, a realm in which the believer has the last word. It is when everybody believes Shingen is dead, not before, that the Takeda clan falls.

But Kurosawa's emphasis on technological determinism strips away the spiritual trappings associated with monumental style. Desser points out the astonishing fact that "Kurosawa has made a Samurai film in which *no one dies by the sword.* . . . There is no 'Bushido' at work anymore, no elaborate ritualistic fights between two deadly swordsmen."[15] Even though *Kagemusha* strips substance from style, demythologizing the epic stature of bushido heroics, the power of style itself remains. The film is built on the persistence of the Japanese heroic legacy in the face of an impersonal, mechanical subversion of the warrior ethos. Oda Nobunaga, who vanquishes Shingen, is portrayed as a flamboyant pragmatist who disdains tradition and embraces Western technology in his rush to domination. Yet, as a warrior, Nobunaga himself avoided the use of guns as personal weapons, even as he outfitted his army with three ranks of *one thousand* gunners who killed *sixteen thousand* at the climactic battle of Nagashino in 1575.[16] A two-tiered army was the result of Nobunaga's personal distaste for guns as instruments unsuitable for demonstration of martial skill and bravery, yet plainly acknowledged as vastly superior long-range killing devices. "Skill had been moved back from the soldier to the manufacturer of his weapon and up from the soldier to his commander," writes Noel Perrin. "Partly for that reason, many of Lord Oda's matchlockmen were farmers and members of the yeomen class called *goshi* or *ji-samurai*, rather than *samurai* proper. It was a shock to everyone to find out that a farmer with a gun could kill the toughest *samurai* so readily."[17]

A deceptively prosaic scene shows a Nobunaga sniper explaining to his daimyo how he was able to hit Shingen with his muzzleloader in the dark. The sniper simply attaches a plumb line to his rifle and marks the spot in the earth when the muzzle is trained exactly on the chair soon to be occupied by Shingen. Word has leaked that Shingen wishes to hear the nightly flute solo that drifts over the walls and comforts the soldiers during their long siege. Ironically, Shingen has turned the flute into an omen: if he hears the flute, the castle will stand; if not, the castle will fall. The sniper tells Nobunaga that all he had to do was set up the rifle according to his measurements and blindly, mindlessly, fire. Writes Joseph Chang,

> Firing, he could be assured that he would hit the seat and any-
> one who held it. The special kind of mindlessness which the
> Zen practitioners would preach had been anticipated by
> another sort, the technological variety which has always trou-
> bled men more concerned with preserving human values than
> in sheer efficiency.[18]

On hearing the sniper's explanation, Nobunaga and Tokugawa agree that Shingen's retreat from Noda castle could be a ruse to lure away the castle occupants. But in the next scene Shingen actually dies in his palanquin. Shingen is dead, but his presence is kept alive. Thanks to the totemic power of the signs with which he is associated—his banners, flags, armor, horses, and especially the telltale gestures of a fortuitous lookalike—the Takeda clan cheats death, and triumphs on borrowed time. But one day the thief is thrown from Shingen's favorite horse, and, like the implacable rhyme about the lack of a nail ("the shoe was lost"), the war is lost and the Takeda kingdom with it. Since *Kagemusha* does not "belong" in the monumental style so much as makes an issue of it, the film reveals itself to be a most critical, yet rueful, vehicle of Japanese cultural identity. *Kagemusha* shows Japanese cultural identity to be bound to the encroachments of Western technology in the sixteenth century no less than in the twentieth, when Tanizaki lamented the passing of shadows. Could there be parallels between the successful banishment of that technology at the dawn of the Tokugawa period and the massive capitulation to it in Showa and before? A parallel involving a singular ambivalence toward the efficiency, rationalization, and irresistibility of Western technology, an admiration for its elegance and repugnance for its applications? Kurosawa and Tanizaki are both conservatives in the best sense by their preoccupation with the machinery of historical mythology. And *Kagemusha* makes painfully clear that the most hallowed icons of Japanese culture and identity are ripe for expropriation.

Ran

If *Kagemusha* exposes the spuriousness of monumental evocations of history, *Ran* is spurious history itself. The film is a kind of limit case because it bears a relation to monumental style as monumental style bears to the propaganda it overshadowed in the late 1930s. If *Miyamoto Musashi* aspires to the monumental style (see chapter 4), *Ran* deforms it, attenuating and inflating it into a carnivalesque ritual unmoored from its sacramental provenance. I have argued that monumental style is an appropriation of the annals of Japanese history, one that uses particular stylistic figures to cast a sacramental light on episodes in the past to inspire people in the present. The classics of prewar monumentalism do this, as does *Gate of Hell*, for different reasons. *Kagemusha*, with its interrogation of the process of monumentalism, still incorporates a great deal of the historical record. *Ran*, in contrast, theatricalizes history.

In this film the story of *histoire* is evacuated by theater, as if history is no longer a past that can be salvaged and recuperated but rather an empty ritual that ransacks a foreign literary hoard. It is just not true that "Kurosawa places *Ran* very firmly and precisely in the Japanese Middle Ages . . . when central government had utterly broken down and Japan was ravaged by the continual strife of warlords."[19] The film's costumes, castles, and sets are recognizably Japanese, but they are abstracted and taken to excess. There are no specific locales, historical personages, or events, and no expository titles to situate the time, place, and predicament. Unlike *Kagemusha*, there is hardly a remnant of any genuine Japanese identity hiding in the wings of *Ran*'s grandiose vision; nor is it simply transplanted Shakespeare that struts and frets across the film's desolate expanses. The film has been likened to noh theater, with its whitened, expressionless faces and mannered movements.[20] But the dead souls who occupy the world of *Ran* bear more resemblance to the wooden puppets of Bunraku theater or even the paper characters of *kamishibai*, for all of their aspect as personages, whether historical or theatrical. *Ran* is a monster, a film that cannibalizes its predecessors in film, in theater, and in history. It is a great film, but not a very human one. *King Lear*, of which *Ran* is an adaptation, is an expressionistic expulsion of royal pathos out into the political and natural worlds. But *Ran*'s King Hidetora plays a cipher, a figure at the mercy of the malevolent, active forces that secretly plot to wrest away his power and wealth. Similarly, Hidetora's elder sons, Taro and Jiro, are subject to the maniacal whims and rages of the demonic Lady Kaede, who completely overwhelms their judgment on appropriate military maneuvers. She is a theatrical descendant of *Throne of Blood's* Lady Asaji, a monster consumed by cold rage and a desire to consume others in blind vengeance for the death of her family at the hands of the Ichimonji clan. She is complemented by the equally inhuman but virtuous Lady Sue, whose Buddhist resignation in the face of all the treachery and carnage around her leaves the king exasperated with disbelief. The other characters follow the Lear story quite closely, including the loyal son Saburo (Cordelia), the fool, the opportunistic warlords Ayabe and Fujimaki (Cornwall and France), and the stalwart retainer Tango (Kent). But *Ran* differs fundamentally from *Lear* in its personification of chaos in an individual character whose machinations drives the story along.

Lady Kaede must rank as one of the screen's greatest villains, her utter rapacity sucking the life from those she has already ruined as well as those whose power she covets. In her the chaos of the film's title resides in its most concentrated form, but once she is dead the inexorable descent into madness, blindness, and desolation continues unabated. More to the point, the film's structure relentlessly demonstrates the triumph of ruin and darkness, concluding with a long shot of a solitary blind figure hesitating on the edge of a precipice formed by the ruins of a once opulent castle, casting about for a lost image of the goddess of mercy. A tragic view of *Ran* can salvage some humanist intent by reciting the value of pity and fear and the cathartic sublimation of destructive impulses. But a tragic view, despite the fact that the film is an adaptation of *King Lear*, falls short. Tragedy presumes some kind of fall from grace, whether due to a Euripidean twist of fate or the absurdity of a tragic flaw. In *Ran* there is no grace, no coherent world from which heroes can fall.

The long prologue, in which the king cedes his authority to his eldest son and the youngest son is banished, establishes a metaphorical level that tyrannizes the impulse to historicity. A sense of abstraction permeates this stunning oneiric sequence, situating it in the realm of myth. It is a mythic, not a historic, conflict that unfolds as Lord Ichimonji Hidetora struggles to maintain his kingly stature in the eyes of his successors and erstwhile rivals. The garish color in the buntings and banners of the grand hunt lend a feverish transience to the proceedings, while the contextless formality of the gathering functions as a parody of conventional courtly settings.

An important aspect of the monumental style is its reliance on traditional Japanese architecture and design to valorize and sanctify the formal protocols of Japanese behavior. The antiquity of the settings—the expansive tatami mats, delicate fusuma screens, the understated tokonoma alcove with its gnomic poems and symbolic flowers, the dark polish of long wooden verandas against the ascetic white of a hushed rock garden—establish the fittingness of Japanese identity with its long historical lineage. This is conspicuously absent in the prologue of *Ran*, whereas it dominates the mise-en-scène of all other monumental films.

Instead, the courtly ritual of inheritance takes place on a vast field of blowing grass, as if some cult or coven were performing its incantations and rituals. The makeshift throne is nothing more than a stool, and the magnificent screens usually surrounding daimyo are replaced by brightly colored bunting flapping loudly in the wind. Instead of royally holding forth on the triumph of the hunt and the joy of relinquishing authority to his heirs, the king promptly falls asleep at the wheel. Instead of seductive strains from the plectrum of skilled geisha, he is entertained by the impertinent cavorting of an androgynous fool. The entire proceeding has an unmistakable artificiality, a sense of transparency in a capricious natural setting, one that exposes these royal posturings as a sham.

The fool, Kyoami, plays a major role in exposing the absurdity of this contextless formality. His routine organizes the figure arrangement and direction of their collective look, parodying the solemn formations of objectified spectatorship. In medium shot the fool occupies the center of the frame and, looking left, sings "What do I hear, coming from over there?" The five nobles sitting on that side of the frame crane their necks and peer in that direction. Then he looks off right, taking along the glances of two nobles sitting opposite. His imitation of a hare is taken up by

The fool and his king: *Ran*. Museum of Modern Art Film Stills Archive.

Saburo, who turns it into a joke at the expense of the visiting lords, Fuji-maki and Ayabe. But as he is chastised by his brothers an insert of Lord Hidetora reveals that he has suddenly fallen asleep. The composition of the subsequent shot is a model of monumental centeredness, with lords and nobles evenly lining the edges of the frame, dominated in the central portion by the snoring king.

By contrast, the most characteristic compositions of Lady Kaede and the treasonous Taro are assymetrically balanced (scene 2). A remarkable diptych following their assertion over Lord Hidetora shows Kaede perched in the position of a *hina ningyo* girls' doll in frame left, with the omnipresent tokonoma scroll at right. The dark rectangles of the tatami stands form assymmetrical blocks in the vertical axis, then a cut to the space immediately offscreen right shows Taro in a mirror image reversal of Lady Kaede's position. Taro is immobile on a raised stand to the right, while the same scroll as in the previous shot is on the left. The angle of view is a 90-degree shift from the profile setup in which the angry Lord Hidetora brusquely signs the agreement with which his children have saddled him. The immobility of Kaede, moreover, contrasts markedly with the immobility of Hidetora's monumental compositions. While these "touchstone" shots of Kaede are still balanced, their asymmetry gives them a dynamic tension in keeping with her association with chaos and destruction.

A still better example of Kaede's precarious control of the frame comes in scene 14, the "sacrament of evil" in which she sees her incestuous lover Jiro off to war. Against his general's advice, Jiro has insisted on preparing for battle with his younger brother Saburo, whose approach simply indicates his desire to find his lost father. Kaede is the one who sees Saburo's approach as a threat, so she plots with Jiro, intoxicating him with visions of uncontested sovereignty over the region. He watches her, in profile, as she kneels before him, solemnly offering him a cup of sake to seal his murderous plans. As with the diptych in which she appears with Taro, her chilling composure lends a statuesque iconography to the gesture: the exquisite courtesan offering up a farewell inspiration to her warlord seated imperiously above, framed by a wooden grillwork as if by a compositional halo.

The shot recalls such representations of Japanese iconography as Juroza playing his flute before a classical screen in *Genroku Chushingura* or the sacramental invocations of the Abe clan the night before their mass immolation. Closer to a real historical reference might be the services undertaken by the Uesugi troops in *Kawanakajima Kassen*, the sake sacrament administered by the officers in expectation of their charges' sacrifice to the greater glory of the clan. Kaede knows too well the seductions of position, disposition, and composition, of influence over the ways in which people are seen and motives are judged. She knows the physical arrangement of things and people that manifest traces of rank and power. Yet for all her Japanese poise and iconocity, she is pure evil, the embodiment of chaos.

The very design of the castle rooms and appointments shows an austerity that is excessive and somehow twisted. The audience chambers in the first castle have wooden floors, not straw tatami. The lady and lord sit up on moveable platforms inlaid with tatami mats and raised from the floor about a foot. These give characters a doll-like, presentational air and has the further purpose of affording a downward glance at any person who seeks an audience. Instead of the delicate translucence of fusuma and shoji, the walls consist of stout wooden grillwork whose vertical shafts recall bars of confinement. There are no live flower arrangements and no standing screens with floral motifs painted on them. The surroundings are in keeping with the martial vocations of their occupants, but they are in stark contrast to the kind of cool, yet sumptuous refinement of samurai dwellings in other jidai geki. The design of these spaces is a kind of overkill of bushido aesthetics, like the unearthly sets in the fantasy sequences of Paul Schrader's *Mishima* constructed by the designer Ishioka Eiko.

The glossy austerity of the castle rooms has its counterpart in the rigid immobility within the shots and the lack of camera movement. For the director of *Seven Samurai* this is indeed a departure. Kurosawa's use of the long shot and long take, according to Rob Silberman, is "an instrument of irony, for if the point of view at first indicates a disengaged, cool indifference, it ultimately seems a reflection of the need to keep a safe distance in a world where, as one character observes, 'Hell is always at hand—which cannot be said of heaven.' "[21] Again, there is an emphasis on artificial presentation as a surrogate for a vital space, a substitute for normal interaction between an organism and its environment. Instead of responding to the stimulation of their surroundings, the players in *Ran* destructively preempt it. A frozen stasis is the modus operandi in the younger generation's keep, a "strategy of withdrawal via the long shot and long take," writes Steven Prince.[22] There is an intensification of horror in this detachment, because it replaces the shock of physical confrontation with a passive acceptance of evil's inevitability.[23]

This is consistent with the makeshift, spurious abstraction of the prologue, which evacuates the detail that concretely situates events in history. The abstracted artificiality of the sets, behavior, and even the battle sequences removes the diegesis from a specific time and space. The neon hues of blood and landscape afford a presentationalism akin to the artificiality of *Gate of Hell*, but while Kinugasa's film is an Orientalist primer of period aesthetics, Kurosawa's is the increasingly remote and hermetic world of grandiose delusions—that is, the archetypal posturings of myth. It is noteworthy that Kurosawa's next film retreats still further into a fantasy cloister with a foray into the contents of his own dreams (*Akira Kurosawa's Dreams*, 1990).

It is tempting to see the metaphorical function of the cloud sequences that punctuate the prologue as a nod to the traditional compositional perspective of Japanese ink painting and later ukiyo-e prints. These works suggest immense distances by interspersing different parts of the scene with wisps of cloud, as in the Zen-inspired landscape paintings of Sesshu and Shubun. Clouds are also used in earlier paintings of the Genji tale and in later eighteenth- and nineteenth-century ukiyo-e to assist the aerial perspective favored by the "blown away roof" composition. The idea here is a deft insertion of cloud cover to conceal perspectival and architectural impossibilities that arise from peering down from on high into the (roofless) houses of the characters. One critic argues that Kurosawa transposes the spatial coherence provided by clouds in thirteenth-century scrolls into a temporal bridge to smooth over breaks between scenes.[24]

Certainly the insistent return to shots of the clouds lend an ethereality and timelessness to the prologue. They may also hint at a Buddhist conception of the illusoriness of the world, a prominent theme running through *Ran*. But finally these connotations are no more than red herrings. Buddhist illusion doctrines supposedly function to bring comfort to suffering in a vale of tears, but the force of the film, particularly its closing shot, emphatically denies the efficacy of such beliefs. The diegesis of *Ran* is the all-too-real world of the nightmare and the lunatic; to say that it is an illusion is true, perhaps, but utterly irrelevant, because there is nothing outside it to function as its crucible.

The weightiest, most monumental images in the film are those of the gates. These huge, creaking barriers both open and constrain vision; their movement and bulk are a colossal symbol of monumental gravity. They recall the groaning weight of history in those touchstone films of Japaneseness, *Rashomon* and *Gate of Hell*. Yet they are also boundaries on a private world of ambition, incest, and patricide. When the king, spurned by his son at First castle, goes to be with his second son Jiro, he is hoping to enjoy commiseration for Taro's impertinence, but instead of comfort he finds only an enormous barred gate. Jiro grudgingly opens up to briefly talk to his father and disingenuously insists he must obey Taro. Stunned, Hidetora turns to go, and the monstrous groaning of the structure testifies to Hidetora's insignificance before the weight of accumulated eons. The gate adds to the impersonality of the drama and the futility of taking initiative for the world's vicissitudes.

Jiro's rationale is this: "Dogs turn on a master who gives up the chase." This lies behind his protest that he is actually discharging his filial duty in obeying Taro and refusing to allow Hidetora his customary retinue of retainers within the castle walls. Jiro's argument makes perfect sense, but it is the kind of specious sense that points to its force, which intimates the worst possible scenario. For in the subsequent scene when Hidetora and his men ride into the undefended Third castle, the gates swing shut again. This time they enfold the king and his men in bloody slaughter. Where moments before the gates were a refuge, now they are a trap.

The gates in *Ran* are quintessentially monumental. They are ancient, massive, and pregnant with ominous possibilities. Their bulk requires a long view to encompass their outsized scale and the painstaking slowness with which they groan open and shut requires considerable duration. Their mythic stature is less recognizably "Japanese," however, than the restful courtyards and verandas of other jidai geki. Nevertheless, they remind us of the colossal ruin of that other gate by which Japanese cinema was "discovered," *Rashomon*. That film is about the ambiguity of the past and its dependence on the motivations of the present. *Ran* evokes the past only to obliterate it by steadfastly denying any guide to its recuperation save the pulsating convulsions of chaos. The gates of *Ran* are the gates of hell.

The gates of *Ran*. Museum of Modern Art Film Stills Archive.

Ran Segmentation
 1. Prologue: King Hidetora cedes authority, Saburo banished
 2. Dispute in First castle with Taro
 3. Rejection at Second castle by Jiro
 4. Jiro's lieutenant occupies Third castle
 5. Hidetora decides to take Third castle
 6. Trapped and ambushed in Third castle, then destroyed; Taro slain
 7. On the heath, Hidetora joins Tsurumaru (Sue's brother)
 8. Lady Kaede emasculates Jiro
 9. King becomes fool and vice versa
          (insert: Kaede orders Sue killed)
10. Waiting on the heath
11. Kurogane's defiant trick
12. Waiting at Fourth castle ruins
13. Saburo's approach, Fujimaki's reinforcements
14. Jiro and Kaede plotting their 'sacrament of evil'
15. Hidetora with Tsurumaru and Sue at ruins
16. Stalemate on the meadow/waiting in ruins
17. Hidetora and Saburo meet on Azusa plain
18. Battle
          (insert: Ayabe destroys First castle)
19. Sue's body; Kaede decapitated
20. Processional; epilogue on ruins

Conclusions

Ran starkly exposes the hollow theatricality at the heart of the monumental style. The film can easily be accommodated in an auteurist framework that substitutes King Kurosawa for the beleaguered Lear. However, the grafting of King Lear onto a monumental evocation of Japanese history calls the Japaneseness of that history into question. For this reason *Ran* is less a film in the monumental style than a film about the monumental style and the Japanese identity it carries. Similarly *Throne of Blood*, despite its debt to noh aesthetics and period setting, is a less than Japanese film. Writes Desser, "The lack of humanity, especially vis-à-vis the *giri/ninjo* conflict is essentially why *Throne of Blood* is not at its core a Japanese film."[25] *Ran* unravels the indigenous associations of monumental style itself. Its excessive spectacle and presentational austerity loosens the tie that binds the monumental style to the Japanese aura most powerfully evoked by representations of its feudal period. Since monumental style is the most elaborate expression of Japanese period representations, demythologizing it is also to debunk the imagination of traditional Japanese history.

Kurosawa has always made aesthetically daring, if not always politically critical, films. In late works like *Kagemusha* and *Ran* there is a stylistic as well as personal imperative in the degeneration of the monumental style. The reason for this is the virus of international contamination inherent in monumental style from the first. Official xenophobia about breakdowns in the ethos of Japaneseness is what led to the monumental style and similar movements in the arts and literature. But this is a somewhat quixotic determination. The cosmopolitan modernism of Japanese national identity is revealed precisely in its attempted indigenization. This is cosmopolitan and modernist in two respects.

First, the notion of national identity is a Western political concept that depends on the differentiating value of one set of national characteristics pitted against another. National identity itself is an idea outfitted for particular communities who sought to extend their spheres of power by trade, colonization, and outright conquest (see chapter 2). How then could a Japanese sense of national identity avoid the essential differentiations inherent in the very concept? Second, monumental style is a case study in the internal differentiations of national identity, insofar as the kokusaku eiga, rekishi eiga, and the stylistic complexes of monumentalism are a deliberate turning away from the traces of classical Hollywood styles in Japanese period film and the chambara (sword fight) films. The monumental style is an imaginary microcosm of how the military authorities would like the Japanese to have seen themselves, but it is also a microcosm of the differentiations within the concept of national identity. Insofar as the monumental style proffered "good and beautiful" images of pure Japaneseness, it performed the very nineteenth-century Western process of carving from history a national essence distinct from others and elevating it as superior. The monumental style exemplifies a double articulation of difference. As a style that repudiates the classical Hollywood system, it works to galvanize a people around the distinctiveness and superiority of their heritage. The occasion for the articulation of this identity, a nationalistic bellows for the flames of war, makes the process that much more cosmopolitan, international, and typical of twentieth-century modernism.

For an example of contemporary monumental style that has come full circle to a liberal cosmopolitanism, consider Teshigahara Hiroshi's *Rikyu* (Shochiku, 1990). This film is a biopicture about the famous tea master Sen no Rikyu (1522–1591), whose religious and aesthetic convictions collided with the shogunate. Rikyu's life and art aptly illustrate the variety of co-optations to which a "pure" aesthetic is subject within a warrior milieu. The film contains many of the historical personages and events in *Kagemusha* and similarly meditates on the paradoxical path of Japanese modernization, marked by repression, xenophobia, and isolation. Whereas *Kagemusha* is about the accoutrements of warfare, *Rikyu* considers discriminations of taste in the tea cult, which have profound political ramifications. The name *Ri-kyu*, whose characters mean "profit" and "rest," was a sobriquet bestowed on him at the request of his patron Shogun Hideyoshi, so that he could help Hideyoshi realize his lifelong dream to serve tea to the emperor.[26] Renowned as a master of *wabicha* (poverty tea), with a radical simplicity of gesture and implement, Rikyu's career nonetheless marked the height of refinement and influence of the tea cult in the highest aristocratic circles. Rikyu's fall from favor and 1591 seppuku thus reveals the Zen-like paradox of aesthetic refinement and political ambition contained in his name. His death also marks the symbolic end of the medieval period, with the initiation of a new, hard-line shogunal hegemony.[27]

Invocations of the sacred in *Rikyu* are made through sound as much as through image. Contemplative close-ups show the preparation and drinking of tea and are overlaid by a steady hissing sound coming from the hot charcoal brazier. A rustic simplicity pervades the room and belies the tea cult's undeserved reputation for effete aestheticism. Despite his suspicion toward Japanese aesthetics on film, Tanizaki might have appreciated the intimacy of these moments.

It is precisely the intimate serenity of the tea sequences that Teshigahara uses as a foil for the political intrigues of the shogunate. Aside from Teshigahara's own status as a noted tea master who presumably wishes to promote his school, the film draws an emphatic line between art and politics. Before we see a single image, the opening title states, "This is the story of the duel between art and politics, of the beliefs of one man against the ambitions of another." If the tea room demands a divesting of one's professional worries along with the longsword (modern tea rituals often require participants to leave watches and cameras outside), political ambition is only too willing to take advantage of that vulnerability. When Sen no Rikyu (Mikuni Rentaro) refuses to poison Hideyoshi's Edo rival, he is banished by the truculent, unpredictable shogun. In a scene where townspeople speculate on the outcome of lordly power struggles, casting lots with toy animals standing in for various daimyo, one woman is sceptical of Hideyoshi, "the monkey": "He's not polished enough to be a ruler."

Played with manic unruliness by Yamazaki Tsutomu, Shogun Hideyoshi recalls the petulant charades of Hikozaemon, mentor to Shogun Iemitsu in Makino's 1940 film (*Shogun and Mentor*, chapter 4). These antics set off the monumental gravity shown by the boy shogun in the earlier film as well as that of Sen no Rikyu. However, unlike the crafty Hikozaemon, Rikyu's gravity is played straight: hagiography commemorating the victimization of art by political machinations. In his better moments Hideyoshi is genuinely sustained by the spiritual nourishment of the tea cult, noh, and brush paintings of Tohaku. But he also craves refinement and status, to brandish high culture over his enemies no less decisively than on the battlefield. With the presence of treacherous Portuguese Jesuits and Hideyoshi's dream of conquering Korea and China, which Rikyu opposes, *Rikyu's* sixteenth century is a site of culture wars no less than civil warring states. The formal audience where Hideyoshi makes overtures to the Jesuits is a hilarious sendup of objectified spectatorship, with Hideyoshi assuring his guests (a hirsute Donald Richie playing the head priest) that he intends to Christianize the continent if they will help him build a formidable navy.

The exemption of the tea cult from the compromises of domestic and foreign politics makes *Rikyu* a form of left-liberal monumentalism. As the monumental style functioned as a crucible of imperial Japaneseness in the 1930s, so in the 1990s it comes to be a rather prim affirmation of artistic purity. In its hissing hermitage of charcoal, pottery, and tea, it summarily dismisses the cultural insecurities of those who cannot find sufficient purity of heart (*makoto*) to resist making instrumental uses of the way of tea. Yet in its straightforward canonization of the master's moral rectitude, *Rikyu* uses the monumental style no less instrumentally than the monumental masterpieces of the 1930s.

To close, we might note the mythological and religious aspects of the monumental style that sound a key note in the screening of Japaneseness. If there is anything distinctive about the prewar invocation of Japaneseness, it is probably in the religious tenor of its calls to duty. The American and British devils were explicitly identified as harbingers of secularism and materialism, a theological enemy no less than a moral and political one. The other Axis powers had their pseudoreligious components, as in the German cult of Wagnerian Romanticism and the Italian glorification of the Futurist machine. However, both Germany and Italy had preexisting institutionalized religions that were to various extents mobilized to facilitate war fever.

In Japan, by contrast, there is no dominant institutionalized religion with a prophetic mandate, that is, a religious tradition capable of criticism and intervention in secular affairs. There are those who contend that Japanese culture is distinctively irreligious, lacking in systematic metaphysical, transcendent values. According to Earl Kinmonth, "Japan had had no Renaissance and no Reformation. There was no concept of one man in a

unique relationship with one god that would provide a rationale for tran-
scending contemporary social conventions."[28] This can be debated, but the
point here is that in the 1930s there appeared to be a spiritual and political
vacuum into which State Shinto was inserted, through revival of traditional
folkways and by coercion from above. Either way, I suspect that this is a
historical peculiarity of the times, a holdover from the "Westernization" of
Taisho liberalism.[29]

The most important thing about monumental style is its appropriation
of the language and pictures of transcendental religious experience, har-
nessing it to an immanent regime of national pride. Even a cynic must con-
cede that the "doctrines" of State Shinto, like the family-state system, the
divinity of the emperor, and the purity of the imperial line, not only gath-
ers the faithful under the rubric of a "Kingdom of God" but also projects an
eschatological vision of the kingdom's outcome. Moreover, there is an
undeniable spirituality, perhaps animism, to the monumental style's atten-
dance on the balance of behavior, the perfection of design, and the contemplation of space. It is tempting to liken this to Paul Schrader's description of Ozu's transcendental style, in that Ozu seems as concerned with the
inanimate object as the psychological subject, but the monumental style is
so immanent, so abundantly present to the senses, that the ethereality and
mysticism of transcendentalism seems wholly inappropriate. (It may be
wholly inappropriate to Ozu as well.)[30]

The religious trappings of monumental style do not stop with period
aesthetics and invocations of warrior traditions. With respect to invocations of Japanese aura in the prewar period, there are still many unexplored
paths. One might, for instance, analyze the stylistic handlings of Japanese
mothers, especially in *gendai geki* (contemporary life films), for ways in
which the mother is apotheosized and linked to patriotic and Shinto objectives. Traditional folk festivals and rituals could be analyzed for ways in
which their religious motivations are put to work in the ideology, style, and
narrative of Japanese film. In the late 1930s the *shomin geki*, or dramas about
the lower middle class, came under suspicion. Why was this, and what
might it have to do with the class dynamics of the Japanese aura? Was it
simply the potentially critical subject matter of the films, or was it their
style and genre as well, with their associations with erstwhile leftist, "tendency" filmmaking? In spite of official disapproval, why and how did it persist through the war years, and how might "common people's drama" have
been monumentally rendered?

What are the religious and mythological connotations of narrative
structure and pace? Why does an intricately plotted, and especially a fast-
paced plot, raise the suspicions of the high priests of monumentalism?

What is it about a slow pace that contributes to a contemplative, perhaps mythological tone? What are the devices of narrative retardation that maintain the gravity of the Japanese aura? Finally, there are many parallels between the monumental style and other nationalist, fascist, or totalitarian cinemas around the world. Is there something about a totalitarian or fundamentalist mentality that calls for a certain aesthetic inclination? Such comparative work would involve a close look at Soviet socialist realism as a style that supposedly invokes an apotheosis of "ordinary" working people without an explicitly religious appeal. On the other hand, Dr. Arnold Fanck's German mountain films and Wagnerian epics (in Fritz Lang, for instance) do contain theological references in support of their mythologization, so the absence of institutionalized religion cannot be a necessary condition of international monumentalism.

In the way I have defined it, monumental style is a cultural sacrament offered to the Japanese people. A sacrament is the enacting of a covenant, or spiritual contract, that sets out the responsibilities of people toward their God. The sacrament also promises salvation in exchange for the faithful devotion of the believer. Salvation, in the monumental style, does not mean everlasting life or individual happiness but rather a sense of belonging to a living entity much larger than the lone, often alienated, self. It promises above all a new way of seeing the world and one's place in it. It penetrates the clutter of ordinary perception to visualize the traces of antiquity and nobility in the slightest movement, in the humblest object. Most profoundly, the monumental style fashions a world where death is not overcome but glorified because it is the best way to show one's loyalty to the kingdom.

Notes

1. Moving Pictures of Japaneseness

1. Contemporary studies of ideologies of Japanese identity include the following: *Japan's Modern Myth*, by Miller, *Japan's Modern Myths*, by Gluck, *The Myth of Japanese Uniqueness*, by Dale. There is also Van Wolferen's massive *The Enigma of Japanese Power* and Buruma's *Behind the Mask*.

2. The best-known works in this country are older studies like Doi's 1973 *Anatomy of Dependence* (*Amae no kozo*) and Nakane's *Japanese Society* (*Tate shakai no ningen kankei*). However, it is more recent, virulent strains of *nihonjinron* that exercise American and European Japanophiles, like Tsunoda Tadanobu's *The Japanese Brain: Uniqueness and Universality* (Tokyo: Taishukan, 1978), Minami Hiroshi's *The Japanese Concept of Self* (Tokyo: Iwanami Shoten, 1983), and Suzuki Takao's "Language Life," in the *Dictionary of Japanese Human Relations* (Tokyo: Kodansha, 1980). According to Miller,

No one likes to appear foolish to others, nor do we generally relish the spectacle of our friends making themselves foolish to others and to the world. . . . Most of us naturally wish that the Japanese would not go on and on making themselves ridiculous in the face of the outside world with all this "unique language" and "unique culture and society" business, in a word, with the whole *Nihonjinron*. But they will not stop.

R. A. Miller, "What Does It Mean to Be a Japanese?" *Asian and Pacific Quarterly* 21, 2 (Autumn 1989), 31. For further analysis of *nihonjinron* see my "Anatomy of Misinterpretation."

3. Edward Said's *Orientalism* (New York: Pantheon, 1978) was a major encouragement in the study of projective fantasies of the Other, but Barthes's *Empire of Signs* (Geneva: Skira, 1970) was an explicit, self-conscious exercise in Japanese Orientalism long before Said theorized it in relation to the Near East and Islam. However, Barthes's book was not published in English until 1982 (Hill and Wang; trans. Richard Howard).

4. The Imperial Rescript on Education was published for international distribution in 1909 by Monbusho (the Ministry of Education) in Chinese, English, French, and German. It has been widely reprinted and can be found, for instance, in Jon Livingston, Joe Moore, Felicia Oldfather, eds., *The Japan Reader*, vol. 1: *Imperial Japan: 1800–1945*, 2 vols. (New York: Pantheon, 1973), 153.

5. Silverberg, "Constructing a New Cultural History of Prewar Japan" and "Remembering Pearl Harbor."

6. Jun'ichiro Tanizaki, *In Praise of Shadows*, 9. See Aaron Gerow's excellent discussion of this passage in "Celluloid Masks: The Cinematic Image and the Image of Japan" *Iris* 16 (Spring 1993), 23–36.

7. Gunning, *D. W. Griffith*, 2.

8. R. A. Brown, "Japan's Modern Myth Reconsidered," *Asian and Pacific Quarterly* 21, 1 (Spring 1989), 41.

2. In the Postnational Neighborhood There Are No Foreigners (Knock on Wood): Nation as Cine-Superstition

1. After Althusser's sense of interpellation, "The nation is to be understood not simply as an abstraction, but as a lived experience made possible by broadcasting technologies, whose achievement was the 'transmutation of the political idea of the nation into lived experience, into sentiment and into the quotidian,' " David Morley and Kevin Robins, quoting Jesus Martin-Barbero in "Spaces of Identity: Communications Technologies and the Reconfiguration of Europe" (*Screen* 30, 4 [Autumn 1989]), 10–34). Stefan Tanaka uses Hayden

White's term, as opposed to Althusser's, in his claim that "people emplot these [national] notions to give their own lives meaning, often in ways quite different from those described by movements, scholars, or governments," review, *Journal of Asian Studies* 53, 2 (May 1994), 505.

2. A good formulation of the brave new global neighborhood is provided by Morley and Robins, who write, "New forms of bonding, belonging, and involvement are being forged out of the global-local nexus. . . . In a world which seems to be increasingly dominated by a global cultural repertoire, new communities and identities are constantly being built and rebuilt" ("Spaces of Identity"). Ed Soja puts it more succinctly in the context of urban "glocalization" (UCLA Seminar, April 1994). See also Soja's *Postmodern Geographies* (London: Verso, 1989), 214–23.

Scan the titles of the chapters in Bhabha's *Nation and Narration* for a taste of postnational rhetoric, an often lyrical defamiliarizing of the seductions of national "security": "The National Longing for Form" (Timothy Brennan), "Irresistible Romance: The Foundational Fictions of Latin America" (Doris Sommer), "Breakfast in America—*Uncle Tom's* Cultural Histories" (Rachel Bowlby), "Telescopic Philanthropy: Professionalism and Responsibility in *Bleak House*" (Bruce Robbins), and "The Island and the Aeroplane: The Case of Virginia Woolf" (Gillian Beer). Tom Nairn's "Internationalism and the Second Coming" (*Daedalus* [Summer 1993], 155–70) is another good example of this ironic millenarianism.

3. For instance, Morley and Robins, "Spaces of Identity," James Donald, "How English Is It?" Victor Burgin, "Paranoiac Space," *New Formations* 12 [Winter 1990].

4. See Angela Dalle Vacche, *The Body in the Mirror: Shapes of History in Italian Cinema* (Princeton: Princeton University Press, 1992), and Marina Warner, *Monuments and Maidens: The Allegory of the Female Form* (London: Weidenfeld and Nicolson, 1985).

5. Forster, "Monument/Memory," 3.

6. Fifteenth Annual Ohio University Film Conference, October 21–23, 1993, Athens, Ohio. The panel Danan chaired was called "From Pre-National to Post-National French Politics." Other panels included "Amnesic Amamnesi: Contemporary Cinema and the (Re)Construction of a National Identity," "(Dis)Locating National Cinema: The Film/Video Construction of Hyphenated-American Identities," "German Cinema: From Before UFA to After DEFA," "Post-Colonial Dilemma: Crisis in the Contemporary Cinema of Hong Kong," and "Italy: From the 'Cinema of Poverty' to the 'Poverty of Cinema.' "

7. "Europudding" is what some have called multinational delicacies like Ridley Scott's *1492: Conquest of Paradise* (U.S., U.K., France, Spain, 1992) and Milos Forman's *Valmont* (U.K., France, 1989).

8. This was formulated most piquantly by Dudley Andrew in his remarks on "Presence du cinema français," Fifteenth Annual Ohio University Film Conference.

9. The point was made by Andrew. To say "no" to the possibility of national-postnational coexistence implies a need to choose between them, as in the explicit national repudiations of first nations (indigenous peoples) or subcultural affiliations (Queer Nation, Nation of Islam, et al.). To say "yes, the national and postnational may coexist" mat also imply a need to choose between different forms of cultural affiliation, but perhaps as a matter for prioritizing rather than mutual exclusion of loyalties.

10. In spite of their dominance of the international film market, American companies are conspicuously infrequent participants in international coproduction arrangements, partly because there is no formal state agency to represent them in the international marketplace and partly because there is no subsidy system to act as an incentive to coproductions (Peter Lev, "From Co-Production to Euro-American Films," Fifteenth Annual Ohio University Film Conference).

11. Quoted in Anderson, *Imagined Communities*, xii.

12. In response to Andrew's talk one professor retorted, "You're not only telling us what to study, but *how* to study it as well!" To which Andrew replied, "As a university professor, it is my duty to strongly advise people what and how to study."

13. "According to one major empirical study, nationalist and ethnic conflict accounted for some 70 percent of 160 significant disputes with a probability of culminating in large-scale violence," Dittmer and Kim, "In Search of a Theory of National Identity," *China's Quest for National Identity*, 8.

14. As a film historian I feel most comfortable choosing examples from popular culture, but with the ubiquitousness of video and computer networking the time when we could confidently assume film as a species of popular "mass" culture is long past. E.g., cult film and its associated fanzines, bulletin boards, video outlets, etc., is elitist no less than Merchant and Ivory productions are in their synthetic upper-crust nostalgia. Merchant-Ivory's popularity *is* their elitism, or snob appeal. Likewise, literature/publishing, art/graphics, music/recording, and architecture/construction all have their meandering borders between the state of the art and the art of the craft.

15. Andrew, "Presence du cinema français."

16. Although its political intent diverges from the European art cinema, the rise of Third Cinema was part of the overall institutionalization of national cinemas in the 1960s. Despite the radical struggles for national liberation, its influences are international in scope: inspired as much by Italian neorealism, John Grierson, and Marxist aesthetics as by regional and local traditions (Jim Pines and Paul Willemen, eds., *Questions of Third Cinema* [London: British Film Institute, 1989], 4–5). Cf. Mandy Merck's definition of art cinema, including "theatrical features which oppose the 'international style' and subjects of Hollywood—films which have historically involved an emphasis on *cultural speci-ficity* (of a nation or social group) and personal authorial 'expression' (the direc-

tor typically being designated as auteur)." See Merck, "Dessert Hearts," in Martha Gever, Pratibha Parmar, John Greyson, eds., *Queer Looks: Perspectives on Lesbian and Gay Film and Video* (New York: Routledge, 1993), 377; my emphasis. My point here is that in the 1960s "dedicated" international cinema, including Third Cinema, came into its own as art, industry, politics, and critical practice. See also Roy Armes, *Third World Filmmaking and the West* (Berkeley: University of California Press, 1987).

17. Andrew and Andrew, *Kenji Mizoguchi*, 29.

18. Allen and Gomery state that cinema studies was probably the fastest growing academic discipline in American universities between 1965–1975 (*Film History*, 27).

19. Pauline Kael on *Pixote*, in *Foreign Affairs* (San Francisco: Mercury House, 1991), p. 497ff.

20. Bakhtin, *The Dialogic Imagination*, 301–31. Paul Willemen's "The Third Cinema Question: Notes and Reflections" is an good example of Bakhtin's importance for non-Western film practice (Pines and Willemen, *Questions of Third Cinema*, 23–27).

21. Yoshimoto, "The Difficulty of Being Radical," describes the impulse to explore and colonize by Western scholars who set the agenda for criticism of non-Western cinema and culture. Instead of revealing the contours of non-Western culture, they [we] reproduce the structures of its domination (338–54). Far from being a problem only for radical film scholars, Stefan Tanaka identifies this as an epistemological blind spot: "Because the development of scholarship on nation-states has proceeded along and in interaction with the nation-state, we often fail to see the extent to which our constructs and vocabulary reinforce that which we seek to overturn," review, *Journal of Asian Studies* 53, 2 (May 1994), 506.

22. "[National cinema] must be read against the local/global interface, which has become increasingly important in the new world order of the 1980s and 1990s. This interface operates in every national cinema, primarily because the film medium has always been an important vehicle for constructing images of a unified national identity out of regional and ethnic diversity and for transmitting them both within and beyond its national borders and also because, from its inception, the history of cinema has always involved a fierce international competition for world markets," Marsha Kinder, *Blood Cinema: The Reconstruction of National Identity in Spain* (Berkeley and Los Angeles: University of California Press, 1993), 7–8. See also Thompson and Bordwell, *Film History*, xxviii, 2, 39, 54–56, 800–4.

23. It was not just the invention of the technology, but the international crisscrossing and artistic cross-fertilization of films themselves, and their audiences—from France and Italy to England and America and back again—that gradually resulted in the self-sufficient narrativization of film culminating in the films of Griffith. Gunning, *D. W. Griffith*, 38–41.

"During this early period, films circulated freely from country to country," until World War I cut short the cross-border movement, according to David Bordwell and Kristin Thompson, *Film Art: An Introduction*, 4th ed. (New York: McGraw Hill, 1993), 453. After the war international cinema proliferated by means of cross-pollination between French impressionism, German expressionism, and Soviet montage throughout the 1920s, at which time it was thoroughly assimilated by Hollywood (470).

24. Musser, *Before the Nickelodeon*, 63. Kinder emphasizes other periods of international competition: the coming of sound, the post-World War II scramble for markets, and the post-cold war era (*Blood Cinema*, 8).

25. Erik Barnouw, *Documentary: A History of the Nonfiction Film*, rev. ed. (Oxford: Oxford University Press, 1983), 11. A similar situation occurred in the early history of photography. Daguerre could take photographic emulsions in 1839 using his daguerreotype reversal process, which he sold to the French government. In 1841 Taylor perfected his negative process in England, allowing for an infinite reproduction of prints from a single negative, and within months exposures were taken in America, Japan, India, Egypt, and the Near East. Museum of Photographic Arts, Balboa Park, San Diego.

26. Bordwell and Thompson, *Film Art*, 454–55. See also Thompson and Bordwell, *Film History*, 48–49. Not that this border crossing went uncontested. By 1907 the French Pathe group had opened offices in London, Moscow, Brussels, Berlin, St. Petersburg, Amsterdam, Barcelona, Milan, Rostov-on-Don, Kiev, Budapest, Warsaw, Calcutta, and Singapore. Of course Pathe had already established a U.S. office in New York by 1904. Litigation against Pathe by Edison was partly responsible for the formation of the Motion Picture Patents Co. in 1908. Thompson, *Exporting Entertainment*, 5.

27. "The economic power of American media, which began with the emergence of Hollywood as a major film-producing center in the 1910s, has been such that some scholars have called it "cultural imperialism." "Hollywood style" is a term apropos not only of films made in the United States, but of many produced in Moscow, Tokyo, and Bombay, as well." (Allen and Gomery, *Film History*, v)

28. As James Donald writes, "A nation does not express itself through its culture: it is culture that produces 'the nation' " ("How English Is It?" 32). However, this could lead to infinite regress: the need to specify preceding nationalizing impulses in every prior cultural apparatus. If one insists that nationhood is produced by cultural technologies, one is still left with the question of provenance. From what other cultural apparatuses does national cinema inherit its nationalizing functions?

29. See David Morley and Kevin Robins, "No Place Like *Heimat*: Images of Home(land) in European Culture," *New Formations* 12 (Winter 1990), especially pp. 18–19, where they discuss the films of Wim Wenders, who says that "Iden-

tity means not having to have a home," making a very un-German divorce between a conscious identity and a fixed abode.

30. Anderson, *Imagined Communities*, xiv.

31. Burch, *To the Distant Observer*, and David Bordwell, Janet Staiger, and Kristin Thompson, *The Classical Hollywood Cinema: Film Style and Mode of Production to 1960* (New York: Columbia University Press, 1985), respectively.

32. As in Pico Iyer's book *Video Night in Kathmandu* (New York: Vintage Departures, 1989), the further afield, the more "ordinary" the movies.

33. Cf. Andrew Higson's understanding

> By Hollywood, I mean the international institutionalisation of certain standards and values of cinema, in terms of both audience expectations, professional ideologies and practices and the establishment of infrastructures of production, distribution, exhibition and marketing, to accommodate, regulate and reproduce these standards and values." ("The Concept of National Cinema," 38)

34. "The Chinese started making movies in the 1930s, and this is explained as the act of money-hungry 'non-Indonesians.' Indonesians regarded film as 'low-class,' but the Chinese didn't care," T. R. White, personal correspondence, National University of Singapore, December 10–11, 1993. Lent, drawing on Y. B. Misbach (1982), also emphasizes the social liabilities of pre–World-War-II filmmakers, seen as immoral, adventurist mountebanks by the middle class. They demanded the higher standards of imported films and traditional Indonesian artforms (*The Asian Film Industry*, 204). See also Salim Said, *Shadows on the Silver Screen: A Social History of Indonesian Film* (Jakarta: Lontar Foundation, 1991).

35. When Usmar's company failed in the early 1950s, he formed a partnership with Djamaluddin Malik in 1954 to combat the pernicious influence of Malaya. "It seems Malaysian films were gaining popularity among the middle classes, and this audience was seen as crucial to success. The Malaysians were soon replaced by the Communists as the enemy of preference, and Djamaluddin and Usmar formed a right-wing group to fight Communism with film" (T. R. White, personal correspondence). Later, when the communists were defeated, Chinese Indonesians and Hollywood again became the villains.

White speculates on the formal and generic consequences of this Sino-Hollywood Orientalism:

> [Indonesian] scholars blame the upper-class tradition on the Chinese and Hollywood (remember, the Chinese, like the Jews in most places, form a wealthy minority in Indonesia, and run many of the businesses). What's ironic is that the "alternative"

> Indonesian filmmakers (such as Teguh Karya) make films that
> are EXACTLY like the mainstream films, but replace upper-class
> characters with lower-class characters; they have EXACTLY the
> same problems (usually romance and disease problems simulta-
> neously) as do the characters in mainstream films, but in squalid
> settings. (personal correspondence, December 11, 1993)

Lent reports that one scholar believes the occupying Japanese improved the quality of Indonesian film by making longer and better photographed documentaries and propaganda films with limited staff and facilities (citing a conference paper by A. Kurasawa [1988]; *The Asian Film Industry*, 204–5).

Other examples of nationalist disavowals of distasteful predecessors include Korea and Taiwan's exclusion of Japan in their accounts of early cinema and Vietnam's disavowal of its pre-1975 film history (Abe Mark Nornes, personal correspondence, February 1994).

36. Anderson, *Imagined Communities*, 44–45. See also Steven Prince, "The Discourse of Pictures: Iconicity and Film Studies," for a critique of current theoretical reliance on Saussurian linguistics (*Film Quarterly* 47, 1 [Fall 1993], 16–26).

37. Cf. Scott Nygren's methodological prescription for cross-cultural studies, which he says must avoid any imposition of "a one-dimensional system of binary oppositions, [lest we] lapse back to empiricist, logocentric, or humanist assumptions already irretrievably problematized by contemporary critical methodology" in "Doubleness and Idiosyncrasy in Cross-Cultural Analysis," (*Quarterly Review of Film and Video* 13, 1–13 [1991]), 84. Note the rhetoric of progress, supercession, and disavowal.

38. Anderson, *Imagined Communities*, 43.

39. Ibid.

40. Gunning, "An Aesthetic of Astonishment," 31–32.

41. Gunning, *D. W. Griffith*, 73, 80–81, 93, 127–28.

42. "Refinement" also in the sense of seeking after middle-class tastes, cf. Charles Musser's *High-Class Moving Pictures: Lyman H. Howe and the Forgotten Era of Traveling Exhibition, 1880–1920* (Princeton: Princeton University Press, 1991). See also Gunning, *D. W. Griffith*, chapter 6.

43. "The desire for middle-class respectability, which arose soon after the first crest of the nickelodeon explosion, ultimately provoked the narrative discourse of film. Were films actually capable of aspiring to the cultural role of respectable narrative arts?" Gunning, *D. W. Griffith*, 89. Of course, there are different national traditions for what counts as respectable narrative art and this sometimes led to conscious "concerted differentiations" from Hollywood. Thompson and Bordwell, *Film History*, 760–61, 797–800.

44. Quoted in Thompson, *Exporting Entertainment*, 94.

45. Gunning, "An Aesthetic of Astonishment," 37.

46. Benedict, *The Chrysanthemum and the Sword*.

47. Burch's italics. *To the Distant Observer,* 114–15.

48. See Anderson and Richie, *The Japanese Film,* 329–31, for a slightly con-descending account of foreign cinematic influences; Anderson's "Second and Third Thoughts About the Japanese Film" is a more sensitive reconsideration of the issue (appended to *The Japanese Film,* rev. ed.). Sato, *Currents in Japanese Cinema,* chapter 2, cites Ince's *Civilization,* Lubitsch's *The Marriage Circle,* Borzage's *Seventh Heaven,* Murnau's *Sunrise,* Goulding's *Grand Hotel,* Sternberg's *The Docks of New York,* Capra's *Lady for a Day,* D.W. Griffith, *The Champ,* and Fitzmaurice's *The Barker* (32–33). Bordwell (*Ozu and the Poetics of Cinema*), cites Fairbanks and William DeMille generally as influential on Japanese cinema (24), and espe-cially Chaplin, Lubitsch, and Lloyd as mentors in the work of Ozu (152). Kurosawa provides a long list of American silent films that influenced him in *Something Like an Autobiography*. The best account of foreign cinema influences in the 1920s and 1930s is Kirihara's *Patterns of Time,* chapters 3–4. He lists Lubitsch, Sternberg, Ford, Clair, Renoir, and Wyler as Mizoguchi's self-proclaimed influ-ences.

49. Frank Lloyd Wright, *An Autobiography,* (New York: Duell, Sloan, and Pearce, 1943), 196.

On the subject of elimination, Ernest Jones writes,

> The intolerance for disorder is closely related to another trait, the intolerance for waste. This has more than one source. It rep-resents a dislike of anything being thrown away (really from the person)—a manifestation of the retaining tendency under con-sideration—and also a dislike of the waste product because it represents refuse—i.e., dirt—so that every effort is made to make use of it. Such people are always pleased at discovering or hearing of new processes for converting waste products into use-ful material, in sewage farms, coal-tar manufactories and the like.

"Anal-Erotic Character Traits," *Papers on Psycho-Analysis* (London: Bailliere, Tindall, and Cox, 1938), 550.

Frank Lloyd Wright and the international style appear in a new light vis-à-vis the following: "The Environmental Assessment Center in Okayama, Japan, announced in October that it had manufactured an experimental sausage out of recycled Tokyo sewage by adding soybean protein and steak flavoring to 'sewage solids.' A company spokesman said, '[S]ewage isn't really such a dan-gerous and dirty thing.' However, he did not foresee commercially marketing the sausage: 'Sewage does have a slight image problem. I don't think people will be content eating something they know has been excreted by humans' "

(*Boston Globe*-Reuters, October 7, 1993; courtesy Allan D. Coleman, November 12, 1993).

50. Herbert Muschamp, *File Under Architecture* (Boston: MIT Press, 1974), 84–5. Cf. Donald Richie, "Learn About Shibui from Japanese Films," *House Beautiful* (September 1960), 109.

51. A. A. Gerow, "The Benshi's New Face: Defining Cinema in Taisho Japan," *Iconics* 3 (1994), 69–86.

52. Kaeriyama Norimasa, leading agitator for the modernization of Japanese film, founder of *Jun'eigageki undo* and editor of its organ *Kinema Record.* Quoted in Gerow, "The Nation as Negation and the Origin of 'Japanese' Cinema," Fifteenth Annual Ohio University Film Conference, 3, 10.

53. Ibid., 8.

54. Ibid., 4.

55. See chapter 2, note 26.

56. Anderson and Richie, *The Japanese Film*, 41. They go on to say, "There is little evidence that these noble intentions were in any way realized."

57. Kirihara, *Patterns of Time*, 43.

58. Ibid., 52.

59. Richie, *The Japanese Movie*, 11.

60. "The story film could provide *a coherent unified commodity*, complete in itself, without need of the explanatory context provided by exhibitors." Gunning, *D. W. Griffith*, 143 (emphasis added).

61. Komatsu Hiroshi, "Some Characteristics of Japanese Cinema Before World War I," in Nolletti and Desser, *Reframing Japanese Cinema*, 240.

62. Richie, *The Japanese Movie*, 16.

63. Komatsu and Musser, "Benshi Search," 88.

64. Komatsu, "Some Characteristics of Japanese Cinema," 252–53.

65. Ibid., 248, 251.

66. Ibid., 248. The same procedures of theatrical 'digests' were used in early French *films d'art* as well as Biograph and other American producers, 1900–1906. Gunning, *D. W. Griffith*, 38–39.

67. Komatsu, "Some Characteristics of Japanese Cinema," 255.

68. Richie, *The Japanese Movie*, 13. Komatsu and Musser state that the first film star was Nakamura Kasen, in a film called *Soga kyodai: kuriba no akebono* (The Soga brothers' dawn hunting party, 1908). Nakamura, too, was a kabuki actor performing a kabuki episode ("Benshi Search," 83).

69. Sato, *Chambara Eiga Ron*, 5; my translation.

70. Anderson and Richie, *The Japanese Film*, 233.

71. Teresa Becker, "*Godzilla* vs. *Rashomon*: Breaking into U.S. Markets," Fifteenth Annual Ohio University Film Conference.

72. Ibid.

73. *Variety*, September 25, 1957, 13.

74. Ibid.

75. Gerow, "The Nation as Negation," 8.

76. Komatsu and Musser emphasize how pre-1912 Japanese film apparatus was positioned as heir to an earlier Japanese exhibition practice, the *Utsushi-e* magic lantern programs, as well as an "enlightening" invention suitable for education, not just gimmickry ("Benshi Search," 84).

3. Approaching the Monumental Style

1. See Siegfried Kracauer, "Propaganda and the Nazi War Film, " Museum of Modern Art Film Library (Ann Arbor: Edwards, 1942); Ruth Benedict, "Race and Cultural Relations: America's Answer to the Myth of a Master Race," National Education Association (Washington, D.C., 1942), and Benedict, *The Chrysanthemum and the Sword*.

2. See, for instance, Nornes and Fukushima, *The Japan/America Film Wars*.

3. Anderson and Richie, *The Japanese Film*, 132.

4. Mosse, *The Nationalization of the Masses*, 10.

5. See Kirihara's *Patterns of Time* for the variety of ways the Japanese film industry relied upon Hollywood, even while restricting its access to Japanese screens. Anderson and Richie's *The Japanese Film*, while emphasizing the continuity between early film and Japanese theater, still renders accounts to Western industrial and stylistic inspiration; see chapter 2, 35–46, and pp. 448–51.

6. I take style to be a work's apparent manner of creation, not the way it actually came to be. Style is proper to human action and behavior, according to Kendall Walton in a lucid article entitled "Style and the Products and Processes of Art" (in Berel Lang, ed., *The Concept of Style* [Philadelphia: University of Pennsylvania Press, 1979]). Insofar as we attribute style to objects, like works of art, we are really characterizing objects according to their apparent manner of creation. Walton is careful to distinguish the apparent genesis of a work attributed to it by some observer from how the work was actually created; the important point is the claim that the concept of style derives from human action, especially from the *process* of creation. Style is an attribute of the work, but only because the work appears to have traces of a certain manner or style of creation. This emphasis accords well with a pragmatic conception of style that prioritizes the *process* of signification in relation to a constitutive situation.

7. Dittmer and Kim, "In Search of a Theory," 18.

> Paradoxical as it may seem, in order to cope with wrenching ambiguities and uncertainties created by China's encounter with the other (Western) world, to fight fire with fire as it were, the Chinese were forced to accept such Western concepts as nation, sovereignty, race, citizenship, and identity. The quest for Chinese *national* identity in a modern sense finally began at

the turn of the century with the popularization among Chinese
intellectuals of such modern terms as *minzu* (literally, "clan people" by connoting the notion of "nation") imported from the
writings of the Japanese Meiji period. (ibid., 251–52)

For wide-ranging discussions of the nation as civic religion, see Hobsbawm,
The Age of Empire, especially pp. 147ff. Anderson also discusses this at some
length in *Imagined Communities*, 11ff. Also see Gellner, *Nations and Nationalism*.

8. "The national essence is, however, by no means fixed in the past, but subject to recurrent reinterpretation" (Dittmer and Kim, "In Search of a Theory,"
18).

9. Quoted in Martin, "Popular Music and Social Change," 333.

10. The *Japan Times* and its earlier incarnation, the *Japan Times and Advertiser*,
is a daily paper serving the foreign community and bilingual Japanese. Its editorial policy plainly caters to an affluent, relatively prestigious readership, but
it contains a daily section summarizing key articles from the so-called vernac-
ular press and gets its stories from the same wire services that other Japanese
papers use. Certainly there is a problem generalizing from this paper and other
English sources about Japanese urban culture, and for this reason I have gathered specific incidents and examples that resonate with implications for popular urban culture, rather than replicating the editorial pronouncements of the
times.

11. Martin, "Popular Music and Social Change," 339.

12. Gluck, *Japan's Modern Myths*, 7, 10. The "east wind" expression figures
prominently in the debate over *shushin*, civil morality, waged by the education
establishment in the Meiji period. It was used by the Tokyo governor in the
1870s to refer to the sublime indifference to ethics instruction manifested by
teachers, administrators, and politicians, not to that of students (p. 116).

13. Bordwell, *Ozu and the Poetics of Cinema*, 34. Specifically, Bordwell compares early Showa Tokyo with Kracauer's description of the German *Angestell-
tenkultur* of the same period.

14. Kasza, *The State and Mass Media*, 70.

15. Fujitake, "The Formation of Mass Culture," 778.

16. An excellent overview of Japanese *modan* (as distinct from "modern" or
"modernization") appears in Silverberg's "Remembering Pearl Harbor."

17. "Historians generally describe the state's wartime campaigns against cafe
culture, permanent waves, and Hollywood as a nativist reaction against Westernization. Yet these policies might also be viewed as part of a clash between
different versions of modernity. Indeed, Protestant moral reformers found
much to support in a wartime regime that advanced their long-standing campaigns against illicit sexuality, smoking, and drinking."

Garon, "Rethinking Modernization and Modernity," 361.

18. Arase, "Mass Communication," 753–54. Fujitake, "The Formation of Mass Culture," 775. Silverberg says that *Kingu* magazine was modeled on the American *Saturday Evening Post* ("Remembering Pearl Harbor," 45).

19. Arase, "Mass Communication, 753–54; Fujitake, "The Formation of Mass Culture," 775.

20. Fujitake, "The Formation of Mass Culture," 776:

> *Chin-don-ya*: troupes of several men in eye-attracting attire, car-
> rying on their backs commodity sale advertisements or waving
> streamers and playing trumpets, drums, etc., as they parade the
> streets; *Kamishibai*: travelling vendors who present sets of serial
> picture story cardboards along with oral commentaries while
> selling millet jelly, seasoned seaweed, candies, etc.

21. Bordwell, *Ozu and the Poetics of Cinema*, 151.

22. Ibid., 188.

23. Fujitake, "The Formation of Mass Culture," 782.

24. Silverberg, "Remembering Pearl Harbor," 34.

25. Tetsuo Najita and H. D. Harootunian, "Japanese Revolt Against the West," in Duus, *The Cambridge History of Japan*, 765.

26. Ibid. However, some of these same writers had enthusiastically embraced "American-style" conventions in prequake Tokyo. Tanizaki, for instance, wrote the script for *Amateur Club* (1920), a slapstick comedy directed by Thomas Kurihara, who had worked in Hollywood with Thomas Ince. The film was the first effort in the newly formed Taikatsu company to provide homegrown product in the American style as an alternative to the stilted the-atricality of Nikkatsu. Tanizaki thus helped to inaugurate the selfsame decade of "Americanism" that he later decried as crass hedonistic materialism.

27. Seidensticker, *Tokyo Rising*, 99, 67–68, 86. This book, the sequel to his earlier *Low City, High City*, is by far the most detailed reminiscence of Tokyo cul-ture and politics since the Meiji restoration, even if it suffers from an impres-sionistic and sometimes opinionated tenor. Bordwell's *Ozu and the Poetics of Cin-ema*, despite its title, is also an invaluable descriptive resource of everyday Taisho and Showa city life, especially pp. 32ff. and 47ff. For a lavish pictorial record of the time, see Iwamoto, *Nihon eiga to modanizumu* (Japanese film and modernism).

28. "Five thousand ordinarilly [sic] sensible people completely lost their sense of propriety Thursday and broke through police cordons, swept aside the offi-cers of the law in a pandemonium, and broke into a mob when Mary Pickford and Douglas Fairbanks stepped out from their train at Tokyo Station at 4:45 pm," reported the *Japan Times* (December 21, 1929). Two days later the Japanese language *Nichi Nichi* reported that "Doug and Mary Left Japan Suddenly Because

of Recent New York Stock Tumble." A few weeks later another article in the *Japan Times* (hereafter *JT*) quotes Fairbanks as saying "It took us five days to recover from the strain of the hospitality shown in Japan" (January 19, 1930).

29. *JT*, November 4, 1929, 4.

30. See Iwamoto, *Nihon eiga to modanizumu*, especially pp. 50–64.

31. *JT*, December 14, 1930, 4.

32. Seidensticker, *Tokyo Rising*, 100.

33. Uenoda, *Japan and Jazz*, 16. Originally published in *Japan Advertiser*, September 11, 1927.

34. *JT*, November 30, 1930, 9.

35. *JT*, February 1, 1930, 4.

36. Fujitake, "The Formation of Mass Culture," 780.

37. Smith, "Tokyo as an Idea," 69.

In the *Japan Times* an article claimed that Japan is rapidly becoming an English-speaking country. About 30 percent of words spoken daily are English, says the author (December 29, 1929, 5). For instance, a train conductor will call out, "All right, Ikimasuyo!" and a group of schoolgirls might chatter about their classmate: "Hana-chan wa good dancer desune. Anokata wa waltz yori foxtrot no hoga umaiwa!" They comment on the appearance of foreigners riding the train: "Seiyojin no style wa iine. Fleshcolor no stockings ga annani yoku feet ni fit shiteru. Dance surukara, poise ga yoinodesune." And a pair of salary men gossip about politics: "Kimi dodai, kono scandal. Shame dane. Bribe wo toru yatsu ga kon-nani oinowa control dekinaikane." The headlines for New Year's Day, 1930, boldly proclaim, "Premier Lauds World Progress in Year's Review; Racial Animosity on the Wane Throughout Universe, He Says; Sees Peace Ahead; Future Is Bright, Declares Prime Minister in Official Statement." In the wake of dizzying Westernization, corruption, scandal, and economic depression, some evidently maintained their sense of humor.

Compare this with the "official antipathy" for foreign morals caused by international tensions in the mid-thirties, resulting in "efforts to uproot from the Japanese language imported words such as *mama* and *papa*. . . . Derivations from the German language, however, were soon on the upswing." See Kasza, *The State and Mass Media*, 139. Richie writes, "When the new Western-style PCL Studio was built [in 1929] it was playfully averred that the initials stood not for Photo Chemical Laboratory but for Pork Cutlet Lard, something which the lean fish-eating Japanese associated with the gross West" (*Japanese Cinema*, 38).

38. Silverberg gives a fine reading on the unstable sexual and national identity of moga and her ultimate recruitment in continental exploits through the suffering of the ill-named "comfort women":

> The mobilization of Chinese and Korean women in *modan*, Japanese-style bars, restaurants, and meeting places on the continent is historically related to the horrors experienced by the

so-called comfort women, the *ianfu* who were forced into sexual slavery by the Japanese military, and to the predecessors/precursors of the *ianfu*, the Korean women restaurant workers first brought to Sapporo, Hokkaido, in the 1920s to serve Korean laborers. ("Remembering Pearl Harbor," 32)

39. *JT*, November 24, 1929, 5.

40. *JT*, January 1, 1930, 4.

41. Mitchell, *Censorship in Imperial Japan*, 200.

42. *JT*, January 12, 1930, 7.

43. *JT*, November 9, 1930.

44. *JT*, November 19, 1930, 4.

45. *JT*, December 14, 1930, 4.

46. Anderson and Richie, *The Japanese Film*, 64.

47. Although this came shortly after the mass arrests of communist youth, early 1932 saw strikes among the benshi and musicians in the Shochiku and Nikkatsu studios over the transition to sound. In 1933 P.C.L., the progenitor of Toho, gave starring roles to Tokugawa Musei, the top benshi of the day, to forestall organized opposition from benshi to the new company's initiation. Organized crime was also involved in strikebreaking and intimidation of labor during this period, as in the celebrated 1937 slashing of Hasegawa Kazuo. Anderson and Richie, *The Japanese Film*, 78–81, 86–88. See also Kirihara, "A Reconsideration."

48. Mitchell, *Censorship in Imperial Japan*, 174.

49. Powell, *Kabuki in Modern Japan*, 7.

50. *JT*, January 12, 1930, 7.

51. *JT*, January 31, 1930, 4.

52. Anderson and Richie, *The Japanese Film*, 68.

53. Iwasaki Akira, "An Outline History of the Japanese Cinema," *Cinema Yearbook of Japan 1936–1937* (Tokyo: Sanseido), 8–9.

54. *JT*, February 9, 1930.

55. Anderson and Richie, *The Japanese Film*, 68.

56. Iwasaki, "An Outline History," 9, and Anderson and Richie, *The Japanese Film*, 70.

57. Anderson and Richie, *The Japanese Film*, 65; Iwasaki, "An Outline History," 8.

58. Anderson and Richie, *The Japanese Film*, 66. In this connection is mentioned Kinugasa's all-talking *Chushingura* (1933, with Tanaka Kinuyo), which, if it were available for viewing, would make an excellent comparison with Mizoguchi's 1941 version.

59. Iwasaki, "An Outline History," 8.

60. Quoted in Phyllis Birnbaum, "Profiles: Modern Girl," *The New Yorker*, October 31, 1988, 48 (on Uno Chiyo).

61. Quoted in High, "Japanese Film Theory," 142.

62. Van Wolferen, *The Enigma of Japanese Power,* 288.

63. See Mitchell, *Censorship in Imperial Japan,* and Kasza, *The State and Mass Media,* for censorship studies based on primary materials.

64. Silverberg, "Remembering Pearl Harbor," 40.

65. Najita and Harootunian, "Japanese Revolt Against the West," 711.

66. Gluck, *Japan's Modern Myths,* 135.

67. Mitchell, *Censorship in Imperial Japan,* 337.

68. Ibid.

69. Ibid., 339.

70. Ibid., 337–38.

71. A good example of (self-)censorship as an enabler of certain forms is the rise of *fuseiji,* or the practice of selectively concealing inflammatory words by simply inserting marks (X-es, dots, or circles) that substituted for the offending passages. As early as 1910, serialized work by such authors as Futabatei Shimei, Morita Sohei and Nagai Kafu were published in book form using *fuseiji* to get around the controversial material stricken from the earlier serialized versions. Of course, it didn't take long for censors to become as leery of *fuseiji* as of actual censorable material. According to Mitchell, "By the mid-1930s the authorities were in a mood to ban it, because editors were growing ever more skillful in using this device to slip through the censorship net" (*Censorship in Imperial Japan,* 280). See also pp. 163–65.

72. Mitchell, *Censorship in Imperial Japan,* 300.

73. Kasza, *The State and Mass Media,* 235.

74. Ibid.

75. Kasza, *The State and Mass Media,* 233; Anderson and Richie, *The Japanese Film,* 128–29.

76. Kasza, *The State and Mass Media,* 233.

77. Ibid., 235.

78. Ibid., 236.

79. Mizoguchi was appointed the national film consultant by the prime minister in 1938 and the following year traveled to Manchuria with five other directors (Andrew and Andrew, *Kenji Mizoguchi,* 11). Anderson and Richie report that Mizoguchi was elected head of the All Japan Film Makers League in 1940; whether this means that Mizoguchi occupied the leadership posts of both the national trade organization and the government advisory position at the same time is uncertain but historically tantalizing ("Kenji Mizoguchi," *Sight and Sound* 25, 2 [Autumn 1955], 77). In 1948, exhibiting the usual fluency in overnight switching from an extreme right to an extreme left (and the other way about), he became president of the Ofuna Local of Nichien, a dominant labor union that controlled film production during this period, at least in certain studios.

80. Anderson and Richie, *The Japanese Film,* 129.

81. Kasza, *The State and Mass Media,* 238–39.

82. Ibid., 238–39, table 21: "Pieces of Film Cut Under the Motion Picture Film Inspection Regulations and the Film Law, By Censorship Standards and Area of Production, 1937–1942." By far the most footage cut is from the "Manners and Morals" category rather than "Public Safety." Within the former category, "Sex-related" offenses make up the vast majority, with "Cruelty/ugliness" a distant second and breaches in the portrayal of "Education" just behind that.

83. Anderson and Richie, *The Japanese Film*, 129.

84. Kasza, *The State and Mass Media*, 237.

85. Ibid., 240.

86. High, "Japanese Film Theory," 135. But it is easy to overemphasize the parallels between the Japanese and Nazi propaganda machines. Don Kirihara points out many differences between them, the most important being that the Japanese film industry was never nationalized, even though it was severely consolidated for tighter centralized control (*Patterns of Time*, pp. 54–55).

87. High, "Japanese Film Theory," 136–37.

88. Ibid., 136. High goes on to describe the "bureaucratic ambush" of the documentarist Kamei Fumio, whose "right" to prior inspection of scripts was withdrawn in the early 1940s, when the authorities came to realize Kamei's films implicitly contained a pacifist message.

89. Ehrlich, "The Artist's Desire," 158. The Education Minister's Prize was also given to Mizoguchi's next film, *Naniwa Onna* (1940), and a Special Education Minister's Prize was awarded to *Genroku Chushingura* (1941–1942).

90. High, "Japanese Film Theory," 148.

91. Ibid., 134. These *bidan* ("human bomb") stories originated in the suicidal heroism of three soldiers who strapped bombs to their bodies and blew up a fortification in the earliest of the Manchurian skirmishes in the early 1930s. Their celebrity was wildly disproportional to their military contribution, and is prophetic of the forms Japanese militarism would take on the homefront. The *kamikaze* pilots of World War II have a long lineage that Westerners tend to forget.

92. Richie, *Japanese Cinema*, 39.

93. High, "Japanese Film Theory," 142.

94. Anderson and Richie, *The Japanese Film*, 129.

95. Ibid.

96. Mellen, *The Waves at Genji's Door*, 152–66.

97. McDonald, *Mizoguchi*, chronology; Mellen, *The Waves at Genji's Door*, 160.

98. Kirihara, *Patterns of Time*, 138.

4. Two Cultures and the Japanese Period Film

1. According to Northrop Frye, shifts in fictional modes are a "change of social context rather than of literary form, and the constructive principles of

story-telling remain constant through them, though of course they adapt to them." See his first essay in *Anatomy of Criticism*, "Historical Criticism: Theory of Modes," 51.

2. Tetsuo Najita and H. D. Harootunian, "Japanese Revolt Against the West: Political and Cultural Criticism in the Twentieth Century," in Duus, *The Cambridge History of Japan*, 735.

3. In film criticism, Bordwell's theory of modes (*Narration in the Fiction Film*) is predicated on the process of narration, defining mode as "a historically distinct set of norms of narrational construction and comprehension" (150). Bordwell takes mode to mean a range of permissible norms and devices occurring within national and historical horizons (e.g., the classical Hollywood mode). Frye, on the other hand, finds modal elements in semantic realms like theme and plot, and therefore can make different modal assignments to the same device, depending on its historical predecessor. Bordwell's emphasis on narration and Frye's expressive classification lend a "hollow," competence-oriented aspect to the Bordwell mode relative to the substantive, performance-oriented tendency in Frye's.

4. High, "Japanese Film and the Great Kanto Earthquake," 83.

5. See Kasza, *The State and Mass Media*, and Mitchell, *Censorship in Imperial Japan*, for the specific means by which official control of popular thinking about the war was attempted.

6. Andrew and Andrew, *Kenji Mizoguchi*, 13.

7. The Library of Congress holds approximately fourteen hundred Japanese films in a collection of audiovisual materials confiscated by the Occupation authorities (Supreme Commander, Allied Powers, i.e., SCAP) in 1945. With the strictures of the Occupation, samurai movies were banned for their "feudal" themes, which were thought to inspire militarism in their viewers. Scores of films were destroyed before the confiscation began. What films that were salvaged are mostly inferior copies of release prints, many of whose reels are out of order, torn, and clipped for study by Occupation researchers. This collection also contains many important *gendai geki*, contemporary genre films, not just samurai movies. For an in-depth study of the Occupation and the Japanese film industry, see Hirano's *Mr. Smith Goes to Tokyo*.

8. Burch says that chambara is distinguished from its theatrical kabuki and shimpa forebears by "the greater realism of the sword-fights" (*To the Distant Observer*, 110). This accords with my emphasis on the "low comedy" norms of jidai geki in the early 1930s, at least with respect to the less realistic theatricality of earlier shimpa-style jidai geki. Burch also concedes that the film is a partial parody of the Ito Daisuke style, which most clearly exemplifies the fast-paced "American-style" chambara (p. 111, n. 4).

9. Silver, *The Samurai Film*, 96.

10. Ibid., 102.

11. This is consistent with Barrett's argument that Musashi's wartime func-

tion was the exhortation to sacrifice personal fulfillment for the state, whereas "Uchida's 'peacetime' Musashi simply represents an antisocial obsession with individual success at all costs" (*Archetypes in Japanese Film*, 52).

12. Andrew and Andrew, *Kenji Mizoguchi*, 38.

13. Anderson and Richie, *The Japanese Film*, 86–88.

14. *Kodansha Encyclopedia of Japan*, vol. 8.

15. I am indebted to the anonymous reader for Columbia University Press for this information.

16. *Kodansha Encyclopedia of Japan*, vol. 4, 182.

17. Ibid.

18. See Smethurst, *A Social Basis;* Peter B. High, "The Transmigrating Hero: Ideological Structures in the Japanese National Policy Film, 1939–1945," unpublished ms., Nagoya University, 16, 24–25.

19. High, "The Transmigrating Hero," 16.

20. Duus, *The Cambridge History of Japan*, 726.

21. Ibid.

22. Smethurst, *A Social Basis*, 178.

23. John Dower, "Japanese Cinema Goes to War," *Japan Society Newsletter*, July 1987, 8. Reprinted in his *Japan in War and Peace*.

24. High, "For Profit and Patriotism," 136.

25. Keene, "Variations on a Theme: *Chushingura*," in Brandon, *Chushingura*, 8–9.

26. High, "The Transmigrating Hero," 23.

27. Both of the 1990 films made to commemorate the death of Sen no Rikyu, Kumai Kei's *Death of a Tea Master* and Teshigahara Hiroshi's *Rikyu*, fall within this legacy. See the discussion of the latter in chapter 8.

5. *Story of the Last Chrysanthemum* (1939): A "Riptide of Reaction"

The phrase "riptide of reaction" is Donald Shively's, in *Tradition and Modernization in Japanese Culture*, 77–119.

1. Andrew and Andrew, *Kenji Mizoguchi*, 31.

2. Barrett writes, "Although the characters in these contemporary [shimpa] plays were usually dressed in the latest Western fashions, they did not differ greatly from their Kabuki counterparts because their love still ended tragically. Still, their heroes, often college students, were even weaker than their feudal predecessors" (*Archetypes in Japanese Film*, 125). The weakness of the vacillating *nimaime* ("second billing" character) is an indication of the character's modernity. The more modern they are, the weaker their love is likely to be, because the *nimaime* will have public responsibilities to fulfill that prevent him from committing suicide or eloping with his beloved.

3. Wakabayashi, *Anti-Foreignism and Western Learning*, 7.

4. Ian Buruma, "The Jingo Olympics: Playing for Keeps," *New York Review of Books*, November 10, 1988, 44–50. Cf. the popular hymn "Onward Christian Soldiers." Buruma analyzes the similarities and differences between Victorian expressions of muscular Christianity through sports and the burst of quasi-religious nationalistic fervor manifested by the Koreans in the Seoul Olympics.

5. In great detail, Van Wolferen's *The Enigma of Japanese Power* analyzes Japanese society as surrogate religion, but this idea can be found in some form in many sociocultural studies of Japan. Takie Sugiyama Lebra, for instance, adapts Durkheim's concept of the "sociocult" for use in Japan, where the group, from family, to neighborhood, to corporation, to nation, is deified, in opposition to the deification of the individual in American ideology (*Japanese Culture and Behavior* [Honolulu: University of Hawaii Press, 1986]).

6. Barrett, *Archetypes in Japanese Film*, 147. See also Kawamura Nozomu, "The Historical Background of Arguments Emphasizing the Uniqueness of Japanese Society," *Social Analysis* 5/6 (December 1980), 4.

7. Robert N. Bellah, *Beyond Belief: Essays on Religion in a Post-Traditional World* (New York: Harper and Row, 1976), 88; quoted in Barrett, *Archetypes in Japanese Film*, 148.

8. Barrett, *Archetypes in Japanese Film*, 191–92. Barrett attributes this idea of theistic-parental transfer to George DeVos, *Socialization for Achievement* (Berkeley: University of California Press, 1975).

9. Van Wolferen, *The Enigma of Japanese Power*, 281.

10. Garon, "Rethinking Modernization," 352, 354–58. In addition to Tomeoka, other prominent Japanese Protestants like Kanamori Michitomo and Nitobe Inazo actively assisted the state in its modernizing, Westernizing efforts through the early 1930s.

11. Wakabayashi, *Anti-Foreignism and Western Learning*, 12.

12. Ibid., 13. This "inoculation" process found its sharpest expression in the strategies of the Meiji restoration: "as the state religion of a new 'civilized' Japan," writes Tsurumi Shunsuke, "Shinto was given a role akin to that of Christianity in Western countries and an increasingly monotheistic character."

13. Tsurumi, *An Intellectual History of Wartime Japan*, 25.

14. Wakabayashi, *Anti-Foreignism and Western Learning*, 13–14.

15. Kirihara, *Patterns of Time*, 139–40. See Ch. 7, n. 25 on the force-sense distinction.

16. Ibid., 151.

17. Ibid.

18. Barrett, *Archetypes in Japanese Film*, 98–99.

19. Ibid.

20. Ibid., 99.

21. Andrew and Andrew, *Kenji Mizoguchi*, 31.

22. Mitchell, *Censorship in Imperial Japan*, 207.

23. People who interpose themselves between combatants in the interest of

conflict avoidance is a quintessentially Japanese image, in all kinds of films, in television, and in everyday life. Karel Van Wolferen, speaking of professional conflict minimizers in diplomacy and business negotiations, calls them, variously, buffers, informants, and apologists (*The Enigma of Japanese Power*, 11–13).

24. See Cohen, "Mizoguchi and Modernism," 110–18.

25. Van Wolferen, *The Enigma of Japanese Power*, 329.

26. Ehrlich, "The Artist's Desire," 164–65.

27. Raz, *Audience and Actor*, 181, quoted in Ehrlich, "The Artist's Desire," 165.

28. See Bordwell on the "screening" function of Mizoguchi's set design, "Mizoguchi and the Evolution of Film Language." Another good example of this is the "wandering camera" in the scene of Lady Asano's chastisement of Oishi in *Genroku Chushingura*. See chapter 6.

29. Seike Kiyosi, "Architecture, Traditional Domestic" in *Kodansha Encyclopedia of Japan*, vol. 1, 81.

30. Ehrlich, "The Artist's Desire," 160.

31. Cited ibid., 160–61.

32. Greenbie, *Space and Spirit in Modern Japan*, 53ff.

33. Ibid.

34. Ibid.

35. Ibid.

36. Seike, "Architecture, Traditional Domestic," 82.

37. Ehrlich, "The Artist's Desire," 161.

38. Greenbie, *Space and Spirit in Modern Japan*, 44. The neurolinguist Greenbie discusses with some approval is Tsunoda Tadanobu, who wrote a book arguing for the uniqueness of the Japanese brain called *The Japanese Brain: Uniqueness and Universality* (Tokyo: Taishukan, 1985; trans. Oiwa Yoshinori).

39. John Dower, *The Elements of Japanese Design: A Handbook of Family Crests, Heraldry, and Symbolism* (New York, Tokyo: Weatherhill, 1971), 35.

40. Arthur Koestler, *The Lotus and the Robot* (New York: Macmillan, 1960).

6. *Genroku Chushingura* (1941–1942)

Major parts of this chapter were published in Ehrlich and Desser, Cinematic Landscapes.

1. Barrett estimates it was filmed more than eighty times between 1907 and 1962, and Anderson says he stopped counting at 220 features dealing with the Chushingura story. See *Archetypes in Japanese Film*, 23, and Anderson and Richie, *The Japanese Film*, 446.

2. See Barrett for a good discussion of this genealogy of *Chushingura* evolution across different media (*Archetypes in Japanese Film*, 26ff).

3. Davis, "Back to Japan," 16–25.

4. David Ansen, on the Arts and Entertainment Network, August 1988. I am indebted to Virginia Wright Wexman for making me aware of this broadcast.

Mellen makes a similar claim in her discussion of Mizoguchi's *Chushingura* in *The Waves at Genji's Door*.

5. Barrett, *Archetypes in Japanese Film*, 23.

6. Nitobe, *Bushido*, 141.

7. High, "For Profit and Patriotism," 141.

8. High, "Japanese Film and the Great Kanto Earthquake," 83.

9. High, "For Profit and Patriotism," 149.

10. Declared by Shochiku's Ushihara Kiyohiko on returning from a trip to Europe, where he saw how Japanese aggression was portrayed in foreign, especially American, newsreels. High, "For Profit and Patriotism," 148.

11. High, "For Profit and Patriotism," 150.

12. Ibid., 150.

13. Zenshinza was a communist kabuki troupe headed by Kawarasaki Chojuro, whose Kokoroza (Soul Theater, after Evreinov) merged with two other kabuki and *shingeki* companies to perform proletarian plays. Zenshinza was formed as a progressive company intent on debunking the reigning kabuki styles and establishments. However, its timing (May 1931), was most unfortunate, this being a period of crackdown against all forms of leftist activism on campus, in arts and letters, and in media/performing arts. The company had to compromise its principles, and soon had a reputation for mounting fine productions of the original *Kanadehon Chushingura*. Zenshinza was the company of choice for the production of Mayama Seika's historically painstaking *Genroku Chushingura*, and it was also the company used for Mizoguchi's screen adaptation of the same play. Mayama's historical theater, like that of the once-proletarian Fujimori Seikichi, was ideally suited to the talents of Zenshinza, and the company continued its collaboration with Mayama through the end of the war. It continued its policy of collective, communalistic production and decision making, true to its original proletarian inspiration, and in 1949 its members voted to join the Japan Communist Party. Powell, "Communist *Kabuki*."

14. Keene, "Variations on a Theme," 14.

15. Mayama had also been in the employ of Shochiku's shimpa division, which presumably made it easy for the film studio to adapt it for the screen. However, he had also been an "idealistic" young Marxist in the 1920s, which complicates the evocation of bushido in Mayama's cycle from the 1930s. The more rousing, headlong expressions of chauvinist loyalty (Tamon's intercessions, Tokubei's suicide) are not congruent with Oishi's understanding of honorable conduct, and may reflect Mayama's distaste for post-1936 bushido militarism. Powell, "The Samurai Ethic." For an in-depth discussion of Mayama's *Chushingura* cycle, see Powell's *Kabuki in Modern Japan*, especially chapter 6.

16. Keene, "Variations on a Theme," 13.

17. Ibid., 16.

18. Ibid., 15.

19. Ibid.

20. Keene, "Variations on a Theme," 17.

21. Andrew and Andrew, *Kenji Mizoguchi*, 107.

22. Ibid., 108.

23. Ibid., 14.

24. Weismann, *The Visual Arts as Human Experience*, 140. Of course photography is a two-dimensional medium, but a tracking shot taken with moving picture photography clearly records its own defining movement in space, even if that space was made solely for the purpose of being filmed. It is possible to maintain, therefore, that the space may be illusory but the movement through it is not. Three-dimensionality in film, therefore, is not an illusion. Cf. Greenbie's definition of architecture and landscape design: "Only humans can maintain a (relatively) permanent physical record of life experience in space. Indeed, one definition of architecture and landscape architecture might be the art of recording human experience in time-space" (*Space and Spirit in Modern Japan*, 44). This is not a bad definition of film, either, at least Mizoguchi's film of *Genroku Chushingura*.

25. Contrast this depsychologizing (Brechtian?) gesture with the characterization of women in the film, who are given the opposite function of magnifying the personal and psychological consequences of the samurai ethos.

A caveat: *Genroku Chushingura*'s opening scene, with its paroxysm of violence and hysteria, is highly atypical of the rest of the film. It is a departure from Mayama's play as well, which does not stage the attack, and in fact does not even bring Kira onstage (Keene, "Variations on a Theme," 13). But this is consistent with the preoccupation with disjunctions of expectations and reality. The scene has an historical aspect, too, given the traditional status of Chushingura as a vehicle for swashbuckling action.

26. Burch, *To the Distant Observer*, 240.

27. Burch even says that symmetry in Japanese architecture is reserved for temple structures, but gives no citation (ibid., 238). If true, this is consistent with my argument that the sequence invites semireligious perceptual concentration and vigilance, despite its spectacular action.

28. Although *shoin* architecture is associated with the aristocracy, the surrounding *kare sansui* dry landscape garden was a product of the upward mobility of *kawaramono*, or outcasts. Outcast gardeners, denied access to the written traditions of stone-setting priests, were compelled to design "withered mountains and water" (*kare sansui*) gardens of astounding creativity and gradually earned the right to become Jishu temple gardeners by examination. Zen priests cooperated with these people, acting as mentors and patrons, to help bring the *kare sansui* style to recognition. Itoh, *The Gardens of Japan*, 80–81.

29. "Gardens," *Kodansha Encyclopedia of Japan*, vol. 3, 10.

30. "Architecture, Traditional Domestic," *Kodansha Encyclopedia of Japan*, vol. 1, 81.

31. Bordwell, *Narration in the Fiction Film*, 242.

32. Burch, *To the Distant Observer,* 238. See also Keene, "Variations on a Theme."

33. Hagen, *Varieties of Realism,* 114.

34. Ibid., 145.

35. Andrew and Andrew, *Kenji Mizoguchi,* 31.

36. Burch, *To the Distant Observer,* 200.

37. To be fair to Burch, he singles out Mizoguchi as a director who likes to use character movement in "contradiction" to the predominant two-dimensionality of the image space. But what Burch sees as a contradiction I see as an essential element of Mizoguchi's stylistics and of the monumental style.

38. Kirihara, *Patterns of Time,* 69.

39. Weismann, *The Visual Arts as Human Experience,* 186–87.

40. Burch, *To the Distant Observer,* 70, 108 (especially n. 18), 116, 118.

41. Cohen, "Mizoguchi and Modernism," Andrew and Andrew, *Kenji Mizoguchi.*

42. Andrew and Andrew, *Kenji Mizoguchi,* 38ff.

43. Burch, *To the Distant Observer,* 238.

44. Ibid., 240–41.

45. Bill Marx, "Secret Agent Man: Walter Benjamin Breaks the Code," *Voice Literary Supplement,* March 1989, 18.

7. Historical Uses and Misuses: The Janus Face(s) of *The Abe Clan*

Major parts of this chapter were published in Film History *7, 1 (Spring 1995), 49–68.*

1. Ogai, "Abe Ichizoku," *The Incident at Sakai and Other Stories,* 48–49. References to the film will be made in English and italicized while references to the novella will be made in Japanese and put in quotations.

2. Dower makes a version of this analogy in his discussion of Japanese family hierarchy as wartime ideology in *War Without Mercy,* 266.

3. Shillony, *Politics and Culture in Wartime Japan,* 2.

4. Ibid., 3–4.

5. Ibid., 2; Miles, *The Search for a New Order,* 3.

6. Ogai, "Abe Ichizoku," 15.

7. Ibid., 15–16. Some writers credit Nogi's suicide with revitalizing Ogai's literary career, which until this time had lain dormant for years.

8. Ibid., 15–16. Many historians consider the Russo-Japanese war, in turn, the turning point in the Japanese accession to its status as a world power. General Nogi, therefore, is a pivotal figure indeed.

9. Ibid., 36.

10. Ibid., 54.

11. Ibid., 15.

12. High, "Japanese Film Theory," 143. This particular objection is quoted in High's article but is not attributed to any individual critic.

13. Ibid., 146.

14. Uchida Kisao, *Cinema Year Book of Japan 1939*, 40.

15. High, "Japanese Film Theory," 15. An interesting irony is that while many Japanese critics denounced *The Abe Clan* for its bushido warmongering, the film looks ambivalent, even pacifist, today (see n. 29). This may indicate not only the film's multivalence, but the persistence well into the late thirties of a more pluralist range of opinion than is commonly thought.

16. High, "Japanese Film Theory," 143, quoted from a February 1938 article by Sawamura collected into *Gendai Eigaron* (Tokyo, 1941). Sawamura also excoriated such masterpieces as *I Was Born But . . .* for their "limpness of spirit."

17. Ibid., 143.

18. Gluck, *Japan's Modern Myths*, 102, 111–15, 138–43; Mitchell, *Thought Control in Prewar Japan*, 19–20; Louis Allen, *Japan: The Years of Triumph* (New York: American Heritage Press, 1971), 84; Peter B. High, "The Transmigrating Hero: Ideological Structures in the Japanese National Policy Film, 1939–1945," unpublished ms., Nagoya University, 30. See also Tetsuo Najita and H. D. Harootunian, "Japanese Revolt Against the West: Political and Cultural Criticism in the Twentieth Century," in Duus, *The Cambridge History of Japan*, 714ff., for a good discussion of the concept of kokutai.

19. Mitchell, *Thought Control in Prewar Japan*, 26, Shillony, *Politics and Culture in Wartime Japan*, 57.

20. Shillony, *Revolt in Japan*, chapter 3.

21. Mitchell, *Thought Control in Prewar Japan*, 30.

22. On the intellectual roots of Showa restorationism, see Najita and Harootunian, "Japanese Revolt Against the West," 713–34. It is important to note that the Showa restoration was a widespread movement with a variety of emphases and goals, cf. Mitchell, *Thought Control in Prewar Japan*, 37–38.

23. Quoted in Morris-Suzuki, *Showa*, 79.

24. Maruyama, *Thought and Behavior*, 69.

25. The force-sense distinction is an important one in the linguistic branch of pragmatics. *Sense* refers to meaning or signification; *force* refers to the pragmatic implications of an utterance. For example, the sense of "It's cold in here, isn't it?" is different from its force, which could involve a request to turn up the heat, among other things.

26. Shillony, *Revolt in Japan*, 56.

27. See Donald Roden, *Schooldays in Imperial Japan* (University of California Press, 1980) on the reception of kokutai ideology in the higher schools, especially 238–42.

28. Shillony, *Revolt in Japan*, 65.

29. Tadao Sato on *The Abe Clan*: "During World War II, when I was a boy, we were taught that central to Bushido is loyalty and devotion toward one's supe-

riors. In *The Abe Clan*, which I saw after the war, it seemed that one's sense of honor takes priority and must be maintained even at the cost of abandoning this loyalty," *Currents in Japanese Cinema*, 47.

30. Ogai, "Abe Ichizoku," 40.

31. Ibid., 51.

32. Ibid.

33. Ibid., 59.

34. Ibid., 63.

35. Ibid.

36. Ibid., 60. Translated in the novella as "Feeling is one thing, duty is another,"

37. Ibid., 52.

38. Ibid., 53.

39. Ibid., 58.

40. Ibid., 43.

41. Ibid., 47–8.

42. Karo shu wa / Tomare tomare to/ Ose aredo/

Tomete Tomaranu / Kono Gosuke kana

The Elders / Urge me to stop/ Yet even so
I cannot, / Not this Gosuke!

Translated by David Dilworth in Ogai, "Abe Ichizoku," 49.

43. Ibid., 48.

44. Ibid. 54.

45. Ibid., 66.

46. Keith Thomas, "Just Say Yes," *The New York Review of Books*, November 24, 1988, 43.

47. A distinction made by Bordwell in *Making Meaning*.

8. Other Manifestations of the Monumental Style

1. See Hirano, *Mr. Smith Goes to Tokyo*.

2. Dudley Andrew, *Film in the Aura of Art* (Princeton University Press, 1984), 184.

3. James Peterson, "A War of Utter Rebellion: Kinugasa's *Page of Madness* and the Japanese Avant-Garde of the 1920s," *Cinema Journal* 29, 1 (Fall 1989), 36–53.

4. Anderson and Richie, *The Japanese Film*, 399.

5. *Variety*, November 25, 1953, review of *Jigokumen* [sic].

6. *New York Times*, review, December 14, 1954.

7. Anderson and Richie, *The Japanese Film*, 274.

8. The Itsukushima torii was built by Taira no Kiyomori in the late twelfth century and placed in the salt flats of Hiroshima bay to appear as if it were floating at high tide. In addition to being a tourist mecca, a major Shinto shrine there houses important national treasures such as the Lotus Sutra, which was dedicated by Kiyomori.

9. *New York Times*, review, December 14, 1954.

10. Joseph S. Chang, "*Kagemusha* and the *Chushingura* Motif," *East-West Film Journal* 3, 2 (June 1989), 31–32.

11. Desser, *The Samurai Films of Akira Kurosawa*, 128.

12. Prince, *The Warrior's Camera*, 279. Actually Prince argues that *Kagemusha* fails to deliver the kind of stylistic self-interrogation exemplified by *Citizen Kane*, but this is because he holds Kurosawa to a "self-reflexive dimension foreign to Kurosawa's work."

13. As does Chang in "*Kagemusha* and the *Chushingura* Motif," 34.

14. From Yoshikawa Eiji's *Musashi: Book 1, The Way of the Samurai* (New York: Pocket Books, 1981), 199.

15. Desser, *The Samurai Films of Akira Kurosawa*, 127, 128.

16. Perrin, *Giving Up the Gun*, 25.

17. Ibid., 25.

18. Chang, "*Kagemusha* and the *Chushingura* Motif," 34.

19. Brian Parker, "Kurosawa's *Ran* and the Tragedy of History," *University of Toronto Quarterly* 55, 4 (Summer 1986), 415.

20. By, among others, Ann Thompson in "Kurosawa's *Ran*: Reception and Interpretation," *East-West Film Journal* (June 1989), 6, and Parker in "Kurosawa's *Ran*," 414. Parker is very good on the noh connection, but overgeneralizes it to mean, broadly, "stylization," "symbolism," and "affectlessness": "Long shots flatten character so that a Noh-like objective aloofness is maintained, in the same way that Noh masks impose a surrender of subjectivism upon the actors wearing them" (414); "Colour is an essential part of the imagery of *Ran*, in fact, and, as in Noh drama, it is used as a notation for immediate symbolic effect" (415).

21. Rob Silberman, review of *Ran*, *Cineaste* 14, 4 (1986), 51.

22. Prince, *The Warrior's Camera*, 289.

23. Ibid.

24. Parker, "Kurosawa's *Ran*," 414. Parker also connects these cloud formations with the "seamless flow and dreamlike rhythms of Noh, rather than drawing attention to the joins with discontinuities, jump cuts, and odd camera angles as [Peter] Brook strove so deliberately to do."

25. H. Paul Varley and George Elison, "The Culture of Tea: From Its Origins to Sen no Rikyu," in George Elison and Bardwell L. Smith, eds., *Warlords, Artists, and Commoners: Japan in the Sixteenth Century* (Honolulu: University Press of Hawaii, 1981), 220.

26. Ibid., 222.

27. Desser, *The Samurai Films of Akira Kurosawa*, 75; *Giri/ninjo*: the clash of human feeling with social obligation that is such a favorite in traditional Japanese drama, especially kabuki (see chapter 5).

28. Kinmonth, *The Self-Made Man*, 332.

29. "In short, the illiberal New Order was more than a conservative or nativist return to premodern or Meiji-era Japan; its modern ingredients of mass mobilization and state controls over the economy flowed, in a sense, from the democratic and socialist currents of the 1920s." Garon, "Rethinking Modernization," 350.

30. Schrader, *Transcendental Style in Film*.

Selected Bibliography

Historiography and Method

Ackerman, James S. "Style." In James S. Ackerman and Rhys Carpenter, eds., *Art and Archaeology*, Englewood Cliffs, N.J.: Prentice-Hall, 1963.

Allen, Robert C., and Douglas Gomery. *Film History: Theory and Practice*. New York: Random House, 1985.

Anderson, Benedict. *Imagined Communities: Reflections on the Origin and Spread of Nationalism*. Rev. ed. London: Verso, 1991.

Bakhtin, M. M. *The Dialogic Imagination: Four Essays by M. M. Bakhtin*. Ed. Michael Holquist. Trans. Michael Holquist and Caryl Emerson. Austin: University of Texas Press, 1981.

Barthes, Roland. *Image Music Text*. Trans. S. Heath. New York: Hill and Wang, 1977.

— *Mythologies*. Trans. Annette Lavers. New York: Hill and Wang, 1972.

Benedict, Ruth. *Patterns of Culture*. Boston: Houghton Mifflin, 1934.

Bhabha, Homi, ed. *Nation and Narration*. London: Routledge, 1990.

Bordwell, David. *Making Meaning: Inference and Rhetoric in the Interpretation of Cinema*. Cambridge: Harvard University Press, 1989.

— "Jump Cuts and Blind Spots." *Wide Angle* (1984), 6(1):4–11.

— *Narration in the Fiction Film*. Madison: University of Wisconsin Press, 1985.

Brecht, Bertolt. *Brecht on Theatre*. Trans. J. Willett. London: Methuen, 1964.

Crofts, Stephen. "Reconceptualizing National Cinema/s." *Quarterly Review of Film and Video* (1993), 14(3):49–67.

Dittmer, Lowell, and Samuel S. Kim, eds. *China's Quest for National Identity*. Ithaca: Cornell University Press, 1993.

Donald, James. "How English Is It? Popular Literature and National Culture." *New Formations* 6 (Winter 1988), 31–48.

Eagleton, Terry. *Criticism and Ideology: A Study in Marxist Literary Theory*. London: Verso, 1976.

Eichenbaum, Boris. "O. Henry and the Theory of the Short Story." In Ladislav Matejka and Krystyna Pomorska, eds., *Readings in Russian Poetics: Formalist and Structuralist Views*. Ann Arbor: Michigan Slavic Publications, 1978.

Forster, Kurt. "Monument/Memory and the Mortality of Architecture." *Oppositions* 25 (1982), 2–19.

Frye, Northrop. *Anatomy of Criticism*. Princeton: Princeton University Press, 1957.

Gellner, Ernest. *Nations and Nationalism*. Ithaca: Cornell University Press, 1983.

Gombrich, Ernst. "Style." In David L. Sills, ed., *International Encyclopedia of the Social Sciences*, 15:352–61. Macmillan, 1968.

— *Art and Illusion*. Princeton: Princeton University Press, 1960.

Goodman, Nelson. "The Status of Style." *Critical Inquiry* 1 (1975), 799–811.

Gunning, Tom. *D. W. Griffith and the Origins of American Narrative Film: The Early Years at Biograph*. Chicago: University of Illinois Press, 1991.

— "An Aesthetic of Astonishment. Early Film and the (In)Credulous Spectator." *Art and Text* 34 (Spring 1989), 31–45.

Hagen, Margaret. *Varieties of Realism: Geometries of Representational Art*. Cambridge: Cambridge University Press, 1986.

— "Cultural Effects on Pictorial Perception: How Many Words Is One Picture Really Worth?" In R. D. Walk and H. L. Pick, eds., *Perception and Experience*. New York: Plenum, 1978.

Higson, Andrew. "The Concept of National Cinema." *Screen* 30, 4 (Autumn 1989).

Hobsbawm, Eric. *The Age of Empire*. New York: Pantheon, 1987.

Jameson, Fredric. *The Political Unconscious: Narrative as a Socially Symbolic Act*. Ithaca: Cornell University Press, 1981.

Kinder, Marsha. *Blood Cinema: The Reconstruction of National Identity in Spain*. Berkeley and Los Angeles: University of California Press, 1993.

Lang, Berel, ed. *The Concept of Style*. Philadelphia: University of Pennsylvania Press, 1979.

— "Style as Instrument, Style as Person." *Critical Inquiry* 2 (1978), 710–736.

Lent, John. *The Asian Film Industry*. Austin: University of Texas Press, 1990.

Michelson, Annette. "Screen/Surface: The Politics of Illusionism." *Artforum*, September 1972.

Morley, David, and Kevin Robins. "No Place Like *Heimat*: Images of Home(land) in European Culture." *New Formations* 12 (1990), 1–24.

— "Spaces of Identity: Communications Technologies and the Reconfiguration of Europe." *Screen* 30, 3 (1989), 10–34.

Mosse, George. *The Nationalization of the Masses: Political Symbolism and Mass Movements in Germany from the Napoleonic Wars Through the Third Reich*. New York: Howard Fertig, 1985.

Musser, Charles. *Before the Nickelodeon: Edwin S. Porter and the Edison Manufacturing Company*. Berkeley and Los Angeles: University of California Press, 1991.

Parker, Andrew, et al., eds. *Nationalisms and Sexualities*. London: Routledge, 1992.

Rosen, Philip. "History, Textuality, Nation: Kracauer, Burch, and Some Problems in the Study of National Cinema." *Iris* 2, 2 (Summer 1987), 69–84.

Schapiro, Meyer. "Style." In Sol Tax, ed., *Anthropology Today, Selections*. Chicago: University of Chicago Press, 1962.

Thompson, Kristin. *Exporting Entertainment: America in the World Film Market, 1907–1934*. London: British Film Institute, 1985.

Thompson, Kristin, and David Bordwell. *Film History: An Introduction*. McGraw Hill, 1994.

Tomashevsky, Boris. "Thematics." In Lee T. Lemon and Marion J. Reis, eds., *Russian Formalist Criticism: Four Essays*. Trans. Lee T. Lemon and Marion J. Reis. Lincoln: University of Nebraska Press, 1965.

Tynjanov, Yuri. "On Literary Evolution." In Ladislav Matejka and Krystyna Pomorska, ed., *Readings in Russian Poetics*. Trans. C. A. Luplow. Ann Arbor: Michigan Slavic Publications, 1978.

Weismann, Donald L. *The Visual Arts as Human Experience*. Englewood Cliffs, N.J.: Prentice-Hall, 1970.

Wells, Susan. *The Dialectics of Representation*. Baltimore: Johns Hopkins University Press, 1985.

Wolfflin, Heinrich. *Principles of Art History*. Trans. M. D. Hottinger. New York: Dover, 1950.

Japanese History and Culture

Anesaki, Masaharu. *Art, Life, and Nature in Japan*. Rutland, Vt.: Tuttle, 1973.

Arase, Y. "Mass Communication Between the Two World Wars," *The Developing Economies* 5, 4 (December 1967), 745–766.

Barthes, Roland. *Empire of Signs*. Trans. Richard Howard. New York: Hill and Wang, 1982.

Befu, Harumi, ed. *Cultural Nationalisms in East Asia: Representation and Identity*. Berkeley: Institute of East Asian Studies, 1993.

Bellah, Robert N. "Japan's Cultural Identity: Some Reflections on the Work of Watsuji Tetsuro." *Journal of Asian Studies* 24 (August 1965).

Benedict, Ruth. *The Chrysanthemum and the Sword: Patterns of Japanese Culture*. New York: New American Library, 1946.

Berger, Gordon M. "Changing Historiographical Perspectives on Early Showa Politics: 'The Second Approach.'" *Journal of Asian Studies* 34 (February 1975), 473–484.

Brandon, James R., ed. *Chushingura: Studies in Kabuki and the Puppet Theater*. Honolulu: University of Hawaii Press, 1982.

Buruma, Ian. *Behind the Mask: On Sexual Demons, Sacred Mothers, Transvestites, Gangsters, Drifters, and Other Japanese Cultural Heroes*. New York: New American Library, 1984.

— "Imperialist Japan." Review essay, *The New York Review of Books*, March 17, 1988.

Casalis, Matthieu. "The Semiotics of the Visible in Japanese Rock Gardens," *Semiotica* 44 (1983).

Christopher, Robert C. *The Japanese Mind*. New York: Fawcett Columbine, 1983.

Craig, Albert M. "Fukuzawa Yukichi: The Philosophical Foundations of Meiji Nationalism." In Robert E. Ward, ed., *Political Development in Modern Japan*. Princeton: Princeton University Press, 1968.

Craig, Albert M., and Donald H. Shively, eds. *Personality in Japanese History*. Berkeley and Los Angeles: University of California Press, 1970.

Dalby, Liza Crihfield. *Geisha*. Berkeley and Los Angeles: University of California Press, 1983.

Dale, Peter. *The Myth of Japanese Uniqueness*. New York: St. Martin's, 1986.

Davis, Darrell William. "Anatomy of Misinterpretation." In Virginia Dominguez, ed., *From Beijing to Port Moresby: The Politics of National Cultural Policies*. New York: Gordon and Breach, forthcoming.

Doi, Takeo. *The Anatomy of Dependence*. Trans. John Bester. Tokyo: Kodansha, 1981.

Dower, John. *War Without Mercy: Race and Power in the Pacific War*. New York: Pantheon, 1986.

Dower, John, ed. *Origins of the Modern Japanese State: Selected Writings of E. H. Norman*. New York: Pantheon, 1975.

— *Japan in War and Peace: Selected Essays*. New York: New Press, 1993.

Duke, Benjamin C. *Japan's Militant Teachers: A History of the Left-Wing Teachers' Movement*. Honolulu: University of Hawaii Press, 1973.

Duus, Peter. *Party Rivalry and Political Change in Taisho Japan*. Cambridge: Harvard University Press, 1968.

Duus, Peter, ed. *The Cambridge History of Japan*. Vol. 6: *The Twentieth Century*. Cambridge: Cambridge University Press, 1988.

Embree, John F. *Suye Mura: A Japanese Village*. Chicago: University of Chicago Press, 1939.

Ernst, Earle. *The Kabuki Theatre*. Honolulu: University of Hawaii Press, 1974.

Fletcher, William Miles III. *The Search for a New Order: Intellectuals and Fascism in Prewar Japan*. Chapel Hill: University of North Carolina Press, 1982.

Friedman, Mildred, ed. *Tokyo: Form and Spirit*. Minneapolis: Walker Art Center/New York: Abrams, 1986.

Fujitake, Akira. "The Formation and Development of Mass Culture." *The Developing Economies* 5, 4 (December 1967), 767–82.

Garon, Sheldon. "Rethinking Modernization and Modernity in Japanese History: A Focus on State-Society Relations." *Journal of Asian Studies* 53, 2 (May 1994), 346–366.

Gibney, Frank. *Five Gentlemen of Japan*. Rutland, Vt.: Tuttle, 1973.

Gluck, Carol. *Japan's Modern Myths: Ideology in the Late Meiji Period*. Princeton: Princeton University Press, 1985.

— "The People in History: Recent Trends in Japanese Historiography." *Journal of Asian Studies* 38, 1 (November 1978), 25–50.

Gordon, Jan B. "Japan: The Empty Empire and Its 'Subjects.' " *Salmagundi*, 61 (Fall 1983), 99–111.

Greenbie, Barrie B. *Space and Spirit in Modern Japan*. New Haven: Yale University Press, 1988.

Grinnell-Cleaver, Charles. *Japanese and Americans: Cultural Parallels and Paradoxes*. Rutland, Vt.: Tuttle, 1976.

Halliday, Jon. *A Political History of Japanese Capitalism*. New York: Pantheon, 1975.

Hasegawa, Nyozekan. *The Japanese Character: A Cultural Profile*. Tokyo: Kodansha, 1982.

Havens, Thomas R. H. *The Valley of Darkness: The Japanese People and World War II*. Norton, 1978.

Hayakawa, Masao. *The Garden Art of Japan*. New York: Weatherhill/Heibonsha, 1973.

Higuchi, Kadahiko. *The Visual and Spatial Structure of Landscapes*. Cambridge: MIT Press, 1983.

Iriye, Akira, ed. *Mutual Images: Essays in American-Japanese Relations*. Cambridge: Harvard University Press, 1975.

Itoh, Teiji. *The Gardens of Japan*. Tokyo: Kodansha, 1984.

— *Space and Illusion in the Japanese Garden*. New York: Weatherhill/Tankosha, 1980.

— *The Classic Tradition in Japanese Architecture*. New York: Weatherhill/Tankosha, 1972.

Kato, Hidetoshi, ed. *Japanese Popular Culture*. Tokyo: Tuttle, 1959.

Kato, Shuichi. *Form, Style, Tradition: Reflections on Japanese Art and Society*. Trans. John Bester. Tokyo: Kodansha, 1981.

Kawasaki, Ichiro. *Japan Unmasked*. Rutland, Vt.: Tuttle, 1969.

Keene, Donald. "The Barren Years: Japanese War Literature." *Monumenta Nipponica* 33, 1 (Spring 1978), 67–112.

— "Japanese Literature and Politics in the 1930's." *Journal of Japanese Studies* 2, 2 (Summer 1976), 225–48.

— "Japanese Writers and the Greater East Asia War." *Journal of Asian Studies* 23, 2 (February 1976): 209–25.

— *World Within Walls: Japanese Literature of the Pre-Modern Era, 1600–1868*. New York: Holt, Rinehart, and Winston, 1976.

Keene, Donald, trans. *Chushingura: The Treasury of Loyal Retainers*. A puppet play by Takeda Izumo, Miyoshi Shoraku and Namiki Senryu. New York: Columbia University Press, 1971.

Kinmonth, Earl H. *The Self-Made Man in Meiji Japanese Thought: From Samurai to Salary Man*. Berkeley and Los Angeles: University of California Press, 1981.

Kokutai no Hongi: Cardinal Principles of the National Entity of Japan. Trans. John Owen Gauntlett. Cambridge: Harvard University Press, 1949.

Kornhauser, David. *Urban Japan: Its Foundations and Growth*. London: Longmans, 1976.

Lebra, Joyce C., ed. *Japan's Greater East Asia Co-Prosperity Sphere in World War II: Selected Readings and Documents*. Oxford: Oxford University Press, 1975.

Livingston, Jon, Joe Moore, and Felicia Oldfather, eds. *Imperial Japan, 1800–1945*. New York: Pantheon, 1973.

Martin, Harris I. "Popular Music and Social Change in Prewar Japan." *Japan Interpreter* 7, 3–4 (Summer-Autumn 1972), 332–52.

Maruyama, Masao. *Thought and Behavior in Modern Japanese Politics*. Ed. Ivan Morris. Oxford: Oxford University Press, 1963.

Miller, R. A. *Japan's Modern Myth*. Tokyo: Weatherhill, 1982.

Mishima, Yukio. *Runaway Horses*. New York: Knopf, 1973.

Mitchell, Richard H. *Censorship in Imperial Japan*. Princeton: Princeton University Press, 1983.

— *Thought Control in Prewar Japan*. Ithaca: Cornell University Press, 1976.

Miyoshi, Masao. *Accomplices of Silence: The Modern Japanese Novel*. Berkeley and Los Angeles: University of California Press, 1976.

Miyoshi, Masao, and H. D. Harootunian, eds. *Japan in the World*. Durham and London: Duke University Press, 1993.

— *Postmodernism and Japan*. Duke University Press, 1989.

Morley, James W., ed. *Dilemmas of Growth in Prewar Japan*. Princeton: Princeton University Press, 1971.

Morris, Ivan. *The Nobility of Failure: Tragic Heroes in the History of Japan*. New York: Holt, Rinehart, and Winston, 1975.

Morris-Suzuki, Tessa. *Showa: An Inside History of Hirohito's Japan*. New York: Schocken, 1985.

Nakamura, Hajime. *Ways of Thinking of Eastern Peoples: India, China, Tibet, Japan*. Ed. Philip P. Wiener. Honolulu: East-West Center Press, 1969.

Nakane, Chie. *Japanese Society*. Berkeley and Los Angeles: University of California Press, 1972.

Napier, Susan J. "Death and the Emperor: Mishima, Oe, and the Politics of Betrayal." *Journal of Asian Studies* 48 (February 1989), 71–89.

Nitobe, Inazo. *Bushido: The Soul of Japan*. Tokyo: Tuttle, 1969.

Nitschke, Gunter. " 'Ma': The Japanese Sense of 'Place' in Old and New Architecture and Planning." *Architectural Design* (March 1966), 116–56.

Nute, Kevin. *Frank Lloyd Wright and Japan*. New York: Van Nostrand Reinhold, 1993.

Ogai, Mori. *The Incident at Sakai and Other Stories*. Trans. David Dilworth and J. Thomas Rimer. Honolulu: University of Hawaii Press, 1977.

Perrin, Noel. *Giving Up the Gun: The Japanese Reversion to the Sword, 1543–1879*. Boulder, Col.: Shambala, 1980.

Powell, Brian. *Kabuki in Modern Japan: Mayama Seika and His Plays*. New York: St. Martins, 1990.

— "The Samurai Ethic in Mayama Seika's *Genroku Chushingura*." *Modern Asian Studies* 18, 4 (1984), 725–45.

— "Communist Kabuki: A Contradiction in Terms?" In James Redmond, ed., *Themes in Drama*. Vol. 1: *Drama and Society*. Cambridge: Cambridge University Press, 1979.

Raz, Jacob. *Audience and Actor*. Leiden: E. J. Brill, 1982.

Reischauer, Edwin O. *The Japanese*. Cambridge: Harvard University Press, 1978.

Richie, Donald. *The Inland Sea*. New York and Tokyo: Weatherhill, 1972.

Schodt, Frederick. *Manga, Manga: The World of Japanese Comics*. Tokyo: Kodansha, 1983.

Seidensticker, Edward. *Tokyo Rising: The City Since the Great Earthquake*. New York: Knopf, 1990.

Sheldon, Charles D. "Japanese Aggression and the Emperor, 1931–1941, from Contemporary Diaries." *Modern Asian Studies* 10 (February 1976).

Shillony, Ben-Ami. *Politics and Culture in Wartime Japan*. Oxford: Clarendon Press, 1981.

— *Revolt in Japan: The Young Officers and the February 26, 1936, Incident*. Princeton: Princeton University Press, 1973.

Shively, Donald H., ed. *Tradition and Modernization in Japanese Culture*. Princeton: Princeton University Press, 1971.

Silverberg, Miriam. "Constructing a New Cultural History of Prewar Japan."

In Masao Miyoshi and H. D. Harootunian, eds., *Japan in the World*, pp. 115–143. Durham: Duke University Press, 1993.

— "Remembering Pearl Harbor, Forgetting Charlie Chaplin, and the Case of the Disappearing Western Woman: A Picture Story." *Positions: East Asia Cultures Critique*, 1, 1 (Spring 1993), 24–76.

Smethurst, Richard J. *A Social Basis for Prewar Japanese Militarism: The Army and the Rural Community*. Berkeley and Los Angeles: University of California Press, 1974.

Smith, H. D. "Tokyo as an Idea: An Exploration of Japanese Urban Thought Until 1945." *Journal of Japanese Studies*, 4, 1 (Winter 1978), 45–80.

— *Japan's First Student Radicals*. Cambridge: Harvard University Press, 1972.

Smith, Robert J. *Japanese Society: Tradition, Self, and the Social Order*. Cambridge: Cambridge University Press, 1983.

Suzuki, Daisetz. *Zen and Japanese Culture*. Princeton: Princeton University Press, 1959.

Suzuki, Takao. *Japanese and the Japanese: Words in Culture*. Trans. Akira Miura. Tokyo: Kodansha, 1978.

Tanizaki, Jun'ichiro. *Naomi*. New York: Knopf, 1985.

— *Some Prefer Nettles*. New York: Perigee, 1981.

— *In Praise of Shadows*. Trans. Thomas Harper and Edward G. Seidensticker. New Haven: Leete's Island, 1977.

— *The Makioka Sisters*. Trans. Edward G. Seidensticker. New York: Grosset and Dunlap, 1966.

— *Seven Japanese Tales*. Trans. Howard S. Hibbett. New York: Knopf, 1963.

Toland, John. *The Rising Sun: The Decline and Fall of the Japanese Empire*. New York: Random House, 1970.

Tsunoda, Ryusaku, Wm. Theodore de Bary, and Donald Keene, eds. *Sources of Japanese Tradition*. 2 vols. New York: Columbia University Press, 1958.

Tsurumi, Shunsuke. *An Intellectual History of Wartime Japan: 1931–1945*. London: KPI, 1986.

Ueda, Makoto. *Literary and Art Theories in Japan*. Cleveland: Case Western Press, 1967.

Uenoda, Setsuo. *Japan and Jazz: Sketches and Essays on Japanese City Life*. Tokyo: Taiheiyosha Press, 1930.

Van Wolferen, Karel. *The Enigma of Japanese Power: People and Politics in a Stateless Nation*. New York: Knopf, 1989.

Varley, H. Paul, and George Elison. "The Culture of Tea: From Its Origins to Sen no Rikyu," in George Elison and Bardwell L. Smith, eds., *Warlords, Artists, and Commoners: Japan in the Sixteenth Century*, pp. 187–222. Honolulu: University Press of Hawaii, 1981.

Vogel, Ezra. *Japan as Number 1: Lessons for America*. New York: Harper Colophon, 1979.

Wakabayashi, Bob Tadashi. *Anti-Foreignism and Western Learning in Early Modern Japan: The New Theses of 1825*. Cambridge: Harvard University Press, 1986.

Wilson, George M. *Radical Nationalists in Japan: Kita Ikki, 1883–1937*. Cambridge: Harvard University Press, 1969.

Wilson, George M., ed. *Crisis Politics in Prewar Japan*. Tokyo: Sophia University Press, 1970.

Wittfogel, Karl August. *Oriental Despotism: A Comparative Study of Total Power*. New Haven: Yale University Press, 1957.

Yamaguchi, Masao. "Kingship, Theatricality, and Marginal Reality in Japan." In Ravindra K. Jain, ed., *Text and Context: The Social Anthropology of Tradition*. Philadelphia: Institute for the Studies of Human Issues, 1977.

Yamamura, Kozo. "Then Came the Great Depression: Japan's Interwar Years." In Herman van der Wee, ed., *The Great Depression Revisited: Essays on the Economics of the Thirties*. The Hague: Martinus Nijhoff, 1972.

— "Zaibatsu, Prewar and Zaibatsu, Postwar." *Journal of Asian Studies* 23, 4 (August 1964), 539–54.

Yoshino, M. Y. *Japan's Managerial System: Tradition and Innovation*. Cambridge: MIT Press, 1968.

Zeami. *On the Art of the No Drama*. Trans. J. Thomas Rimer and Yamazaki Masakazu. Princeton: Princeton University Press, 1984.

Japanese Cinema

Anderson, Joseph, and Donald Richie. *The Japanese Film: Art and Industry*. Rev. ed. [1959.] Princeton: Princeton University Press, 1982.

Andrew, Dudley, and Paul Andrew. *Kenji Mizoguchi: A Guide to References and Resources*. Boston: Hall, 1981.

Andrew, Dudley, and Michael Raine, eds. *Iris* No. 16 (Spring 1993), issue on image theory, image culture, and contemporary Japan.

Barrett, Gregory. *Archetypes in Japanese Film: The Sociopolitical and Religious Significance of the Principal Heroes and Heroines*. Selinsgrove: Susquehanna University Press/London: Associated University Presses, 1989.

Belton, John. *Cinema Stylists*. Metuchen, N.J.: Scarecrow, 1983.

Bock, Audie. *Japanese Film Directors*. Tokyo: Kodansha, 1978.

— *Naruse: A Master of the Japanese Cinema*. Chicago: Film Center of the School of the Art Institute, 1984.

Bordwell, David. *Ozu and the Poetics of Cinema*. Princeton: Princeton University Press, 1988.

— "Mizoguchi and the Evolution of Film Language." In Stephen Heath and Patricia Mellencamp, eds., *Cinema and Language*, pp. 107–15. Los Angeles: American Film Institute, 1983.

— "Our Dream Cinema: Western Historiography and the Japanese Film." *Film Reader* 4 (1979), 45–62.

Bordwell, David, and Kristin Thompson. "Space and Narrative in the Films of Ozu." *Screen* 17, 2 (Summer 1976), 41–73.

Branigan, Edward. "The Space of Equinox Flower." *Screen* 17, 2 (Summer 1976), 73–92.

Burch, Noel. "Approaching Japanese Cinema." In Stephen Heath and Patricia Mellencamp, eds., *Cinema and Language*, 79–96. Los Angeles: American Film Institute, 1983.

— *To the Distant Observer: Form and Meaning in the Japanese Cinema.* Berkeley and Los Angeles: University of California Press, 1979.

Cinema Year Book of Japan, 1936–1937. Tokyo: Sanseido, 1937.

Cinema Year Book of Japan, 1938. Tokyo: Kokusai Bunka Shinkokai, 1938.

Cinema Year Book of Japan, 1939. Tokyo: Kokusai Bunka Shinkokai. 1939.

Cohen, Robert. "Textual Poetics in the Films of Kenji Mizoguchi: A Structural Semiotics of Japanese Narrative." Ph.D. diss., UCLA, 1983.

"Toward a Theory of Japanese Narrative." *Quarterly Review of Film Studies* 6, 2 (Spring 1981), 181–200.

— "Mizoguchi and Modernism: Structure, Culture, Point of View." *Sight and Sound* 47, 2 (Spring 1978), 110–18.

Davis, Darrell William. "Kurosawa's *Kagemusha*: In Praise of Shadows." *Transactions of the Asiatic Society of Japan*, forthcoming.

— "Back to Japan: Militarism and Monumentalism in Prewar Japanese Cinema." *Wide Angle* 11, 3 (July 1989), 16–25.

Desser, David. *The Samurai Films of Akira Kurosawa.* Ann Arbor: UMI Research, 1983.

Ehrlich, Linda. "The Artist's Desire: Eight Films of Mizoguchi Kenji." Ph.D. diss., University of Hawaii, 1989.

Ehrlich, Linda, and David Desser, eds. *Cinematic Landscapes: Observations on the Visual Arts and Cinema of Japan and China.* Austin: University of Texas Press, 1994.

Galbraith, Stuart IV. *The Japanese Film Encyclopedia: A Filmography and Personnel Directory.* Jefferson, N.C.: McFarland, 1995.

Gerow, A. A. "The Benshi's New Face: Defining Cinema in Taisho Japan." *Iconics* 3 (1994), 69–86.

High, Peter B. "The Transmigrating Hero: Ideological Structures in the National Policy Film, 1939–1945." Unpublished ms., 1988.

— "A Propaganda of Real Human Emotions: The 'Humanist' War Films of 1938–1940." Chubu University: Kokusai kankei gakubu No. 4:6 (1987), 82–92.

— "For Profit and Patriotism: The Japanese War Film, 1930–1935." Nagoya: Nagoya University *Kokusai kenkyu* No. 3:6 (1986), 119–53.

— "Japanese Film Theory and the National Policy Film Debate: 1937–1941." Chubu University: Kokusai kankei gakubu No. 2:3 (1986), 133–49.

— "Japanese Film and the Great Kanto Earthquake of 1923." Chubu University: Kokusai kankei gakubu, No. 1:3 (1985), 71–84.

— "The Dawn of Cinema in Japan." *Journal of Contemporary History*, 19, 1 (January 1984), 23–57.

— "The War Cinema of Imperial Japan and Its Aftermath." *Wide Angle* 2, 1 (1977), 19–21.

Hirano, Kyoko. *Mr. Smith Goes to Tokyo*. Washington, D.C.: Smithsonian Institution Press, 1992.

Iwamoto Kenji, ed. *Nihon eiga to modanizumu, 1920–1930*. Tokyo: Libroport, 1991.

Kasza, Gregory J. *The State and Mass Media in Japan, 1918–1945*. Berkeley and Los Angeles: University of California Press, 1988.

Kirihara, Donald. *Patterns of Time: Mizoguchi and the 1930s*. Madison: University of Wisconsin Press, 1992.

— "A Reconsideration of the Institution of the Benshi." *Film Reader 6* (1985), 41–54.

— "Kabuki, Cinema, and Mizoguchi Kenji." In Stephen Heath and Patricia Mellencamp, ed., *Cinema and Language*, pp. 97–106. Los Angeles: American Film Institute, 1983.

Komatsu, Hiroshi, and Charles Musser. "Benshi Search." *Wide Angle* 9, 2 (1987), 72–90.

Kurosawa, Akira. *Something Like an Autobiography*. Trans. Audie Bock. New York: Knopf, 1982.

Leach, James. "Mizoguchi and Ideology: Two Films From the Forties." *Film Criticism* 8, 1 (Fall 1983), 67–78.

McDonald, Keiko. *Mizoguchi*. Boston: Twayne, 1984.

— "Form and Function in *Osaka Elegy*." *Film Criticism* 6, 2 (Winter 1982), 35–44.

Mellen, Joan. *The Waves at Genji's Door: Japan Through Its Cinema*. New York: Pantheon, 1976.

Misono, Kyohei. *Katsuben Jidai*. Tokyo: Iwanami Shoten, 1990.

Nolletti, Arthur Jr., and David Desser, eds. *Reframing Japanese Cinema: Authorship, Genre, History*. Bloomington: Indiana University Press, 1992.

Nornes, Abe Mark and Fukushima Yukio, eds. *The Japan/America Film Wars: WWII Propaganda and Its Cultural Contexts*. Switzerland: Harwood Academic, 1994.

Peterson, James. "A War of Utter Rebellion: Kinugasa's *Page of Madness* and the Japanese Avant-Garde of the 1920s." *Cinema Journal* 29, 1 (Fall 1989), 36–53.

Prince, Steven. *The Warrior's Camera*. Princeton: Princeton University Press, 1991.

Richie, Donald. *Japanese Cinema: An Introduction*. Hong Kong: Oxford University Press, 1990.

— *The Japanese Movie: An Illustrated History*. Rev. ed. Tokyo: Kodansha, 1981.

— *Ozu*. Berkeley and Los Angeles: University of California Press, 1974.

—— *Japanese Cinema: Film Style and National Character.* New York: Anchor, 1971.

Sato, Tadao. *Currents in Japanese Cinema.* New York: Kodansha, 1982.

—— *Chambara eiga ron: Onoe Matsunosuke kara Zatoichi made.* Tokyo: Film Art Theater Series, 1978.

—— "War As a Spiritual Exercise: Japan's National Policy Films." *Wide Angle* 2, 1 (1977), 22–24.

Schrader, Paul. *Transcendental Style in Film: Ozu, Bresson, Dreyer.* Berkeley and Los Angeles: University of California Press, 1972.

Silver, Alain. *The Samurai Film.* Woodstock, N.Y.: Overlook, 1983.

Thompson, Kristin. "Notes on the Spatial System of Ozu's Early Films." *Wide Angle* 1, 4 (1977), 8–17.

Thompson, Kristin, ed. *Film History* 7, 1 (Spring 1995).

Yoshimoto, Mitsuhiro. "The Difficulty of Being Radical: The Discipline of Film Studies and the Postcolonial World Order." In Masao Miyoshi and H. D. Harootunian, eds., *Japan in the World*, pp. 338–54. Durham: Duke University Press, 1993.

Filmography

Monumental Style

Abe Ichizoku (The Abe Clan), 1938; Toho, Kumagai Hisatora.

Genroku Chushingura, parts 1–2 (The Loyal Forty-Seven Retainers of the Genroku Era), 1941–1942; Koa Uzumasa Studios and Shochiku, Mizoguchi Kenji.

Iemitsu to Hikozaemon (Shogun Iemitsu and His Mentor Hikozaemon), 1941; Toho, Makino Masahiro.

Jigoku Mon (Gate of Hell), 1953; Daiei, Kinugasa Teinosuke.

Kagemusha (The Shadow Warrior), 1980; Toho, Kurosawa Akira.

Kawanakajima Kassen (The Battle of Kawanakajima), 1940; Toho, Kinugasa Teinosuke.

Ran (Chaos), 1985; Toho/Serge Silberman Production, Kurosawa Akira.

Rikyu, 1990; Shochiku, Teshigahara Hiroshi.
Zangiku Monogatari (Story of the Last Chrysanthemum), 1939; Shochiku, Mizoguchi Kenji.

Prewar Jidai Geki (Period Drama)

Ahen Senso (The Opium War), 1943; Toho, Makino Masahiro.
Ashigaru Kichiemon (Kichiemon the Footman), early 1930s; Nikkatsu, Satogi Ichiro.
Beni Komori (The Red Bat), 1931; Nikkatsu, Tanaka Tsuruhiko.
Chuboku Naosuke (Faithful Servant Naosuke), early 1930s; Nikkatsu, Uchida Tomu.
Edo no Asagiri (Morning Mist in Edo), 1938; Nikkatsu, Nishina Norihiko.
Edo no Hanaoi (Hollyhock Crest of Edo), 1940; Nikkatsu (incomplete).
Edo no Taka (Falcon of Edo), 1938; Shochiku Konoe Sushiro.
Edogawa Ranzan (Edogawa Family Revolt), 1937; J. O. Studios (Toho), Shimamura Kenji.
Enmusubi no Takadanobaba (Romantic Love of Takadanobaba), 1938; Shochiku, Itsushima Tadanobu? (photography), with Fujii Mitsugu.
Enoken no Ganbari (Enoken's Persistent Tactics), 1939; P.C.L., Nakagawa Nobuo.
Enoken no Kondo Isamu (Enoken's Kondo Isamu), 1935; P.C.L., Yamamoto Kajiro.
Gonza to Sukeju (Gonza and Sukeju the Palanquin Carriers), 1940; Shochiku, Furuno Eisaku.
Goto Matabei (Matabei Goto), 1935; Nikkatsu, Shiratori Masaichi.
Heiroku Yume Monogatari (Dream Tales of Heiroku), 1940; Toho, Aoyagi Nobue.
Hitohada Kannon (The Mercy Goddess of Hitohada Shrine), 1937; Shochiku, Kinugasa Teinosuke.
Iwami Jutaro (Jutaro the Strong Man), 1937; Daito, Ishiyama Minoru.
Jingisu Kan (Genghis Khan), 1943; Matsuda Sadaji, Ushihara Kiyohiko.
Jitsuroku Chushingura (The True Story of the Loyal Retainers), 1928; Nikkatsu, Makino Shozo.
Kaigara Ippei, part 1 (One-Handed Kaigara), 1930; Nikkatsu, Kiyose Eijiro.
Komatsu Riyuzo, part 2 (Komatsu Riyuzo), 1930; Nikkatsu.
Kurama Tengu (Kurama Tengu, Robin Hood of Japan), 1940; Nikkatsu, Matsuda Sadaji.
Mito Komon, part 2 (Mito Komon), 1932; Nikkatsu, Tsuji Kichiro, Arai Ryohei.
Miyamoto Musashi (Miyamoto Musashi), 1940; Nikkatsu, Inagaki Hiroshi.
Musashibo Benkei (Musashibo Benkei), 1942; Toho, Watanabe Kunio.
Sugata Sanshiro, part 2 (Sugata Sanshiro), 1945; P.C.L.-Toho, Kurosawa Akira.
Tange Sazen (The Famous Tange Sazen), 1940; Toho, Hagiwara Ryo.
Tange Sazen: Koigusa no Maki (The Famous Tange Sazen: Lovesick), 1940; Toho, Nakagawa Nobuo.

Yakko Gimpei (The Servant Gimpei), 1938; Shochiku, Osone Tatsuo.

Prewar Gendai Geki (Contemporary Drama)

Atarashiki Kazoku (A New Family), 1938; Shochiku, Shibuya Minoru.

Atatakaki Kaze (Warm Wind), 1940?; Shochiku, Oniwa Hideo, producer.

Byakuran no Uta (Song of the White Orchid), 1939; Toho-Man'ei (Manchuria), Watanabe Kunio.

Chikara no Shori (Victory of Might), 1935; Nikkatsu, Uchida Tomu.

Chokoreto to Heitai (Chocolate and Soldiers), 1941; Toho, Take Sado.

Daini no Niji (The Second Rainbow), 1938; Shinko, Koishi Eiichi.

Gekiryu (Swift Current), 1944; Toho, Ieki Niyoji.

Gion no Shimai (Sisters of Gion), 1936; Dai-Ichi, Mizoguchi Kenji.

Gonin no Sekkohei (Five Scouts), 1938; Nikkatsu, Tasaka Tomotaka.

Haha o Kowazuya (Mother Should Be Loved), 1934; Shochiku, Ozu Yasujiro.

Hijosen no Onna (Dragnet Girl), 1933; Shochiku, Ozu Yasujiro.

Ichiban Utsukushiku (The Most Beautiful), 1944; Toho, Kurosawa Akira.

Kagami Jishi (Mirror and Lion: Kabuki Lion Dance with Onoe Kikugoro), 1935; documentary, Kokusai bunka shinkokai (Society for International Cultural Relations), Ozu Yasujiro.

Kaigun (Navy), 1943; Nikkatsu, Tasaka Tomotaka.

Keisatsu Kan (Policemen), 1933; Makino, Uchida Tomu.

Kodo no Nippon (Imperial Way of Japan), 1940; Toho? documentary.

Naniwa Ereji (Naniwa Elegy), 1936; Dai-Ichi, Mizoguchi Kenji.

Nipponjin (The Japanese), 1938; Shochiku, Shimazu Tasujiro.

Nishizumi Senshachoden (The Story of Tank Commander Nishizumi), 1940; Shochiku, Yoshimura Kimisaburo.

Otoko no Gaika (Man of Triumph), 1940; with Yamane Hisako, Satomi Aiko, Shimura Ayako, Hamabusa Yuriko.

Oyako Zakura (Zakura Father and Son), 1944; Nikkatsu, Koishi Eichi.

Rikugun (Army), 1944; Shochiku, Kinoshita Keisuke.

Tsuchi to Heitai (Mud and Soldiers), 1939; Nikkatsu, Tasaka Tomotaka.

Wakaki Hi (Days of Youth), 1929; Shochiku, Yasujiro Ozu.

Index